A LIFE OF
ITS OWN

BOOKS BY ROBERT GOTTLIEB

with Peter Wiley

Empires in the Sun: The Rise of the New West
America's Saints: The Rise of Mormon Power

with Irene Wolt

Thinking Big: The Story of the Los Angeles Times,
Its Publishers, and Their Influence on
Southern California

Robert Gottlieb

A LIFE OF
ITS OWN

The Politics and
Power of Water

HARCOURT BRACE JOVANOVICH, PUBLISHERS

SAN DIEGO   NEW YORK   LONDON

Library of Congress Cataloging-in-Publication Data
Gottlieb, Robert.
A life of its own: the politics and power of water/Robert Gottlieb.
p. cm.
Bibliography: p.
Includes index.
ISBN 0-15-195190-X
1. Water resources development—Government policy—West (U.S.)
2. Water resources development—Government policy—California.
3. Water resources development—Government policy—United States.
I. Title.
HD1695.A17G68   1988
333.91'15'0973—dc19   88-11135

Map by EarthSurface Graphics

Design by Dalia Hartman

Printed in the United States of America

First edition

A B C D E

For Marge, Casey, and Andy
"All we really need . . ."

CONTENTS

Preface xi

ONE THE ECLIPSE OF THE WATER
     INDUSTRY: AN INTRODUCTION 1

  1 UNHOLY ALLIANCES:
     A CALIFORNIA WATER WAR 3
     Scurrilous Attacks 3
     Contending Interests 5
     "The Final Solution" 14
     Strange Bedfellows 20

TWO THE PLAYERS 35

  2 FORMATION, CONSOLIDATION, AND CHALLENGE:
     THE WATER INDUSTRY IN TRANSITION 37
     "Soldiers for America" 37
     The Role of the Feds 40

The Iron Triangle   46
Last of the Big Projects   52
The Water Industry in Turmoil   58
Hit List   63
The Uncertainties of the Reagan Years   65

3   AGRICULTURAL EMPIRES:
THE FARM-WATER CONNECTION   75
AgOreo's Reluctant Portfolio   75
The Rise of Irrigation   79
The Subsidy as King   84
The Farm-Water Lobby   90
Desert Politics   94
Center Pivot Crisis   103
The Continuing Quest for Cheap Water   109

4   THE URBAN-DEVELOPMENT COMPLEX:
THE POLITICS OF GROWTH   113
Moon over Honey Springs   113
From Private to Public   116
The Growth Machine   123
End of the Pipeline   128
Urban-Suburban Rivalries   136
Beat the Peak   143
New Approaches, Old Objectives   149

THREE   NEW ISSUES, CHANGING FACES   153

5   THE WATER QUALITY BATTLEGROUND:
ENTERING THE AGE OF TRACE ORGANICS   155
Image Development and Behavior Modification   155
The Search for Safe Water   158
The Industrial Factor   162
The Disinfection Quandary   168
Groundwater Crisis   177
The Leaching Fields   187
Privatizing Water Quality   192

6   THE OUTSIDERS: WATER INDUSTRY
    CRITICS, OUTCASTS, AND NEW PLAYERS   199
    Robert Redford's Search for Consensus   199
    Preservationists, Conservationists,
    Utopians, and Reformers   202
    The Environmental Decade   209
    The Third Wave   213
    The Outcasts   219
    The Rural Opposition   228
    Community Politics   234

FOUR   WATER POLICY CONFRONTS
       ITSELF: A CONCLUSION   241

7   A NEW ERA? PROSPECTS FOR CHANGE   243
    The Water Industry in Trouble   243
    Opening Up the Process   246
    The Problem of Equity   253
    The Interrupted March Toward Privatization   257
    Troubled Markets   261
    Values and Ideologies   272

Acknowledgments   281

Notes   283

Index   320

PREFACE

Water policy touches our lives in an enormous number of ways. It affects the water we drink and the food we eat. It is central to irrigation and urban growth. It addresses water quality and toxicity associated with increasing kinds of industrial hazards. It is linked to our mighty river systems, deep-water lakes, and shallow streams. It establishes in legal, political, and economic terms what to some is sacred but to others is nothing more than a commodity to buy or sell, transfer or lease. Control over water has ultimately become tantamount to controlling the destiny of the land and the people who settle on the land.

Yet water policy–makers, members of a distinct entity that calls itself "the water industry," are an obscure group. Little known to the public and the press, they speak to one another in a technically dense and often inaccessible language, making decisions that are central to our day-to-day lives.

This water industry is a combination of private interests and public agencies. The private groups, led by agriculture, have dominated over the years, with other contending parties—including recreation, mining and energy, navigation, and more recently

urban-development interests—also playing critical roles. These
groups are the *benificiaries* of water development, taking advantage
of its generous subsidies and extensive facilities.

The public agencies, on the other hand, predominate in supplying this most basic resource. They are organized in a variety of
forms, from municipal water and sewer departments to county water
authorities and irrigation districts, each of which has varying powers,
from the ability to levy taxes and charge user fees to the ability to
make formal or informal land-use decisions. Water agencies, in
fact, function at times as de facto land planners for their service
areas.

These agencies have primarily been engineering and construction oriented. They have needed access to a great deal of capital to
develop their facilities and build their infrastructures. They have
thus relied on a wide variety of financial players, from bond-rating
houses to investment bankers and individual consultants. The agencies have also relied heavily on water lawyers, who have been a
central fixture at water-industry gatherings. There they have joined
to set the course of water development with the engineers and
construction people, land development and real estate operators,
irrigators from large to no-so-large land holdings, and, of course,
the federal and local water agency officials themselves. These representatives from public agencies and private interest groups have
come to consider their activities as a coherent and integrated whole,
a discrete "water industry."

For more than seven years, I was a direct participant in the
water industry. I attended its conferences, gossiped at its cocktail
parties, learned its ways of thinking and its organizational culture.
I witnessed some of the maneuvering and sat behind closed doors
and listened while policies were shaped and a public posture
formulated.

Often I was not a welcome guest. As a critic and activist, I was
frequently on different sides of issues, and I related to a different
set of constituencies. In the course of those seven years, I became
a kind of insider-outsider—speaking the language, intrigued with

the politics—but never really belonging to this self-described "water community."

My first encounters with the water industry took place more than fifteen years ago. I was then researching the role of the Chandler family, publishers of the *Los Angeles Times*, for a book on this powerful Southern California family and their newspaper. The *Times* and its owners had been instrumental in shaping the development of Southern California. The manipulation of water policy had also been crucial to that activity. Part of the research led me to the glass-and-concrete headquarters of the Los Angeles Department of Water and Power, and, a few blocks to the north, to the home of the Metropolitan Water District of Southern California, known as MET. There I began to discover the world of the water industry with all its influence and intrigues and its crucial role in the politics and economics of the region.

Los Angeles is not the only city where the water industry plays such a paramount role. Salt Lake City, Phoenix, Tucson, Denver, Albuquerque, and Las Vegas, have all been dependent or are becoming dependent on imported water supplies, including some that travel thousands of miles. Similarly, an irrigated agriculture, which stretches from California's Central Valley to the cotton fields of Arizona's Pima and Pinal counties and more recently to the Sand Hills of Nebraska, has depended on water development as the basis for its expansion. Places like Chicago and Cincinnati have developed water rate and discharge policies that have allowed expanding industries to consolidate their position and avoid paying the costs associated with their undesirable by-products. These urban, industrial, and agricultural forces have thrived in part because the water industry was there to help them, identifying development objectives as central to its mission.

Water, of course, has long been an essential resource in the *regional* development of this country, both East and West. The growth of the cities along the Atlantic seaboard during the nineteenth century was linked to the availability of an abundant and continuing supply of water, while the new industrial order required water for both production and discharge purposes. Much of the focus on water development in the twentieth century has centered on the lands west of the 100th meridian, the line roughly dividing the water-short areas of the West where rainfall averages under twenty inches a year from the wetter regions of the East where the problems are defined more by the need to get the water off the land rather than onto it.

It was in the western sunbelt that the water industry became a dominant player in what can be characterized as a resource-development complex. This complex of interests subsequently became the subject of research by me and my longtime writing partner, Peter Wiley, for our book *Empires in the Sun: The Rise of the New American West*. As we explored the activities of the water industry, I realized I would eventually want to undertake a more detailed look at this curious and powerful group.

While Peter and I were finishing up *Empires*, I received a call one day from Dorothy Green, a water activist who had been monitoring the activities of MET and the Southern California water industry. I had interviewed Dorothy several months earlier about her background and her battles with MET and its water-industry allies. I had been intrigued by how she, a housewife from West Los Angeles, had become engrossed in an obscure though fascinating subject where citizen participation had been so minimal. Her activities paralleled that of other like-minded water critics in cities such as Phoenix and Denver. They all faced the difficult task of taking on little-known water agencies who had become adept at influencing press and public officials alike.

These citizen activists appealed to my sense of equity and concern for quality of life issues, and aroused my interest as a writer in finding out more about their confrontations with such an elusive body. Now Dorothy Green was asking me to become a participant as well as an observer by applying for an opening on the Metropolitan Water District board of directors for the City of Santa Monica where I lived.

I couldn't resist the opportunity. I approached members of the Santa Monica City Council, alerting them that as an outsider and critic of the water industry I would not likely be perceived as a welcome addition to the MET board. The council was then sharply split between two political factions—one liberal, with populist overtones, and a second more conservative faction. For the liberal-cum-populist grouping who supported me, MET, though not well known, seemed to represent those distant and powerful forces of development this faction had fought on a local level. But I also received the support of one key member of the more conservative faction. She was sensitive to the environmental consequences of water development and had also become particularly disturbed over the years by the ways in which this urban water district had functioned in what she saw as an arrogant and aggrandizing manner. This council member became the swing vote and ultimately my strongest backer. On a four-to-two vote, I received the appointment. I took my seat in December 1980 and immediately plunged deeper into the world of the water industry.

December 1980 was an exciting and critical juncture in the politics of water in several ways. Shortly before my appointment, water-industry critics had succeeded in gathering enough signatures to place on the ballot a referendum to approve or disapprove a group of facilities for expansion of the California State Water Project. These projects included the Peripheral Canal, a forty-three-mile-wide canal designed to send water around the Sacramento Bay Delta in Northern California to the farms and cities of Central and Southern California. A water-industry priority, these dams and ditches had already become highly controversial.

That was also the transition time between the Carter and Reagan presidencies. The water industry had joined other interest groups like the oil companies, utilities, and military contractors in presenting wish lists to the new president. James Watt had just been named secretary of interior and the water industry had every reason to believe, given his previous work at the Denver-based Mountain States Legal Foundation, that he would become their champion. William Gianelli, another water-industry veteran, had been named to head the other big federal water agency, the Army Corps of Engineers. In contrast to the difficult Carter years, with their hit lists of water projects, talk of water reform and cost sharing, and environmentalists entering the corridors of power, the Reagan victory seemed a godsend. The water industry had become convinced that, in the words of the Mormon hymn, All Was Well.

But, as it turned out, all was not quite well. The Reagan years would become a time of turbulence in water politics, as new issues, new players, and new realities became part of the debate. The long-standing expectations about continuous water development would give way to public fears about the quality of existing water supplies. Irrigated agriculture, the linchpin of the water industry, would face its most serious crisis since the Depression, which had forced major changes in farming and the character of rural life. And the urban forces of expansion, in the wake of the rapid growth of cities and suburbs especially since World War II, would also face escalating problems not easily resolved.

These changing conditions were not readily perceived or accepted by a group long set in its ways. The very obscurity of the discourse concerning water issues created a kind of priesthood culture among the members of the water industry. They had a strong sense of who belonged and who intruded. Though I was clearly an intruder, my new position as a director of the largest and most expansive water district in the country exposed me to the dynamics of this self-contained interest group. As an insider-outsider, I became at once a participant-observer, acting on the very issues I had begun and would continue to research.

This book is a product of that connection between research and action. It is an exploration of the players and the issues and the social realities they engender. My first major experience on the water board turned out to be a classic water war—a metaphor of the changing times. As such, I have presented it in the first chapter as a way to set the stage for a description of the water industry's role. The emergence of the water industry can also be viewed in part from the vantage point of the history of the big federal water agencies, the Bureau of Reclamation and the Army Corps of Engineers. Though the water industry has always been predominantly local in composition, it has thrived in its relationship with Congress and the federal agencies, although those ties, as described in chapter 2, have today become more problematic.

Water policy has also been a reflection of the strategies and objectives of the dominant players, particularly agriculture and urban interests—the subjects of the third and fourth chapters. Water development to a great extent has its historical roots in the rise of irrigated farming. The early conception underlying the water projects was social in character, encouraging small-scale land ownership and a protective stewardship of the land. That eventually gave way to water-related programs that reinforced the business or industrial form of agricultural activity through a range of subsidies and major water importation schemes. But agriculture today is in relative decline, thus creating a shift in power and emphasis within the water industry itself.

As agricultural fortunes ebbed, water development became an increasingly important component of the continuing trend toward urban expansion. Major urban-development interests, at first in the East and then particularly in more recent times in the arid West, have viewed access to new water sources as central to their plans. The patterns of urban growth became a function of the nature and scope of regional water development. With future expansion still a priority, the urban wing of the water industry has eagerly sought out the most effective ways to accomplish long-standing objectives.

While the players within the water industry maneuver and reposition themselves, they have at the same time been obliged to confront a different set of issues and a growing array of critics of their overall water policies, as the fifth and sixth chapers describe. As concerns regarding new forms of contamination have emerged, the public has shifted its focus to the quality of the water rather than its availability. Water quality has become both an urban and a rural issue, affecting as much industry as municipalities and agriculture. These issues in turn have forced the water industry to contend with differing interpretations of the role and purpose of the water agencies themselves and the policies they pursue. Social movements have sought to address the ways in which these water policies are established and objectives are defined. The water industry has been challenged, and the outcome is still in doubt.

The conflicts in the water arena today are conflicts over values as well as policies, as discussed in the seventh and concluding chapter. The water industry's desire for a more effective public posture and greater efficiencies has not diminished its lack of democratic input and the range of inequities that bias its decisions. The recent flurry of interest in the Reagan years over *private* solutions, enlisting the private sector or the "market," has only compounded this conflict over values and objectives. Water policy remains at once a question of political choices and the direction of change.

As the outlines of this book took shape, I became more aware than ever how water generates strong responses in both its absence and its presence. By focusing on the water industry, I've attempted to chronicle some of the factors that determine why this resource has been so central to the development of our industrialized and urbanized society. Though water politics have become most associated with regional interests in California and other western states, the issues of the water industry—urban expansion, the role of irrigation and the industrialization of agriculture, the quality of the drinking-water supply, and pollution of waterway systems—are national in scope and importance.

To explore the way in which water has been used and misused becomes a way of ultimately exploring certain forms of politics and power in our society. It tells us how key decisions get made and who gets to make them. It suggests the limits of democratic participation when powerful public agencies and private interests merge. It reveals the nature of the values involved in the options selected. It can also tell us much about the prospects for change and the resistance to it. And if, as the Ute Indians say, water has a life of its own, it becomes crucial to understand how those who wish to control this basic resource can, by their actions, affect our lives.

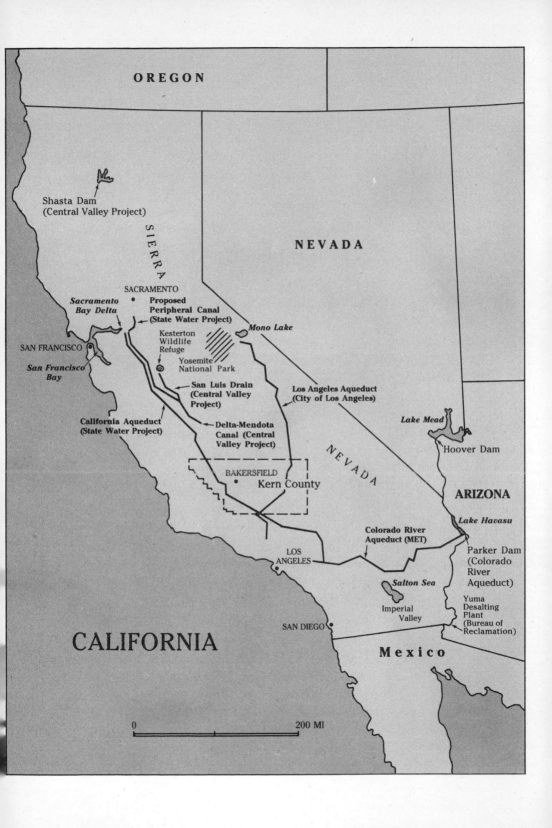

OREGON

NEVADA

Shasta Dam
(Central Valley Project)

SIERRA

SACRAMENTO

*Sacramento
Bay Delta*

Proposed
Peripheral Canal
(State Water Project)

Mono Lake

Kesterton
Wildlife
Refuge

SAN FRANCISCO

Yosemite
National Park

*San Francisco
Bay*

San Luis Drain
(Central Valley
Project)

Los Angeles Aqueduct
(City of Los Angeles)

Lake Mead

California Aqueduct
(State Water Project)

Delta-Mendota
Canal (Central
Valley Project)

Hoover Dam

NEVADA

BAKERSFIELD

Kern County

ARIZONA

Lake Havasu

Colorado River
Aqueduct (MET)

Parker Dam
(Colorado
River
Aqueduct)

LOS
ANGELES

Salton Sea

Imperial
Valley

Yuma
Desalting
Plant
(Bureau of
Reclamation)

CALIFORNIA

SAN DIEGO

Mexico

0   200 MI

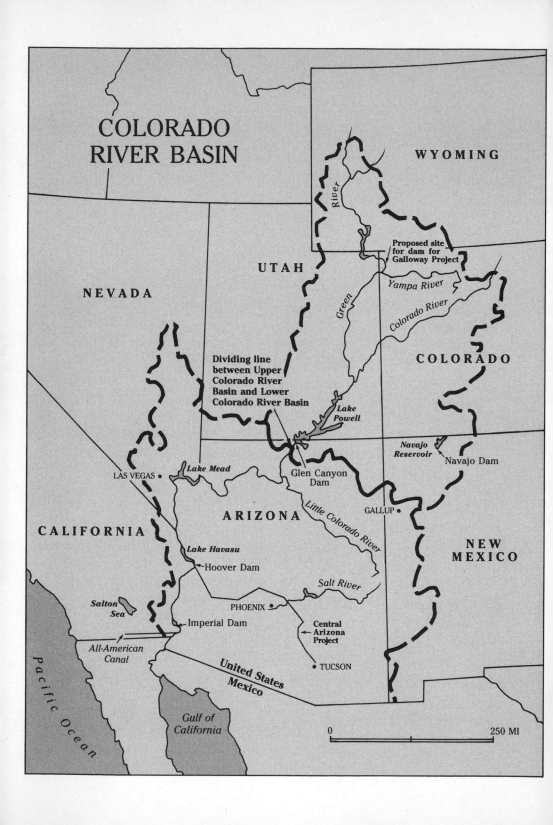

COLORADO RIVER BASIN

WYOMING

UTAH

NEVADA

River

Proposed site
for dam for
Galloway Project

Yampa River

Colorado River

COLORADO

Dividing line
between Upper
Colorado River
Basin and Lower
Colorado River Basin

Green

*Lake
Powell*

*Navajo
Reservoir*
Navajo Dam

Lake Mead

LAS VEGAS •

Glen Canyon
Dam

CALIFORNIA

ARIZONA

Little Colorado River

GALLUP •

NEW
MEXICO

Lake Havasu

← Hoover Dam

*Salton
Sea*

Imperial Dam

Salt River

PHOENIX •

Central
← Arizona
Project

*All-American
Canal*

*United States
Mexico*

• TUCSON

Pacific Ocean

*Gulf of
California*

0   250 MI

PART ONE

The Eclipse of the Water Industry: An Introduction

Chapter 1

Unholy Alliances:
A California Water War

SCURRILOUS ATTACKS

The mood in the Metropolitan Water District board room in down-town Los Angeles was tense. There were signs that not everything was going well with the campaign, that the presumption of an assured victory was perhaps premature. The directors sat back in their swivel chairs, perched in the horseshoe shaped three tiered structure that lay slightly elevated from the rest of the meeting room. They were awaiting the end of the meeting, less than three months to election day in June 1982.

The senior member of the elderly 51-member board (their average age was sixty-seven), was a crusty eighty-eight-year-old named Preston Hotchkis—landowner, insurance company executive, and long-standing figure of power who bridged the worlds of the water industry and those of the larger business and political elites of the region. On cue, Hotchkis, or "Pres" as he was known to his fellow directors, asked for recognition from the chair just as the meeting was about to come to an end. It was a setup, I was later to learn, and I was the target.

"It has just come to my attention," Hotchkis declared, "that one of our board members has been engaged in scurrilous attacks

3

against the rest of us. I wish you'd let everyone know what's going on, Mr. Chairman."

There was a pause as attention turned to the chairman, Earle Blais, a burly man who always seemed to hover over his audiences with his booming sing-song voice and imposing presence. Blais waved a letter—a fundraising appeal I had signed for the opposition campaign in the Peripheral Canal referendum—and proceeded to lash out at this latest example of perfidy and betrayal.

In the letter I had singled out the MET board of directors—whose fifty other directors listened intensely to Blais's excoriation—as representative of the structure of power in the water industry. These board members reflected a cross-section of the water industry: agriculture, real estate, construction and engineering interests, utilities, law firms, banks, insurance companies, and, of course, the water agencies themselves. This group of board members acted as a kind of water-development complex, de facto land planners heavily influencing the shape and pattern of their region through their decisions.

I had attacked the water industry in this letter and on other occasions for defining water policy as the pursuit of development goals for the direct and indirect benefit of its members. Water in Southern California, indeed in the West and in many ways throughout the country, set the terms of development, whether the new real estate subdivisions in urban areas or the massive irrigation that increasingly characterized the farm economy.

This was the final straw, Blais thundered. I was the renegade, beyond the pale; my critique of the water industry a form of "McCarthyism" as one of the directors exclaimed. Blais ordered the legal staff to investigate my actions. Consensus had been breached and an enemy had entered the ranks.

The breakdown of consensus extended beyond the horseshoe structure on Sunset and Beaudry in downtown Los Angeles. The Peripheral Canal referendum was to be a pivotal moment in the fortunes of the California water industry, the last hurrah of the Consensus Group, as one of its coalitions was called. Economic, environmental, and regional pressures were all coming to bear on the situation, threatening to unravel the ties that had been established between development forces through much of the twentieth century. The political divisions that had emerged revealed weaknesses from which the water industry would never quite recover.

The fight over the Peripheral Canal was a fascinating affair, filled with unholy alliances, strange bedfellows, the power of ideas, the evocation of basic needs, and ultimately a new interest on the part of the public in an issue that has always been presented as obscure, technical, and divorced from politics. It was a rare moment to both observe and experience.

CONTENDING INTERESTS

The stakes in this particular California water war were exceptionally high. Through much of the twentieth century, water development had helped to shape the direction of irrigated agriculture and urban growth in the state. Various interests in different regions and with different needs had a common objective in making available a large, continuing, and secure water supply. A powerful and dominant agricultural industry had visions of more lands being brought into production and of expanding markets—all made possible through inexpensive water for irrigation. The big cities of the southern part of the state had become aggressive and forceful "water seekers" (as one analyst called them) who had long made the equation that additional water development meant continuing rapid growth. Through the years, contending yet affiliated interests had considered future water development, with its potential economic, environmental, and social costs, as not only a given but a kind of birthright. Water *belonged* to those who claimed it and developed it. Now the limits of that development were coming into focus, as the costs were becoming clearer and the terms of such development no longer accepted as *automatically* as when the water industry could manipulate policy with little resistance. During the 1970s and early 1980s, the search for a new water supply had commenced once again, but the route had become riddled with obstacles and unforeseen difficulties.

California water politics had long been an intense affair. Its players, who have defined themselves in both regional and interest-group terms, have alternately created coalitions and played hardball in their lobbying and influence peddling. The two major players have been the sprawling urban interests of the south and the powerful and diverse agricultural groups of Central California. Urban Southern California, consisting of a host of real estate, industrial, and financial interests allied with a variety of water agencies, has been led by the Metropolitan Water District—MET. The Central California agricultural interests have been dispersed throughout the great Central Valley, a huge, dry land mass stretching from the Sacramento Bay Delta in the north to the Tehachapi mountains in the south. The southern end of the valley includes the giant corporate farms of Kern and Kings counties, heavily dependent on the California State Water Project. These have been the biggest users of water in the state system since it reached the Kern area in the late 1960s.

Further north, on the east side of the valley, in places like Fresno and Tulare counties, can be found the beneficiaries of the federal Central Valley Project. These include primarily medium- and large-sized farming units, many of whom, like the J.G. Boswell Company, are among the oldest and most aggressive players in the water industry.

At the center of California water politics has been the Bay Delta, a system of marshes, islands, and water channels that links the Sacramento River and its tributaries to the north with an outlet to San Francisco Bay and the Pacific Ocean. Since the construction of the CVP commencing in the 1940s, and the State Water Project in the 1960s, the Delta has also served as a conduit for "exporting" water to the south. This had consisted of millions of acre feet* of

* One acre foot is the equivalent of 326,000 gallons, or a little more than 43,500 cubic feet of water, about the annual amount used by a family of five in a dry climate.

6

water pumped uphill into the vast stretches of irrigated farms in the valley and onwards through the California aqueduct over a second chain of mountains into the six-county service area of MET, home today of nearly fourteen million people. These two projects are among the most massive resource-development efforts of this century. They consume extraordinary amounts of electricity (the State Water Project is the largest single user of electricity in the state), involve miles on miles of concrete, and have transformed California into an agro-industrial power and heavily urbanized environment.

The Delta, a base for important farming and industrial interests, is also the home of striped bass and dozens of other species of fish and a range of wildlife that have settled in the region's marshes and estuaries. It has become a prime recreational area: located a short distance from the Northern California Bay Area urban complex, it attracts those who hunt and fish and thousands of other northerners who journey there on weekends and see the Delta as an extension of the Bay Area.

The Delta has become pivotal in recent years because it gives rise to contrasting visions of the role of water. There are those in the south and central part of the state, members of the water industry, who see the flow of water to the sea as wasted water, water that could be harnessed and "developed." Others, northerners and an assortment of environmental groups, many of whom are based in the north, see the flow to the Bay as intended. They want this flow to remain uninterrupted, flushing out the salts (some of which have been created by the Delta's own agricultural and industrial development), to allow the fish and the birds to flourish rather than be sucked into pumps or lose their source of nourishment. Finally, there are those from both north and south, critics of the water industry, who suggest that the issues are also about values and priorities for people and the effects of water development on urban and rural communities.

All these different forces came together in June 1982 in what turned out to be one of the most unusual of political campaigns. Some of the players had already been engaged in the incessant maneuverings of the water industry more than thirty years previously

7

when the question of a State Water Project had first come to the fore. The two key players, then as in 1982, were MET and the Kern landowners. Both of them had identified a need for additional water and for their own reasons explored the possibility of a project to be built by the State of California, bypassing the federal government, which had become the traditional sponsor of water projects throughout the country.

By the 1950s, much of the Central Valley had benefited from the federally financed and operated Central Valley Project. The westside of the valley, however, was not connected to the CVP. The landowners in the area, including the huge Kern County Land Company and several oil companies, saw an opportunity to irrigate more of their acreage. Production had already increased on the westside thanks to a boom in the use of local groundwater that had occurred after World War II. But that water was in limited supply and the landowners faced the threat of overdrafting, or overusing, the resource, which could seriously harm the quality of the water. The Kern landowners formed their own association and started lobbying in Sacramento for a project that would provide their area with additional water for irrigation, without restrictions in terms of the size of the units of land receiving the water and it was hoped, at a price competitive with the low-priced, heavily subsidized water delivered by the CVP.

MET too, for its own reasons, was also interested in a state water project. The fast-growing Southern California region was experiencing its most extensive and expansive boom. In urban Southern California, water had long been key to the growth pattern. Since the early 1950s, MET had played a crucial role in centralizing water development throughout Southern California, especially in providing water to new growth areas. Each successive land boom after World War II from San Diego to Orange to Riverside and Ventura counties could be traced to annexation to MET and the provision of "imported," or nonlocal, water. "Land is just land until it gets water on it. When it gets water, its assessed value and its sale value increase materially," longtime MET chairman Joseph Jensen had said of his region.

8

Through the 1950s both MET and the Kern landowners actively maneuvered inside and outside the state legislature. They were warily eyed by Northern Californians who particularly resented the growing clout of their regional neighbors to the south and worried about the designs on a water system that ultimately flowed out to San Francisco Bay. Proposals were floated and then shot down until a new governor, Pat Brown, himself a Northern Californian, came up with legislation known as the Burns-Porter Act. This package of facilities and regional trade-offs, which finessed its way in 1959 through a skeptical legislature, described the art of coalescing interests or "distributive politics" at its most intricate and complex levels.

"Pat Brown deserves the credit," recalled William Gianelli, a key Brown appointee during the early stages of the State Water Project and later Ronald Reagan's top water man in both Sacramento in the 1960s and then in Washington as head of the Army Corps of Engineers. "On the one hand, he had something for everybody: lots of water for the south and the farmers, some projects for the north, and some things for the Delta farming and industrial interests," Gianelli mused. "But he also outfoxed those like Kern and MET who wanted to put their own stamp on the package and had blocked efforts up to then."

In the give-and-take of the maneuvering to pass Burns-Porter, the Kern farmers received perhaps their most important concession—the elimination of any acreage restriction such as provided by federal reclamation law—in return for what appeared to be a full-cost payment structure. In the federal projects like the CVP, beneficiaries, if they wanted to receive the subsidized water, were limited to 160 acres, though many larger landowners, particularly in California, had found ways to get around the law. With the new state project, Kern landowners, several of whom held large-sized holdings in the thousands of acres, were relieved to be rid of the 160-acre restriction. With the acreage restriction now removed, Kern landowners immediately began to seek ways to modify the proposed price of their project water, which was significantly higher than CVP water.

9

MET, on the other hand, was most concerned about future growth and wanted an assured water supply in the case of drought or the inability of the state to complete the project. MET was initially unhappy with the way the contracts for the project had been drawn. It continued to debate the issue in the weeks and months preceding a 1960 bonding election that was to provide authorization for funding the project. "It was like a cat and mouse game," one longtime MET employee recalled, "with Jensen and Pat Brown and their various staff meeting constantly." The big water district, which was seriously divided on the issue, decided to formally support passage of the bonds only a few days before the election took place.

The 1960 bonding election was in some respects a prelude to the Peripheral Canal election twenty years later. To the electorate in the south, the passage of this $1.75 billion bond measure was deemed essential by its promoters in the press and by the water industry and its allies. If not, the argument went, Southern California could go dry—a powerful image that has been continually raised in California and in western water battles. If the bonds passed, the project advocates, including the *Los Angeles Times*, asserted, then it would be possible for the region's cycle of growth to continue. Growth, "Los Angeles' primary industry," as *Fortune* magazine had once commented, was on everyone's lips, reflected on billboards, in newspaper commentaries, and in the expectation that the boom this time might be permanent. Assuring growth through water development was thus considered a popular position, and support for the State Water Project equivalent to endorsing the future of the region.

The arguments in the north were no less evocative and powerful. The *San Francisco Chronicle* matched the *Los Angeles Times* with hostile diatribes about blank checks for its southern neighbors and passionate appeals to save a northern birthright—the water at its area of origin. If they need water, thundered the *Chronicle*, let them bring icebergs from Alaska, or better yet, slow down their infernal growth machine.

This was regional politics, a longtime factor in the state, at its most intense. In fact, the bond election turned out to involve more regional than interest-group conflict. It was a close election, with only one-hundred-fifty-thousand votes separating the successful pro-Project side from their opponents. There were lopsided percentages in both the north and the south reflecting the regional divisions, with the larger number of voters from the south providing the margin.

Once the north-south divisions had faded, a number of unanswered questions still remained after the bonding authority had been established. Pat Brown and others in the water industry were well aware that the $1.75 billion was far from sufficient for completing the project. Both urban and agricultural interests wanted to contract for massive deliveries of water. Everyone in the water industry assumed that all the water being requested—a phenomenal four-million-plus acre feet of water each year—would eventually be used. Continued rapid growth, both urban and agricultural, was considered a given.

To meet those anticipated requests, a big obstacle had to be tackled—to get the water effectively through or around the Sacramento Bay Delta. Through much of the twentieth century, the Delta had become a multipurpose waterway. It had served at different times navigational interests (particularly the Ports of Sacramento and Stockton), agricultural development in the Delta (which in turn was heavily dependent on a fragile system of levees creating artificial islands and pockets of potentially fertile land), recreational interests (which coveted the fishing areas and wildlife), and industrial activities (much of which required a continuing supply of water). Now the forces from the Central Valley and urban Southern California wanted to import their substantial amounts of water through the Delta on its course southward.

It soon became clear that this newly authorized State Water Project would require construction of a "Delta facility." Without this facility—either a Peripheral Canal to take water around the Delta or another facility to take water through the Delta—the area's fragile system of lateral canals, levees, and ditches would substantially limit the amount of water that could be pumped south. A Delta facility also made possible future water development of the

11

majestic and untamed rivers of Northern California such as the Eel, the Smith, the Klamath, and the Trinity. It thus provided the key for current and future cycles of urban and agricultural growth and expansion.

But in the early 1960s all this remained to be seen. Kern and MET, though allied together as advocates of water development, were wary partners. Compromises were finally arranged on the contracts resolving differences over price and contract guarantees. Kern got much of what it wanted in terms of the price of its water and agreed to sign the contract. The system was designed so that Kern could receive the water it wanted immediately while paying far less than its full costs, while MET would pay to have an entitlement to the water, though it still wouldn't need most of it for years to come.

For Kern, the deal set the stage for a whirlwind of activity that changed the shape of the region. Major corporate interests took over some of the big landholdings in the area and aggressively moved into the land-development business. With the arrival of the State Project water in 1968, the amount of irrigated acreage in the county shot up by more than two hundred thousand acres in less than a decade to nearly a million acres under production by 1980. Whole new cropping patterns were established, led by King Cotton, which had come to dominate the valley in ways inconceivable just two decades earlier.

For MET, the deal offered some ambiguous lessons. Though the district saw itself as a major player in Sacramento and Washington, it had a begrudging admiration and at times fear of the political clout of agriculture. Some of the most powerful legislators in Washington and Sacramento represented agricultural districts. They were at the center of the water policy–related subcommittees, lobbying, maneuvering, and ultimately shaping the agendas on the issue. While Kern landowners claimed economic poverty to obtain price breaks, they used their considerable political muscle to continually put MET's urban bloc on the defensive.

MET ultimately accepted the deal, arguing that inclusion of Kern was essential for the project. The big urban district was most

12

concerned with its future guarantees of water. MET planners foresaw, when its full entitlements to the state water became available by 1990, a vast urban land mass stretching from Ventura County to the north to the Mexican border on the south, with a population of more than twenty-three million people. The water district was willing then to trade these water-supply guarantees for a less favorable financial arrangement. Later internal MET memos estimated that Kern received several million dollars in subsidies due to the pricing structures of the project.

By the 1970s, a new crop of MET leaders had emerged who had become comfortable with these arrangements. Those like Howard Hawkins, Earle Blais's predecessor as chairman, were far more inclined to support Kern's claims that it needed the subsidies to make its participation in the project viable. Hawkins, a silver-haired politician who owned an agricultural fertilizer company in the San Gabriel Valley to the east of downtown Los Angeles, would continually interject at board meetings his support for the "farmers," and symbolized personally the link between the urban and agricultural wings of the water industry.

By the late 1960s and early 1970s, as State Project water flowed into Kern County, the concentration of land ownership and changing cropping patterns took a quantum jump. The "farmers" of Kern County hardly resembled even their contemporary counterparts in the Midwest. Companies like the Houston-based Tenneco (which acquired the massive and powerful Kern County Land Company in 1967 just prior to the introduction of state water) and Prudential Life Insurance (which invested in a substantial joint venture operation that focused on specialty crops like olives) defined their "farms" as land-development interests. The reduced price of water, established through the deal with MET, allowed these new investors to take risks and profitably engage in new plantings and expand existing acreage. The introduction of this new water supply, originally justified as a means to raise the level of the groundwater in the area and eliminate the problem of the overdraft, became the springboard for new irrigated production. Ironically, it extended, in the process, the very problem of overdraft.

13

By the mid-1970s, the land-development interests of Kern County and urban Southern California were pleased with this new system. Buoyed by the prospects of expanding markets, favorable tax laws, and an aggressive effort by the federal government to stimulate production and dominate international markets, the state's big water projects had helped expand California's form of industrialized agriculture into one of the biggest and most powerful industries in the state. Meanwhile, real estate and development interests in places like San Diego, Riverside, and Orange counties rapidly extended the parameters of growth in the region, made possible in part by the prospects of an unlimited water supply. The big water projects, it appeared, were capable of making such growth in California, already the equivalent of the world's seventh-largest country in terms of GNP, continuous and permanent.

"THE FINAL SOLUTION"

Earle Blais liked to call it "the final solution." By 1976, talk was in the air of building a Peripheral Canal, to lay the groundwork for sustaining the urban and agricultural expansion of Central and Southern California. During the late 1960s and early 1970s, the discussions about a Delta facility had stalemated. Ronald Reagan was governor in this period, and his administration was high on rhetoric but short on performance. Reagan and his leading water official, Bill Gianelli, the director of the Department of Water Resources that managed the State Water Project, were strong advocates of expanding the system to the Eel River, a process dependent on constructing a Delta facility. But Gianelli, with the concurrence especially of the agricultural contractors, was in no rush. The Kern landowners in particular had already borrowed heavily to put in their own local connecting systems in order to receive the State Project water.

The water industry advocates within the Reagan administration were also concerned with the growing political clout of a newly emergent and contentious environmental movement. Dam building was under attack for disrupting the environment and its potential to cause permanent damage to the free-flowing rivers of the north. The environmentalists had already scored one important victory in the early 1970s by stopping construction of the Dos Rios Dam in the north. Furthermore, they had successfully made common cause with Gianelli's adversary in the administration, Norm "Ike" Livermore, Reagan's secretary of resources, intensifying the conflict between the water development advocates and their critics.

By the time Governor Jerry Brown took office in January 1975, the pressures to construct a Delta facility had begun to mount once again. With agricultural production levels high, the local distribution systems in place, the possibility of further appreciation of the value of the land stronger than ever, and urban-development interests tied to MET still locked into their conception of future rapid growth, the water-industry coalition for expansion seemed as potent as ever.

And then came The Drought. The dry summer of 1976 turned into the even drier winter months of the 1976–77 rainy season, when the reservoirs are supposed to fill up again and the river flushes out the Delta on its way to the Bay. The problem became even more pronounced when the dry spell continued into the summer and fall, and the new director of the Department of Water Resources, a cautious and respected water lawyer named Ronald Robie, prepared to enforce the shortage-related provisions contained within the project contracts.

According to these contracts, MET was supposed to obtain all its water in the first year of a drought, while Kern and the other agricultural contractors were to have their deliveries cut back by 50 percent. But MET, despite the drought in the north, still had available an abundance of water sources. While the Sacramento River system was dry, the Colorado River system, MET's other major water supply, was not. As it turned out, MET was able to draw a substantial amount of water from the Colorado, well above what it had recently been receiving.

In the midst of the drought, MET, on request from Kern and the other agricultural contractors, agreed to give up its State Project water despite the contract provisions. MET then proposed a 10

15

percent across-the-board cutback within Southern California. This cutback was designed more for political than water supply purposes. Regional antagonisms in the dry north were as great as ever and MET knew those jealousies could undermine the campaign for a Delta facility.

Yet even with MET giving up its State Project supply, the agricultural contractors still needed to cut back as much as 45 percent of what they had formerly been receiving. Some of that amount had been in the form of cheap "surplus" water, as provided in the compromise deal with MET. As the system's largest user, Kern was particularly vulnerable to cutbacks.

For both Kern and Met, while the drought brought a scare, it also provided an opportunity. MET speakers immediately took to the hustings to transform the drought into a powerful weapon in the push for Blais's final solution—"the missing link" as it was referred to by the MET staff. A Delta facility, they argued, was essential if the south was to avoid in the future the traumas that Northern Californians were currently experiencing. The "missing link" was both insurance against shortages and assurance of future growth.

The concern about the drought in Kern also helped refocus efforts around a Delta facility. "The drought forced us to think about what might happen in a future drought," commented Gene Lundquist, a water-industry leader from Kern. "It brought us together after we had been fighting among ourselves over who would get the surplus water. We now knew we needed a long-term solution, and a Delta facility would unlock not only the State Project supply but ultimately the rivers of the north."

The drought set the stage for a new and fierce political debate not only regarding a Delta facility but over the future of water politics in the state. MET and the Kern landowners led the effort to create a powerful water-development coalition, while various other players, including the Delta farmers, environmental groups, and Northern California officials joined in the jockeying and maneuvering to influence legislation being considered by the state legislature. The water-development advocates emphasized the need for more water

16

exports to the central and southern parts of the state while the environmentalists and the northerners worried about further exports harming the Bay and Delta environments, including the fish population. The Delta farmers, meanwhile, were most focused on keeping the water flows *within* the Delta rather than *around* it through a Peripheral Canal. Water through the Delta was free water to these farmers who had banded together to form an effective lobbying bloc.

One of the keys to the debate was the evolving ambiguity of Jerry Brown. Along with a host of other western Democratic governors elected at the time, such as Colorado's Richard Lamm, Brown had been heavily backed by environmental groups. While his top water person, Ron Robie, had maintained ties with the water industry as an assistant to Assemblyman Carley Porter (of the Burns-Porter Act), his deputy, a biologist named Gerald Meral, had been a senior staff member of the Environmental Defense Fund, the leading environmental group monitoring the State Water Project.

Yet Brown avoided constituency pressures like the plague. Even environmental groups, including EDF, had problems sorting out Brown's agenda. On the one hand, the Brown administration seemed genuinely concerned with the problem of overdraft in the Central Valley, a condition that had been exacerbated in the drought. Brown advisors tentatively explored the possibility of a variety of groundwater management programs, partly to alleviate the overdraft. These programs required a system of controls to govern the use of the groundwater. Once such a system was installed, then water could be stored in the ground during the wet winter months, when there was more than enough for both the Delta and Bay environments as well as the agricultural interests south of the Delta. Then, during the dry summer months, these landowners could pump the water that had been stored; they would then need less imported water when the supply in the State Project was scarcer and the Delta and the Bay were most in need of fresh water flowing to the sea. Such an approach would also help the overdraft situation in the Central Valley by reducing over time the amount pumped from the ground.

The groundwater management program, however, was anathema to the agricultural interests. Already wary and mistrustful of Jerry Brown, they insisted that they and they alone would determine when and how much to pump. Such a decision, they insisted, had to be bound not by management objectives, but by economic factors—in other words, the cheapest way to do it. They invoked the fear of state intervention as a rallying cry throughout the Central Valley to mobilize against groundwater management and continue the push for a Delta facility and additional supplies.

Though nervous about Brown's nontraditional, anti-constituency political approach, the Kern and MET interests were still able to maneuver the governor into a position of supporting a facility and accepting the arguments for additional supplies. Like his father before him, Jerry Brown sought a version of distributive politics—something for everyone. But included in his package of trade-offs were some environmentally inspired caveats. Brown was not successful in adding provisions for mandatory groundwater controls, but he was able to issue an executive order on the subject of conservation, which kept the agricultural landowners' fears about groundwater management alive. Brown did get in some provisions that would make it tougher but not impossible to go after the Eel and the other wild and scenic rivers of the north. And he made the completion of a Delta facility contingent on the success of a series of fish screens. These were designed to protect the fish from being swallowed by the giant pumps of the State Project system.

The centerpiece, however, was the Peripheral Canal, the facility that received the most attention and generated the greatest controversy. It was to be built in three stages, taking the water from the Feather River in the north around the Delta to the pumps at the town of Tracy, at the base of the Delta. There the water would be pumped uphill into the Central Valley and on toward urban Southern California. For MET and the Kern landowners, this much-sought-after Delta facility represented the road to future expansion.

This package proposal was considered "the best anyone could get under the circumstances," as Jerry Meral later commented not only about the approach of a number of environmentalists but the water industry as well. Though the environmental movement had been strong enough to ward off earlier water-development proposals during the 1970s, several of its leaders in organizations like the Sierra Club felt some kind of water-development legislation was "inevitable." Furthermore, these groups worried about the changing political environment, symbolized by Ronald Reagan's strong campaign for the presidency. Brown's advisors, led by Meral, pushed hard on this theme of changing political times and were ultimately able to convince, at least at first, a significant number of environmental leaders to sign off on the package deal.

The water-industry groups were also divided over and uncertain as to how far to deal with Jerry Brown. Some water-industry leaders were convinced that the only way to accomplish water-development objectives was by eliminating or at least neutralizing environmental objections. Others were less inclined to accept any restrictions on water-development goals and opposed both the mitigation measures, such as the fish screens, or limitations on developing new supplies, such as the rivers of the north. But the coalitions put together by MET and the Kern landowners held long enough to pull in the votes the legislature needed for passage.

When Jerry Brown signed the Peripheral Canal legislative package into law in August 1980, he declared, in terms reminiscent of his father, that a new era was about to dawn for California. Expansion would be linked to environmental protection. The water industry could lock arms with environmentalists and a new consensus could emerge. "For the first time," Brown said at the signing ceremonies, "a water project already authorized is now constrained by a deep commitment to environmental values." But at the very moment that the Peripheral Canal package was being signed into law, forces were emerging to challenge this grab bag of tradeoffs. In the process, the water industry would be torn asunder, and the future terms of water politics, so carefully crafted for more than three generations, would be transformed.

STRANGE BEDFELLOWS

It was a strange gathering at the outset of what would be an even more unusual campaign. Seated around the table in a nondescript conference room at the Airport Marina Hotel in Sacramento in April 1981 was a motley crew, the constituent parts of the "strange bedfellow" coalition, the term Jerry Brown and the press used for the opponents of the Peripheral Canal. Lukewarm coffee in paper cups, half-eaten stale Danish, and long rambling memos and policy papers were strewn about. The tired and bleary-eyed coalition members warily heard one another out as an attempt was made to shape the campaign. The group had come together to discuss strategy for the forthcoming referendum. Just a few months earlier, the eight-hundred-thousand-plus signatures they had gathered had been filed with the secretary of state's office opposing the canal package, enough signatures to require a referendum to vote up or down the Peripheral Canal legislative package.

I was at the meeting as a newly installed member of the Metropolitan Water District board of directors, the only one of fifty-one directors opposed to the canal facilities. I was there with a contingent from Southern California, including water industry critic Dorothy Green. Tim Brick, a community activist in the area of resource politics who would later also become a member of the MET board, was there as well.

Seated across the way were a handful of environmentalists from the north, including Michael Storper, a Berkeley intellectual who was representing the environmental group Friends of the Earth. Storper specialized in explaining the intricacies and inequities of the State Project, and had calculated and quantified the subsidies in that system.

The two cochairs of the group were also from the north. Besides representing different constituencies and points of view, they had developed an intense rivalry and personal antagonism. The one who would emerge triumphant from this feud was Sunne McPeak, a supervisor from Contra Costa County. Sunne had already become an experienced infighter and had decided that water would be her political ticket. Her antagonist, Lorell Long, who considered herself a part of the environmental and public interest constituency, was equally prepared for battle. Their feud in the early stages of the campaign, which expressed itself in personal terms, masked some more significant differences that would emerge during the next several months.

At the head of the table sat two water lawyers from Stockton, both representing a variety of agricultural interests and water districts in the Delta. The two—Tom Zuckerman and Dante Nomellini— were quite different personalities but worked so closely together and overlapped so completely in points of view and campaign objectives that they came to be called, interchangeably, "Zuccolini." The Delta interests had been involved in the signature-gathering phase and had developed an uneasy but effective working alliance with the environmentalists from the north and the water industry opponents from the south.

This tentative alliance had been extended even further when McPeak and Zuccolini proposed bringing in two of the most powerful and free-spending agricultural interests in the state, the J.G. Boswell Company and the Salyer Land Company. The two companies had together established during the 1970s and early 1980s a political alliance in the various legislative battles around a Delta facility. After much hand wringing and soul searching (Boswell-Salyer after all had been most opposed over the years to any environmental measures such as groundwater management or the fish screens), the environmental/public interest group forces had agreed to the Boswell-Salyer participation. At this strange-bedfellows meeting, the Boswell-Salyer tandem was represented by John Sterling, a cagey, soft-spoken general counsel for Boswell, and John Penn Lee, a more flamboyant southerner who was vice-president of the Salyer company.

The Boswell-Salyer tandem had been a forceful presence within water industry politics for more than a decade. They were particularly adept at using campaign contributions as a tool to affect policy outcomes. "Money," John Sterling once commented, "makes politics." In one notable instance, Boswell-Salyer had used the power of political contributions to help block Delta-related legislation by influencing the votes of a couple of key Southern California legislators.

Their position was based on a series of gambles. They wanted no environmental conditions, no talk about groundwater management, and no interference with the water—free water—that flowed into the Delta where Salyer, for one, had land holdings. Since the Peripheral Canal would take water around the Delta rather than through the Delta, it would mean a reduction of the water available to the Delta interests. But even Boswell, with its substantial land holdings south of the Delta, only wanted a Delta facility without the environmental features of the canal package, even if they had to wait a while for it. Both companies felt that such "unrestricted" facilities would eventually come to pass, and they set out to block any compromise deal, even if it meant allying with their historic opponents.

The Boswell-Salyer group were also adept at playing this kind of "realpolitik" and they said as much to the people seated across the way at that Sacramento motel. It was an unbeatable combination they suggested to their longtime environmental antagonists: our money and your troops; our insider dealing and your credibility; our media and campaign consultants and your themes and issues. It was an offer hard to refuse. At the very next meeting of the finance committee of the anti-canal forces, the various interest groups each pledged to fundraise a certain amount. The northern environmentalists suggested one figure (fifty thousand dollars), the southern public interest grouping another (twenty-five thousand dollars), the Contra Costa representatives still another (one hundred thousand dollars), and so on. After everyone spoke, it was Boswell-Salyer's turn. John Sterling was there and he paused so that everyone would listen. "We'll do half," he said dramatically. "We'll match whatever the rest of you raise—all together." In fact, he would be true to his word, as Boswell-Salyer ultimately provided as much as 60 percent of the total—more than $3 million.

The Boswell-Salyer stance was just one of several calculated gambles that characterized this campaign. During 1979 and 1980,

22

Jerry Brown had met with various coalitions of the water industry, most especially the Consensus Group, which had been put together in part by Earle Blais and MET assistant general manager David Kennedy. The Consensus Group included nearly every representative of the water industry. The California Business Roundtable and the State Chamber of Commerce were involved, as were the Farm Bureau and various CVP agricultural interests. The Kern landowners were participants, as were various water district representatives, including those from the Delta. Even Boswell-Salyer had been involved in the coalition's early meetings but they soon dropped out. The two farm companies, in fact, had ultimately developed a reputation through their overt lobbying and maneuvering as the "peck's bad boy" of water industry politics.

By 1980, however, after the canal package had been successfully put together and passed the legislature, it appeared that Boswell-Salyer might have isolated themselves. Some water industry participants, such as the Farm Bureau, had been dubious about the deal with Jerry Brown, but had reluctantly gone along. But then MET joined Jerry Brown in campaigning for an environmental initiative providing protection for the scenic rivers of Northern California that appeared on the November 1980 ballot. Passage of the initiative had been a precondition of the Peripheral Canal legislative package becoming law. When the environmental measure narrowly passed, some of the agricultural interests began to have second thoughts. They had assumed that everyone in the water industry would oppose or at least remain neutral on these environmental provisions. Brown would then have to yield, they presumed, and go along with a less environmentally restrictive measure. MET on the other hand had decided that the deal with Brown was the best shot the water industry had to get a Delta facility, particularly since it was judged that Brown's compromise would, at the least, split the environmentalists or even bring them around to a position of support.

The environmentalists were at first badly divided. The leadership of the Sierra Club initially endorsed the package, as did a sprinkling of other groups. Brown appointee Gerry Meral became one of the most visible supporters of the canal package and continued to be effective in influencing environmental groups, especially their Sacramento lobbyists.

But the environmental constituencies would have none of it. On three successive occasions the Sierra Club membership over-ruled their executive committee and voted to oppose the canal. Groups like the League of Women Voters were sharply divided, but the anti-canal forces seemed more impassioned and ultimately in-fluential with the membership. Like the divisions in the water in-dustry, the environmental and public interest groups were hard pressed to find easy consensus.

It was in this setting that I, along with other strange bedfellows, plunged into the campaign. Those of us from the south—the south-ern opposition, as we were called—immediately landed on the lec-ture circuit, challenging the substantial and well-organized speaker's bureau and public information apparatus of MET. MET in fact had developed over the years what amounted to a powerful prop-aganda machine. Press releases would appear verbatim in dozens of newspapers, public officials would line up to endorse MET po-sitions, business organizations such as local chambers and Rotary Clubs would await the word on when to mobilize, and editorial writers eagerly anticipated the next pronouncement on such subjects as the likelihood of drought, Southern California's shrinking water supply, and the missing link.

To counter this MET juggernaut, the southern opposition, functioning a bit like a small guerrilla force behind enemy lines, questioned MET's assumptions about future shortages and pointed to the increasing costs of further development. Implicit in our po-sition was a different concept of the role and value of water in an urban setting, a different notion of priorities. While MET, through its various policies had stimulated expansion without evaluating costs or the nature of the development, we appealed to a powerful "slow growth" sentiment that had emerged even within a growth-oriented Southern California. We did this by discussing how to reshape the urban design. We talked about the needs of the inner city and not just new subdivisions on the edge of development, about the quality of life within the city rather than expansion at the city's limits. We also highlighted the difference between the water industry's position, which emphasized supply and the further construction of dams and ditches, and our position, which focused on the demand side of planning. We argued that the water industry had to fundamentally reorient its policies.

What became most striking to us during this period were the indications that MET's consensus bloc in the south was not mono-lithic. We discovered that audiences in the south were receptive, especially with respect to insider information about how the water industry operated. One revealing example was a thirteen-page memo that was to be circulated to Wall Street bond buyers at a 1981 bond buyers' conference. The bond buyers, of course, read the newspapers and the dire predictions of future drought and massive shortfalls if the canal were not built. What if you don't win the election, the bond buyers were likely to want to know? Would that mean trouble ahead? Such trouble, obviously, could also mean a lower bond rating. Have no fear, the MET bond buyers' memo answered, there will be no crisis. We have alternatives to the canal. Even more to the point, it went on, the district did not expect any shortfall for many years to come.

The bond buyers' memo instantly became the hottest item on the campaign circuit. The Northern California newspapers jumped at the chance to discuss it in front-page news articles and lead editorials. Even the *Los Angeles Times*, supportive of the canal in its editorial pages, and careful in its news pages to appear even-handed (given in part the conflict-of-interest charges stemming from the company's ownership interest in the Tejon Ranch, one of the biggest landowners in Kern County and a major supporter of the canal), ran a sidebar on the memo.

What made the bond buyers' memo so potent was the sharp contrast with the position put forth by MET and other proponents who insisted that shortages could be anticipated as early as 1985 and certainly by 1990 without the canal. MET had, in fact,

25

launched the Water Watch campaign during the summer of 1981, a $625,000 ad campaign used to continually reiterate the message of potential shortfall. The bond buyers' memo contradicted that public posture.

To make matters worse for MET, its spokesmen, such as Dave Kennedy, later dismissed the memo suggesting that it represented the mistaken assumptions of a staff member who had been rebuked. In fact, as the staff member, chief financial officer Gerald Lonergan, would later reveal, the memo was a collective product of MET staff. "I was brand new at the time," Lonergan later recalled. "When I got the bond buyers' questions, I farmed them out to people like Kennedy and others. These were the definitive responses. It was the party line. But then Earle [Blais] said it was no longer the party line and I was hung out to dry." Six months after the initial publicity on the memo and the charges and countercharges about it, an identical memo circulated among MET committees in preparation for another session with bond buyers. This memo had also been approved by top MET management, including Kennedy. When this memo was once again made public, it further disrupted MET's central strategy.

While the southern opposition was making headway in the south, the campaign, almost despite itself, was getting an even better response in the north. The opposition's formal campaign efforts in the north were relatively limited, despite the substantial suspicions and concerns in the community about the canal package. Much of the lack of organization could be attributed to the relative absence of ongoing grassroots activity among the environmental groups (many of whom were staff-based and relied more heavily on their lobbying, litigation, and technical expertise) or the activities of other opponents, such as the public officials like McPeak. Fishing and recreational groups were an exception: their large membership coveted the Delta as a scenic and waterway resource and they were deeply engaged in the anti-canal campaign.

Despite the uneven organizational focus, however, the enormous outpouring of interest and concern in the north was extraordinary. It could be felt in every setting, from talks at senior citizen groups or women's clubs, discussions on radio talk shows, or lectures at the establishment Commonwealth Club. The northern view that the Delta was a *local* resource was clearly one reason. The feelings about the Bay were equally intense, as was the residual mistrust of the south, a mistrust that dated back to the turn of the century.

But it wasn't just the concern for issues and the strong emotions that was striking about the campaign in the north. Unlike in the south, water had become a tangible and identifiable issue in Northern California, one that had entered the general political discourse, perhaps influenced by the experience of the 1976–77 drought that had affected the north much more severely than the south. People were not only knowledgeable about the issues, they constituted a kind of common information exchange, a pool of research, word-of-mouth speculation, and shared assumptions. It was a kind of populist outpouring, rejecting the presumption that only a limited handful of experts could reliably make decisions given the technical nature of the issue. It provided in its own way the most direct challenge of its decisions and orientation the water industry had ever experienced.

The outpouring of the north reinforced the more subversive elements of the campaign in the south that had also begun to challenge the anti-democratic bias of water policy–making. A common refrain by MET directors and their business allies in and out of the water industry was that an issue such as the Peripheral Canal was too complex, too important to be left to the public through an electoral device such as a referendum. This time, however, despite the formidable campaign machinery for the proponents in the south and their argument about relying on the experts and the public officials, the public was not entirely responding to all the buttons being pushed.

One poll undertaken by MET in this period showed that the major concern of Southern Californians was not the supply-oriented issues of drought and shortages but the quality of the water they were drinking. MET and the water industry as a whole were also beginning to lose some credibility because of the emphasis on supply. The exhortative nature of their appeal about a grim future without additional facilities, which had always worked in the past, was losing some of its edge. At one particularly memorable debate before an auto workers' group, one of the business leaders of Citizens for Water, the pro-canal campaign group, stung by the criticism of the prediction of future supply shortages, appealed to his audience: "Whom do you believe?" he asked his audience. "Are you prepared to dismiss what every elected official, every newspaper, every water agency, every business organization in Southern California is telling you?" he exclaimed. "Yes!" shouted several of the hard hats to the delight of the rest of the audience. Many of those auto workers might well have voted for the canal, but they no longer automatically concurred with the water industry perspective about the need for new facilities to accommodate growth.

As the campaign intensified, the opponents, despite their internal divisions, attempted to develop central themes to attack the canal. With McPeak allied with Boswell-Salyer and the Delta farmers, they sought to steer such themes toward an attack against Jerry Brown and the environmental compromises in the canal package. To that end, the Boswell-Salyer faction insisted that a pair of self-assured, media-oriented consultants named Sal Russo and Doug Watts, who had long-standing ties to agriculture and were beholden from the outset to Boswell-Salyer and their checkbook politics, be hired as campaign managers. Russo-Watts then hired Ronald Reagan's pollster, Richard Wirthlin and his Orange County polling firm DMI (Decision-Making Inc.), to check out voter attitudes.

The language of the poll questionnaire lent itself to the anti-Brown and anti-environmental message, but the results undercut that approach. Instead, voters in the north overwhelmingly talked of their environmental fears around the Delta and the Bay, and their mistrust of the south. And to everyone's surprise, there was more interest in the south on the cost, equity, and environmental issues. To win this campaign, as it was now abundantly clear, Boswell-Salyer and Russo-Watts had to adopt to an environmental and economic argument. Cost in the south and environment in the north were the obvious campaign themes. It was also clear from other aspects of the poll, as John Sterling had to admit at one meeting, that bashing away at corporate farmers in Kern County would likely win votes. "Bash away," Sterling declared, ready to finance a campaign that would include attacks against his one-time water industry compatriots.

Still, there were limits to how far the Boswell-Salyer/Farm Bureau grouping would go. By a certain point in the campaign, some of us from the southern opposition had become symbols of those limits. The more we hammered away at the theme of the water industry, the more uncomfortable our campaign allies became. And we also violated some rules of the traditional campaign game, by continually criticizing the strategies of our own allies like Boswell. This campaign has become a risk for all involved, we told audiences, since Boswell-Salyer's long-term goals (a Delta facility that would go through rather than around the Delta with no environmental restrictions) were substantially different from those of the various environmental and public interest groups. The same tension around goals could be said of the Jerry Brown/MET/Kern County tandem. Our allies in this campaign, we argued in public, were as dangerous as our adversaries.

Some of the meetings of the "executive committee of the strange bedfellows," as we began to call ourselves, were raucous indeed. I remembered a passage from Isaac Deutscher's biography of Leon Trotsky, when the mercurial Trotsky began negotiating a peace treaty with the Prussian generals at Brest Litovsk during World War I. While the generals mistrustfully eyed Trotsky, the irresponsible Bolshevik wagged his finger, looked the Prussians in the eye and began exhorting the German proletariat to throw off their shackles and stimulate an uprising as the only real way to end the war. The generals just looked on in amazement. And when some of us spoke of populist themes and of restructuring the water industry, we could see the bewilderment of these modern-day Prussians. At a critical juncture in the campaign, Boswell-Salyer, McPeak, and Russo-Watts engineered a coup, insisting some of us be taken off the executive committee of the opposition campaign structure.

This action, however, didn't change the thrust of the campaign and it never did stop the southern opposition. A key participant in this group, Tim Brick, not only remained on the executive committee but became the campaign manager for the campaign in the south. The southern group intensified its efforts and continued to find interested audiences and constituent groups, spending Boswell-Salyer's money in the process.

The campaign of the canal opponents reflected the substantial opening created by public input and continuing internal turmoil; the proponents' campaign was smoother but ultimately less effective. For one, there was never any substantial environmental input to the pro side, despite the deals with Jerry Brown. Brown immediately began to distance himself from his own compromise as he shrewdly perceived the populist overtones the campaign was generating. For months he dallied with the question of when to call the election for the referendum, finally deciding to place it on the June 1982 ballot, at the time of the next general election. That decision had a crucial impact on the outcome, for it allowed up to eighteen months of campaigning, a length of time that strengthened the grass roots character of the election. And, as the campaign heated up, Brown, who had decided to run for the Senate in 1982, made his distancing official by taking a neutral position on the referendum.

The pro side was also plagued with early overconfidence (there were, after all, more voters in the south), a defensiveness about the Boswell-Salyer incursions on water industry unity, and reliance on traditional methods of lining up the vote. The proponents in effect ran two campaigns: one unofficial campaign by the water agencies, led by MET (which was constrained by state law from advocating in an election), and another, official, campaign put together by such business interests as Newhall Land and Farming, the Irvine Company, the Kern-based oil companies like Getty and Shell, and utilities such as the Southern California Gas Company. This official campaign was slow in getting off the ground. It took a while to get their fundraising machinery in shape, in part because the business interests in the south felt the referendum could easily be defeated. While some money had been raised in the early stages, there was still a listlessness to the fundraising effort. It was only after Boswell-Salyer's big contributions began to surface, that a gas company executive, Robert McIntyre, was enlisted to undertake a more intensive fundraising drive.

To win the campaign had seemed a simple effort at first: line up the money, the endorsements, and the press. And the issues seemed equally simple: supplies are being cut off; growth, in order to continue unabated, requires more water. Without the canal and with the certainty of drought there will be shortages. Those arguments, it was felt, would not only get out the votes but create some passion about the subject in the south to match the passions being stirred in the north. A parallel campaign structure emerged: MET and the agencies out on the water industry speaker circuit, Citizens for Water getting the money to finance the media campaign.

Everything seemed to work smoothly for a while, and early polls indicated a victory for the proponents. But by early 1982, the early confidence first turned into fears about slippage and then incomprehension as the polls suggested that the canal package might be defeated. A sense of betrayal began to permeate the pro side's campaign, a feeling that voters in the south were not sufficiently believing the message about drought and the requirements for growth while those in the north had reached a point of no return in their opposition to this set of facilities.

The election results confounded everyone's expectations. In the south, the canal side pulled substantial majorities in San Diego (73 percent) but smaller percentages in Los Angeles, Orange, and Riverside counties (61, 62, and 59 percent, respectively). The canal package was even defeated in the Santa Barbara area where environmental sentiment was the strongest in the southern part of the state. But once north of the Kern County line, the percentages against the canal were phenomenal: San Francisco (95 percent), Marin (97 percent)—even Santa Clara, which was supposed to receive a share in the benefits (89 percent). The feelings in the north against the canal outstripped any previous margins recorded in a statewide initiative or referendum in California. All told, thirty-five counties in Northern California voted against the canal by majorities

31

of 90 percent or greater. It was not just a landslide (62 to 38 percent were the statewide totals) it was a catastrophic repudiation of the water industry's message of growth and expansion and method of distributive politics.

Within a week after the election, the MET board convened at its regular monthly session. The mood was less somber than puzzled. Board directors were not so much angry as a bit shaken. The results from the north were the immediate subject of hallway gossip ("even my brother-in-law from up there had been angry with me") and reflection. But there was a deeper anxiety, not directly articulated, about how to interpret the situation, what to do next, how to move on.

Within six months a series of storms would pass through the South Coast Basin, causing floods, short tempers (the infrastructure tends to break down when it rains in Southern California), and a water crisis caused not by too much use but by too few sales of imported water, generating insufficient revenues to pay for the high fixed costs of the State Project. Water issues would remain in the news the next few years, but less about supply issues and canals and a lot more about such things as drinking water quality, selenium-laden disfigured birds, or overdrafted groundwater basins in places like West Texas. There was a drought in 1985–86, the year Southern California was supposed to lose much of its Colorado River water to Arizona; this one, though, wasn't centered in Los Angeles, but twenty-five hundred miles away in New York City. That same year, several Kern County landowners, instead of talking about the rivers of the north, were seeking to *sell* some of their own water entitlements in the face of an agricultural crisis that had by then reached the industrialized farms of California. This activity continued even after consecutive dry years in California in 1987 and 1988 put talk about drought back on the front pages of the press. And even some environmentalists, once the scourge of the water industry, were talking about a new approach they called "the third wave" that would lead them back into negotiations with the water industry where a new set of deals would be arranged.

The water industry was in flux and you needed a scorecard to keep up with the players, old and new. The Peripheral Canal campaign of 1982 would eventually begin to fade although the water industry would continue to try—and fail—to obtain legislation for a Delta facility. The canal election, however, still provided an important demarcation point, one of several episodes that had served as a signpost. And it had provided me and others with an education, a rite of passage into an obscure and self-contained policy-making universe that had been made a little more visible, a little less divorced from its audience. That process of education continues today, though the policy outcomes remain unpredictable.

PART TWO

The Players

Chapter 2

Formation, Consolidation, and Challenge: The Water Industry in Transition

"SOLDIERS FOR AMERICA"

The speaker at the rostrum, thin, slight, yet intense in his manner and delivery, jabbed his finger toward the high ceilings of the Grand Ballroom and began to engage his water industry audience in what amounted to a kind of political evangelism. It was a special moment at a special conference: the fiftieth anniversary of the National Water Resources Association (NWRA), one of the more powerful water industry lobbying groups, with members from the seventeen states on the Pacific side of the 100th meridian. Over the years, NWRA had achieved semi-official status with the federal government's Bureau of Reclamation. Its annual meetings had become occasions for leading figures of the bureau, the Army Corps of Engineers, and key officials of the Interior Department—including, at times, the secretary—to give speeches, hold backdoor meetings, and renew ties.

The setting this year was the Hotel Utah in Salt Lake City on a crisp October day in 1982 just a few months after the Peripheral Canal election. It was an appropriate setting. Many a water deal had been cut in the Mormon-owned hotel, even prior to the creation of the Bureau of Reclamation in 1902. The forbidding and magisterial Brigham Young had held forth in these quarters during the heyday of the Great Basin Kingdom in the 1860s and 1870s, invoking the crucial role of water delivery systems in shaping the social organizations of the community. His was a powerful vision of cooperation and centralized authority, a kind of theocratic agriculturally based communism, where the ditch was commonly held and water rights segregated from individual ownership.

Now, a century later, another self-styled secular preacher was holding forth, telling of the accomplishments of the Reagan administration and the coming tasks for all. James Gauis Watt had been actively solicited as keynote speaker for the NWRA fiftieth anniversary. This was friendly territory for the Interior Secretary. He was about as close as one could get to being the administration's point man on water policy, chairing the President's Cabinet Council on Natural Resources as well as heading a department that played such a powerful role in western and national water-policy areas. Watt was speaking to a responsive and even solicitous group of water businessmen and agency officials, whose representatives had come to Washington in the winter of 1980 to join the legion of industry and special interest groups ready to anoint the Reagan administration as one of their own. Watt himself had been especially embraced for his identification with the cause of water development. And this beleaguered water industry, which had already made something of a comeback during the contentious Carter years, stood ready to be further revived.

The speech at the Hotal Utah seemed to fit the bill. "The battle is not yet over," Watt's voice rose and fell in cadence with each point made and gesture delivered. "We have struggled, clawed, and fought our way to where we are now. And it is sad therefore to see what we now have to confront." He began to focus on the enemies: environmentalists first and foremost, Congress, Democrats, and, generically, those "types who don't believe in water resource development." "Liberals don't believe in water resource development," Watt thundered. He spoke of the coming congressional elections as a referendum on whether the results would "turn us back to the anti-West, anti-water, anti-agriculture days," or instead ratify all the big changes he claimed the Reagan revolution had already brought about and would continue to make.

"You men and women in this room," Watt's hands reached out to his audience, "it is in your power to be soldiers for America." Ronald Reagan's America, Watt implored, joins those qualities of respect and vision for water resource development with faith in God. The enemies have decreed that there is no more political gain in water development; what we are battling, Watt concluded, are all those "who lack the vision for America in the twenty-first century."

It was a rousing speech, classic oratory that was part-political, part-religious, and pure vintage Watt. He got many cheers, and hundreds of delegates mingled afterward to shake his hand and tell him that their America did indeed coincide with his definition of America. Yet for all the crusading talk and its political combativeness, a tinge of malaise could be felt in the air. There was an uneasiness among the delegates, reflected in part by some of Watt's other remarks and the recognition that what Reagan and Watt had to offer was, as one Colorado water official put it, "a whole lot of rhetoric and almost nothing in terms of additional funding."

Watt had also heralded the "production and accomplishment" of the first two years of the Reagan administration in his speech, but he had indeed offered little by way of new projects or even any increase in the authorizations of the big water projects already under way, such as Utah's own Central Utah Project, the multibillion-dollar Garrison Project from North Dakota, or the Central Arizona Project. Watt was aware of the discontent: at times he angrily lectured his audience that even here he had received abuse from those who should be appreciative. But Watt had some explaining to do as well for such Reagan initiatives as cost-sharing on water projects and the absence of any new water projects. Don't blame us, he appealed, blame it on the deficit, which he claimed had been inherited from that assortment of enemies out to limit America's vision.

There was an uneasiness in the hall that day after Watt left the hotel and other speakers from the Reagan administration offered much the same upbeat rhetoric but limited possibilities of development. Here was a moment of triumph, a fiftieth anniversary celebration with an administration that had declared that the cycle of expansion through water development was once again in place. Yet at this moment of political confidence and self-congratulation, those enemies had not only regrouped, but the terms of the debate had begun to shift. The water industry delegates appeared a bit disoriented, caught between this expectation of continuing water development raised by Watt and the changing realities represented in part by his administration's confusing policy signals. Nevertheless, the delegates went about focusing on business as usual. The same resolutions were passed, as they were year in and year out, the same deal-making was taking place over cocktails, the tours for the spouses were once again arranged. Something, however, was out of sync, and it wasn't clear whether this disjuncture was just a passing phase.

THE ROLE OF THE FEDS

Since its emergence in the nineteenth century, the water industry has primarily functioned as a *local* center of power. It has represented regional agricultural and urban interests and attempted to promote the expansion of those interests through water development projects. As irrigated agriculture increased in scale and the cities grew in size, the water industry turned to the federal government as a source of capital and the construction and engineering resources necessary to sustain that expansion. The history of water politics, then, has primarily involved that interplay between local interests and the federal agencies who became instrumental in shaping the structure of water development as we know it today.

The two key agencies within the federal government in the area of water development have been the Army Corps of Engineers and the Bureau of Reclamation. They have primarily served as an economic resource, establishing programs in such areas as irrigation, trade, commercial development, power generation, flood control, and navigation, among others. Though other agences such as the Soil Conservation Service have played a modest role in water development, it has been the Big Two, the corps and BuRec, who have become the central players in federal water policy.

Mammoth agencies in terms of their staff size and annual appropriations, the Big Two have initiated and controlled vast programs that became essential to certain regional interests in the country, most especially in the South and the West. By the scope of their activities and relationship to their local constituents, these agencies, along with the local beneficiaries and their congressional supporters, came to constitute the water industry on the national level.

The Army Corps of Engineers is one of the more intriguing agencies of government, a national bureaucracy with extensive local ties, a professional engineering group with a nonprofessional mode of decision making. Established in 1802 as an engineering body with both military and civilian functions, the corps, housed in the Department of the Army, was the premier construction agency of government through the nineteenth and much of the twentieth centuries. As a military unit, the corps, both in wartime and peacetime, has been involved in a vast range of military-oriented engineering projects, from constructing barracks and bridges to seaports and airstrips. In its civilian duties, where it became best known, the corps was on the front lines of government-subsidized economic development, from maintaining the navigational channels of the Mississippi, to the construction of the locks on the Erie Canal, to the dredging of channels in nearly every major river system east of the 100th meridian.

The corps became particularly adept at expanding its base of operations. As early as 1824, when Congress stipulated that the corps should enter the navigational area, to as late as 1972 when the Clean Water Act stipulated that the corps be the agency responsible for reviewing and issuing permits in wetlands areas, the corps has been assigned an increasing range of jurisdictions and activities. More than any other agency, it became, through its long and extensive ties with key congressional committees, associated

41

with the concept of the pork barrel, linking local interests with federal programs.

Through much of the nineteenth century, the corps's activities covered a wide geographical area, though it was heavily involved in particular regional activities, such as development on the Mississippi. In its first century, however, it played a limited role in the promotion of irrigable acreage. It serviced farmers of the South and parts of the Midwest by establishing new markets through enlarging the transportation corridors on the big river systems, but not through extensive water development programs such as storage or flood control. As commercial and industrial interests began to look West, however, the corps's approach was seen as inadequate by western representatives and irrigation advocates interested in establishing a new water development agency. The Colorado River, the central river system of the arid West, was hardly navigable—countless expeditions from the 1860s to the turn of the century had already discovered that. Yet if the West were to be settled—a key policy of the federal government in the Civil War and post–Civil War era—then a thriving system of agriculture had to be established. In states like Colorado, Utah, Arizona, and California that meant a system of irrigation.

During the last quarter of the nineteenth century, a complex and multifaceted irrigation movement emerged in the West, seeking to define the terms of development and the forms of government intervention necessary to sustain that development. Key economic forces such as the railroads, mining, banks and other financial institutions, budding agricultural communities, and a variety of other commercial and industrial groups, promoted their notion of how to organize and control the flow of water.

Debates over development focused on three contrasting approaches to the land and the water: cooperative; private; and one that sought a public/private partnership. The cooperative model was primarily associated with the Mormon farming communities of the Great Basin Kingdom, especially the communitarian United Orders that flourished in the 1870s and 1880s. Though championed for a time by the western explorer John Wesley Powell as the most appropriate model for the Colorado River Basin, the Mormon experiment was severely undermined by the federal government as part of its larger campaign to rid the West of this autonomous and alternative society. The Mormons, their economic assets seized and their social organizations disrupted, never did link up with other radical and populist movements of the time, and ultimately came to terms with the larger society by accepting the dominant mode of capitalist social and economic organization.

The concept of private ownership and development was widely adopted by the great majority of settlers who arrived in the West ready to transpose their eastern ways onto the land and the water. Various legislative efforts to encourage western settlement, beginning with the Homestead Act of 1862 and the Desert Land Act of 1877, reinforced the patterns of land speculation and trade in water rights based on the assumption of private ownership. Speculation was particularly rife in the 1870s and 1880s, with the federal programs resembling massive giveaways, contributing to attempts to monopolize the land and control the water.

It soon also became clear, by the turn of the century, that throughout the arid West, the land was considered worthless without the water, either for irrigation or even urban subdivision. Getting the water to the land did not involve simply laying an irrigation ditch or drilling a well. Diversion projects were more complex and costly. The strongest promoters of rapid development, particularly the railroads who held title to much of the land not owned by the federal government, were keenly aware of the economic costs of subsidizing western irrigation or urban settlement. The National Irrigation Congresses of the 1890s, led by the railroads and including both populist and expansionist advocates, became the champions of public intervention and partnership with local private entities. If the federal government could finance the construction of the dams and ditches and subsidize the terms of repayment, the West would boom. Irrigated agriculture would make possible the development of new population and commercial centers, which in turn would create new markets for a potentially expansive farming economy. With the passage of legislation establishing the new Reclamation

43

Service in 1902 (later the Bureau of Reclamation), the coalition of forces that pushed for its passage and now dominated the West eagerly anticipated the results.

From the outset, the Reclamation Service, unlike the more eastern- and southern-oriented corps, saw itself as an agency with a mission. In its first twenty years, it rapidly established itself as a powerful force in western development, constructing a number of water development projects from Wyoming to Arizona, and beginning to survey possible future sites. Wrapped in the cloak of populism (because of a provision in its charter that allowed it to serve only those landowners who held title to 160 acres or less), BuRec became the advocate and champion of irrigation as a social force. Various popular movements in the West saw the creation of the Reclamation Service and the consolidation of irrigation as a means of establishing the underpinnings of a new society at once democratic and expansionist.

The bureau, however, was immediately beset by contradictory impulses in carrying out this mission. Limited to operating in the seventeen states west of the 100th meridian, the bureau from the outset was heavily influenced by local economic interests who benefited from bureau projects. Its head planning office was located in Denver. Most of its division chiefs heading up regional offices were westerners who had been born and raised on western farms before becoming engineers. The bureau's social purpose, furthermore, was immediately compounded by two early features that influenced its mode of operation. First, the bureau was dominated by its engineers, who soon developed a kind of cult of expertise that narrowed the sources of public input and influence on its policies. Second, the bureau's policies regarding the terms of repayment provided generous subsidies to local beneficiaries while at the same time it expanded its constituency from small farmers to larger landowners and eventually, by the 1930s, expanding metropolises.

Almost from the outset, bureau officials became intertwined with various local interests, and ultimately came to be perceived as an extension of the locally based water industry. In the early years of maneuvering between the City of Los Angeles and the farming interests of the Owens Valley over the construction of the Los Angeles Aqueduct, for example, the Reclamation Service became rife with conflict-of-interest problems. A bureau employee, J.B. Lippincott, who represented himself as a federal agent to Inyo farmers, was secretly on the payroll of the Board of Water Commissioners of the City of Los Angeles, which was then actively acquiring land and water rights along the Owens River in hopes of controlling the water source for the aqueduct it wanted to build. The bureau ultimately sided with Los Angeles, the more powerful party in that dispute, which had argued that since more people would be able to use the water, there would accrue a greater set of benefits by constructing such an aqueduct and foregoing development of the thinly populated Owens Valley.

In its desire to ring the Colorado River and its tributaries with storage facilities and distribution systems, BuRec explicitly stretched the definition of its small farmer constituency to include both urban centers and larger landowners. In the space of five years between 1933 and 1938, BuRec exempted from acreage restrictions two major service areas: the Imperial Valley in California and the Colorado Big-Thompson area on the eastern slope of the Continental Divide. These decisions were made by others—Hoover's secretary of the interior in the case of Imperial and Congress in relation to the Colorado—but they were part of a larger shift taking place, transforming BuRec's mission into one of partnership with an aggressive and increasingly self-confident western water industry.

These changes in BuRec were obscured for a time by other considerations that shaped its agenda, especially its "public works" function in providing employment during the Depression. During the 1930s, BuRec projects such as Grand Coulee Dam in Washington were heralded as serving primarily a social purpose in stimulating local economies and creating jobs in the severely depressed Pacific Northwest and other western regions. During the 1940s, BuRec continued to maintain some of its social reformer reputation as the 160-acre issue flared up once again, this time with respect to the Central Valley Project in California. BuRec was bitterly attacked in Congress in this period by legislators either beholden to the large landowning interests in California or conservatives who saw an opportunity to attack the New Deal and its aftermath. In one striking incident, legislation was passed in 1947 taking away the pay of the Reclamation Commissioner and the head of the Bureau's regional office in California as punishment over the 160-acre conflict. BuRec also locked horns on a couple of occasions with the army corps over jurisdictional battles, with large landowning interests and conservative critics touting the corps as the "apolitical," more accommodating agency for the local interests.

While these battles received press and public attention, the BuRec was quietly strengthening and extending the reach of water development in alliance with its erstwhile antagonists among the water industry. Its pricing policies, aggressive plans for development, and overall thrust toward construction of new facilities were far more significant in the long run than the more highly charged debate around acreage restrictions for federally reclaimed water. By the 1950s, the bureau had effectively lost any pretense at social reform, as it comfortably settled into its role of project dispenser and its regional offices came to be influenced by powerful elites at the local level. These relationships were particularly developed in California where irrigated agriculture had become a major power in the state and bureau expenditures were most extensive. Though still locked in occasional bureaucratic conflict, the bureau and the corps now resembled each other in both definition and scope of activity. The two federal agencies were motivated in part by the engineering bias that dominated their activities and partly by the complex relationships they had established with both their funding sources and their constituencies. The Corps and the bureau had become as much a functioning participant in the water industry as its financial underwriter.

THE IRON TRIANGLE

At the heart of the system of water development throughout much of the twentieth century, both east and west, has been the Iron

Triangle. This three-way interlocking network of interests—Congress, the water agencies, and the local water industry groups—held sway over several generations of water projects. It was difficult to buck the system: annual appropriations were rarely established on the basis of project merit, let alone evaluated on anything but the narrowest and frequently manipulated definition of cost-benefit analysis. Instead, projects were most often selected on the basis of who had the clout to make it happen: a local congressional figure, a member of the House or Senate appropriations committees, local water-industry representatives, or industrial or agricultural groupings with the political and economic muscle to initiate the process of project approval.

The Iron Triangle system especially dominated the authorization and funding for the projects of the army corps. As far back as 1901, a water development lobbying group, led by Mississippi River interests, was established to monitor and promote corps projects. This National Rivers and Harbors Congress consisted of local business and political figures, contractors, trade and industry bodies, key members of Congress (who were honorary members of the group), and corps officers (who were ex-officio participants). The group was especially supportive of the corps and actively blocked any attempts to diminish its power and independent relationship with congressional and water industry backers. The rivers and harbors lobbyists would initiate and pass judgment on projects even before they were introduced in Congress or formally reviewed by the corps. The corps would then evaluate each project, mindful of the position of both the lobbying interests and of various members of Congress and their committees. Legislation would subsequently be introduced as part of an omnibus public works bill. Much of the time, these bills primarily contained continuing authorizations with a handful of "new starts." Many congressional districts, particularly those whose representatives sat on key committees, would have their own particular projects included. The system worked so effectively that at its heyday in the early 1960s, the chairman of the House Appropriations Committee would boast that "every state and practically every congressional district" was included in that year's bill. "There is something here for everybody," the chairman boasted, "and no project of merit has been omitted."

This was "pork barrel" politics in its most blatant form, a system so effective that the Iron Triangle became, in effect, a "subgovernment." Through the first six decades of the twentieth century, the selection, funding, and construction of the corps's projects was thoroughly dominated by the Iron Triangle. Once a project made its way through the early screening by lobbyists, their corps allies, and key congressional figures, it was rarely attacked on the floor of Congress. An unspoken rule called "logrolling" was established: Thou Shall Not Attack a Project from Another District. Conversely, a legislator was able to demonstrate effective district work by pointing to the authorization and construction of a locally based project. The threat to deny such projects became a powerful political weapon. It was used liberally, for example, by Lyndon Johnson, who delighted in twisting a legislator's arm by suggesting that spending levels for a favored dam in a legislator's district might well reach the budget cutting room floor unless LBJ's own program was supported.

Corps projects were also notorious in their range of subsidies and lack of management controls. They invariably favored a structural or engineering approach to a nonstructural policy (for example, the use of dams rather than zoning to manage flood-plain areas). Cost-benefit criteria, which were imposed on the corps at the height of the Depression in 1936, were frequently manipulated so that benefits would exceed costs, a precondition for project authorization. Projects were selected through the Iron Triangle processes and only afterward justified through cost-benefit analysis. The corps was able to inflate the benefit side of the ratio by using extremely low inflation indexes for construction costs and other expenses, adding in recreation benefits that were then quantified, and generally exaggerating various project benefits. The corps was particularly egregious in overestimating the benefits of their flood control, navigation, and hydroelectric projects.

Up through the 1940s and early 1950s, the corps remained the

favored agency among local interest groups, even with some westerners. The corps had a lower discount rate for its interest payments
than the Bureau of Reclamation and had a liberal cost-sharing
formula that provided substantial financing by the federal government in several areas, like the construction and operation of reservoirs, navigation projects, and flood control facilities. Congress,
furthermore, provided only a cursory review of the "feasibility" of
the corps' projects prior to their initial authorization, which helped
smooth the way for logrolling. But the bureau was still the force to
reckon with in the West, and by the time Floyd Dominy, a sharp-
tongued, hard-boiled BuRec veteran assumed the mantle of commissioner in 1959, the relations with local interests and various
western lobbying groups such as NWRA had become quite close.

This was particularly true of the bureau's ties with the agricultural interests of the Central Valley in California where relations
between the federal bureaucracy and the locals had not always been
cordial. The CVP had originally been conceived during the late
1920s as a state financed and operated system. The Central Valley
landowners were wary of the bureau, its 160-acre provision, and
social mission, and were convinced a state-run system would more
effectively serve their needs.

Legislation authorizing the Central Valley Project was passed
in 1933, in part because it could be justified as a vast employment-
oriented public works bill. But the lack of funds within the state
treasury ultimately shifted the project to Washington. Federal authorization was similarly conceived in public works terms, and the
first $20 million allocated for the project came from the Federal
Emergency Relief Appropriations Act of 1935.

While the local landowning interests fretted about New Deal
reformers intruding on their turf, the bureau in fact had already
undergone a crucial change in certain operational features. By the
mid-1930s the bureau had effectively abandoned its requirement
that the lands which benefited from bureau projects should bear the
costs of reclamation. The early subsidies such as interest-free repayment—initiated as a mechanism to encourage small family farm
settlement in the West—were now expanded to include what be-

came known as the power subsidy. The rapidly expanding power component of bureau projects such as Hoover Dam provided an enormous revenue base to help defray overall project costs.

The focus on power was also linked to a second major change in bureau policy: the delivery of water and power to cities as well as farms. The inclusion of cities in bureau projects both established a new constituency for bureau projects and added a new dimension to the repayment picture. This third major change in bureau policy—the costs of irrigation were no longer to be exclusively assumed by farmers—laid the groundwork for a major shift in the impact of reclamation. Whereas bureau projects in the first couple of decades of the Reclamation Service were crucial because landowners or irrigation districts could not come up with the capital to finance construction of projects, now bureau projects were also attractive because they had become a source of substantial subsidies.

The 160-acre battles in the 1940s obscured this shift for a time. When the first stage of the CVP was completed with the construction of Shasta Dam in 1944—hastened in part by the war-related requirements for additional power—local landowners had begun their protracted battles with the bureau over interpretation of the 160-acre law. California congressmen linked to these landowners introduced legislation exempting CVP from the acreage limitation, similar to earlier exemptions in the Imperial Valley and Colorado Big-Thompson projects. New Dealers in Congress, with support from the bureau, successfully resisted these attempts and the landowners ultimately shifted their strategies to maneuvering around the law. A variety of techniques were successfully employed by large landowning interests such as DiGiorgio and the Southern Pacific to maintain their holdings either through phony leases, deceptive sales, and promises about divesting holdings that were never kept. By the time the second stage of the CVP was completed in 1951 with the construction of the Friant-Kern and Delta-Mendota canals, the bureau and the farmers had begun to bury the hatchet.

Through the 1950s and early 1960s those ties were cemented when certain key congressional figures from the Central Valley such as Bizz Johnson and Bernie Sisk became major power brokers in the House and advocates of bureau projects, especially in California. In the early 1960s, with Sisk, Johnson, and key valley Congressman John McFall leading the way, the bureau had proposed and had authorized a key addition to the CVP: the provision of water as well as construction of a drainage system for the area served by the powerful new Westlands Water District in Fresno and Tulare counties in the heart of the Central Valley.

The bureau's relation with Westlands came to symbolize the triumph of the Iron Triangle with respect to this western-oriented and socially conceived bureaucracy. Westlands became at once the largest and most powerful water district in the country whether measured by irrigated acreage or total water use. Westlands landowners—some of the largest in California, such as the Salyer Land Company—were notorious violators of the 160-acre provision, violations that the bureau now greeted with a wink of the eye. These "paper farmers," as one seminal *San Francisco Examiner* article characterized these landowners, placed new lands in irrigation, often planting such crops as cotton, which were chronic surplus crops. The key to the operation in Westlands was the bureau commitment to build a drain that would remove highly saline and contaminated runoff (which could not drain effectively in the Westlands soil) and eventually transport it to the Delta and San Francisco Bay.

During the 1970s and 1980s, the Westlands drain became a cause célèbre among critics of the bureau. They accused the bureau of doing the bidding of the local landowners and their congressional allies and questioned the policy's environmental impact. The ecological disaster at the Kesterson Wildlife Refuge, where the drain had been temporarily located, heightened those criticisms. Images of deformed and dying wildlife, caused by concentrated levels of selenium resulting from the contaminated run-off, placed both the bureau and Westlands on the defensive. The bureau was charged with negligence and a possible intentional disregard of the seriousness of the problem.

At the core of the criticisms were the cozy relationships the bureau had established with Westlands and other local water interests. These close ties, characterized in part by a revolving door between Westlands and bureau and Interior Department officials, was a central component of the Iron Triangle system that had already become firmly established during the Dominy period of the 1960s.

The Dominy years also saw the consolidation of this new definition of bureau projects as sources both of construction capital and subsidized water. In a 1968 article for a trade publication, Dominy touted the value of bureau projects, not for underwriting small family farms but as the promoter of a subsidized irrigated agriculture in the West dominated by large farms and, increasingly, a corporate structure of ownership. Bureau-sponsored agriculture, Dominy boasted, has meant "new farms, new jobs, and increased production." Blasting bureau critics, especially those who critically analyzed cost-benefit ratios of the bureau projects, Dominy trumpeted that it was "fortunate that progress was not held in check while economists debated over the refinements of economic evaluations."

The period from the 1940s to the late 1960s represented the triumph of the Iron Triangle and of an approach that emphasized grand solutions and big projects as the bureau contribution to the long-term water needs of the West. But while Dominy was boasting of the bureau's successes in his December 1968 excoriation of his critics on the role of irrigation, these very same critics were becoming more effective at challenging the policies of both the bureau and the corps. The era of the Iron Triangle was ready to give way to a new period where the rationale for water development seemed to lose its force and new questions about quality, environmental consequence, and economics were coming to the fore.

LAST OF THE BIG PROJECTS

Today, even water industry figures call them "dinosaurs," but during the 1950s and 1960s, projects conceived under the Iron Triangle system were considered and justified as essential prerequisites for local regional growth. Though there were a fair number of small projects linked to specific needs like flood control or small-scale irrigation, the post–World War II period witnessed the design of some of the largest, costliest, and subsidy-laden water development projects ever conceived. It was in this period that the bureau came up with plans to regulate and capture the entire flow of the Colorado River. It wanted to ring the Colorado River Basin states with dozens of dams, canals, and hydroelectric plants to serve agriculture and, increasingly, urban centers. The army corps, similarly, had focused on major river systems, especially the Mississippi, where its construction plans would have major impacts on the wetlands, river flow, parks, archeological sites, and large land areas throughout the country, and especially in the South.

This was the era of such projects as Tennessee-Tombigbee, North Dakota's Garrison, the Central Arizona and Central Utah projects, and Glen Canyon Dam in the Four Corners area of the Southwest—projects that were breathtaking in their scope, and, as critics charged, devastating in their costs and impacts. To get these projects authorized was no longer a simple matter, despite powerful congressional support, water industry coalition lobbying, and the continuing legacy of growth-oriented policy-making. To the arguments around cost-benefit ratios were added arguments over environmental impacts. The key battlegrounds were shifting to questions about whether to build projects in scenic areas affecting parks or wild flowing rivers, with the disputes becoming increasingly difficult to resolve.

Still, most of the projects got through, with some trade-offs and modifications. For example, the package of Upper Basin Colorado River projects, authorized in 1957 as the Colorado River Storage Project, required one significant change: the elimination of a dam in the Dinosaur National Monument at the intersection of Utah, Colorado, and Wyoming. The campaign to save Dinosaur brought together for the first time in the post–World War II period a national mobilization of conservationists and citizen groups who had no direct economic stake in the outcome. These groups effectively contested the plans of the water industry and its system of distributive politics and economic trade-offs, highlighting in the process the narrow, wasteful, and self-interested character of water development. The water industry, however, was still able to successfully maneuver to replace the power production and revenues from Echo Park Dam slated to be built at the Dinosaur National Monument. In its place, Glen Canyon Dam, near the Arizona/ Utah border, was enlarged, becoming the primary hydroelectric facility and source of project revenue. Water industry critics, such as Sierra Club executive director David Brower, accepted this modification as a way to save a national park. But those who knew the little-explored Glen Canyon area were outraged at the critics' accommodation, and Brower, in a powerful self-criticism, later vowed to never sacrifice a "scenic resource" again.

During the early and mid-1960s, criticism of the big water projects became more extensive. During most of this period the water industry maintained the upper hand, however, helped out in part by the continuing dominance of regional coalitions of agricultural, industrial, and development interests setting the growth agendas in their areas.

In the battles around the big projects, the water industry was able to rely on regional factors: drought in the Northeast, economic decline in the South, agricultural expansion in the Plains States, boom conditions in the Southwest and the Mountain States, and the emergence of California as a national and international power, with its vast export-oriented agriculture and expanding urban megalopolises. Each of those regional factors became an incentive for water development. And while the critics of the big water projects were able to either postpone authorization (Garrison), slow down construction schedules (Tennessee-Tombigbee/Central Utah Project), or modify the package of projects (Central Arizona Project), the need for water development still seemed to set the parameters of debate.

Even when the debate became contentious, the terms essentially remained the same, such as the highly charged conflict during the mid-1960s over the bureau's package of facilities that included as its centerpiece the long-sought Central Arizona Project. To get the CAP authorized, project backers needed to accommodate two quite different sets of players: other water industry interests who wanted to include additional facilities or exclude certain aspects of the package, and water industry critics, led by the Sierra Club, who were particularly outraged at one aspect of the legislation: a plan to build a hydroelectric plant in the Grand Canyon.

The dealings among the different regional interests once more required the fine art of distributive politics. Colorado interests, championed by the chairman of the House Interior and Insular Affairs Committee, Wayne Aspinall, were able to obtain a series of additional dams, including one, the Animas–La Plata project in southwestern Colorado, that during the 1970s and 1980s came to symbolize expensive bureau projects with shifting objectives. California, the nemesis of Arizona in their competition for Colorado water, became willing, after a defeat in the courts on the division of the river, to revise its long-standing attempts to prevent passage of the legislation. In offering to do so, the California delegation obtained a provision that Arizona and not California would take the first cut when shortfalls on the river occurred. Finally, Pacific Northwest interests, led by the chairman of the Senate Natural Resources Committee, Washington Senator Henry Jackson, added language in the bill that forbade the bureau from even studying for at least ten years the idea of transferring water from the water-rich Northwest to the water-short Southwest.

These trade-offs occurred behind the scenes, far removed from the public eye. Not so with the battle over the Grand Canyon dam. The Sierra Club and its allies, mindful of the Glen Canyon deal they now regretted, launched a massive public campaign. They ran newspaper ads, undertook organized letter-writing efforts, and traveled on the media circuit to save what they considered the greatest scenic resource of all.

For a brief period, the campaign resembled a war. The Sierra Club lost its federal tax-exempt status, which in turn brought about an enormous public response in the form of donations and memberships. The bureau and its allies at first refused to budge. The issue was power generation and the revenues it generated to subsidize the project. Without a major hydroelectric facility the project could become too costly for the beneficiaries. Interior Secretary Stewart Udall, an Arizona loyalist who had served in Congress representing the Tucson area, was concerned about the conservationist campaign. Udall, who had a reputation as a strong supporter of wilderness and had helped put together the 1964 Wilderness Act, eagerly sought a compromise. But conservationists, bolstered by the growing signs of opposition to the water industry's agenda, had adopted a position of no compromise over scenic resources, the core of their concern.

The Interior Secretary finally settled on an ingenious solution. Instead of locating the dam in the Grand Canyon the bureau would opt to participate—in order to obtain the power—in expanding the Mojave coal-fired plant serving several southwestern and California utilities. The conservationists tacitly accepted the plan since the Grand Canyon had been saved and no river system was involved; instead the coal mining and power plant were located in the desert area of the Four Corners region in Indian territory. It was another deal the conservationists would later regret, but at the time it enabled the water package to pass in Congress in 1968. And it became, having exhausted the art of distributive politics, the last of the big deals.

In the maneuvering for the CAP facilities, water industry critics were able to add a provision establishing a National Water Commission. This proposal had been linked to the ban on studying any water transfer from the Northwest. The commission was to review issues of water development and, it was hoped, set the terms for the future water agenda. There had been other water commissions authorized by Congress in the recent past, including the Senate Select Committee on National Water Resources, established in 1959, and the Water Resources Council, originally set up as an ad hoc cabinet committee and then given statutory power through legislation in 1965.

These earlier water councils had basically expanded on the traditional water industry approach: anticipated supply shortages required additional development. This included an increased focus on interbasin transfers—transporting water from one river system to another. The two councils were also interested in greater efficiencies in water development, increased secondary water treatment to protect water supplies, and a more pronounced engineering rationality to the projects, all of which was intended to reinforce water development objectives.

The National Water Commission was designed, however, in a somewhat different manner. Its review was to be more inclusive than that of the previous commissions. The staff selected for the NWC were drawn from the growing ranks of water-related academics in the fields of political science, economics, and resource planning, many of whom had already focused on the inefficiencies and negative "externalities" of traditional water development projects. Efficiency in fact became the byword of the National Water Commission study, taking the concept a significant step further than the earlier commissions.

The NWC analysts for one were strongly critical of interbasin transfers. They drew on economic arguments to advocate nonconstruction-oriented solutions to future water supply requirements. They showed how the big projects, with their vast array of subsidies, bred marginal users. They advocated a number of different approaches, such as a change in pricing policies and the creation of "markets." These in turn could help reallocate existing supplies, benefiting primarily urban areas most in need of new sources.

The National Water Commission Report was published in 1973 without much fanfare and attention, particularly from the water industry. Its comments about "inefficiencies" were duly noted but never acted on. Yet the report provided an interesting commentary on the state of water policy and its shifting focus. Commission staffers were able to point to a whole set of issues largely ignored by the water industry that were nevertheless finding their way onto the water agenda. These included environmental concerns such as "instream uses" designed to protect free-flowing rivers as scenic and recreational resources. They also included a group of problems that fell under the category of "water quality." These ranged from drinking-water standards to polluted lakes and rivers. The report, while pointing to the growing concerns around quality, was also critical of the inefficiencies in the existing water pollution regulations.

These concerns, including the environmental and pollution

issues, were being raised by a different and more forceful set of constituencies who had joined the attack against the plans of the federal bureaucracies and the water industry. By the 1970s, the water industry would no longer be able to control the agenda. The politics of water, focused now on the annual budgets of the big federal agencies and the pace of construction, became more contentious than ever. The Iron Triangle system was not nearly as effective in pushing through legislation or keeping the budgets of the bureau and the corps intact. Water policy was beset by uncertainties. The next decade, called by some the Environmental Decade, would force the water industry into a broad and extended retreat.

THE WATER INDUSTRY IN TURMOIL

The period between 1970 and 1974 witnessed an extraordinary outpouring of new legislation with an "environmental" focus. These included key bills, such as the Clean Water Act and the Safe Drinking Water Act, that addressed water issues. This and other environmentally oriented legislation reflected the growing recognition that water quality and environmental protection were fast surpassing supply issues as a public concern.

Yet water supply issues remained an area of contention. Long-standing projects of both the bureau and the corps, most of which were authorized and many just in their initial stage of construction, came to be challenged. A number of new environmental groups immediately became players in the water debates over quality and supply. Although this newly restructured environmental movement was in part an outgrowth of activity and protest on the community level, much of the focus of the nationally based environmental organizations—both new and old—centered on Washington.

To the water industry and the federal agencies, this new environmental focus appeared to question and contest the very basis of water development activity since the turn of the century. The environmental organizations, empowered by court interpretations of such key legislation as the National Environmental Policy Act,

58

actively incorporated litigation as a tool to complement their legislative initiatives. Instead of accepting the parameters of the debate around water development and the pressure to accommodate and compromise as the earlier conservationist groups had done, the new environmentalism appeared at first to be adversarial and uncompromising. In the eyes of the water industry, the new environmentalists of the 1970s seemed determined to delay or kill outright all the projects that had been so central to the agenda of development.

The environmentalists were not the only problem for the water industry. Many of the projects were becoming increasingly costly, particularly in the highly inflationary 1970s. At the same time, annual expenditures for the bureau and the corps were being more closely scrutinized, both by the administration and Congress. In the Nixon and Ford periods, the Office of Management and Budget, which had at times, in earlier years, cast a somewhat critical eye on the water development projects, became more assertive. Many of the completion dates of projects like the CAP or the corps' Tennessee-Tombigbee, were stretched out, while new project authorizations were also becoming scarcer. The corps, for one, was no longer able to obtain funding for its traditional annual water omnibus bill consisting of new and continuing authorizations.

While both the bureau and the corps remained strong champions of water development, the two agencies responded somewhat differently to the challenges they were facing. The bureau posture in the early 1970s, even after the departure of the unreconstructed Dominy in 1969, was essentially defensive in nature. Like much of the western water industry, the bureau assumed these attacks were just momentary. Although they reserved their strongest rejoinders for the environmentalists, BuRec officials also remained wary of the fiscal conservatives at OMB and elsewhere.

By the mid-1970s, regional divisions also came into play. Congressional representatives and other political figures from the northeastern and midwestern states established caucuses to focus on funding inequities that favored their sunbelt rivals. Water projects became one of the items that were scrutinized. The "frostbelt" states argued that water development represented a transfer of federal funds to the sunbelt. These projects not only stimulated a thriving—and geographically competitive—agriculture but also made possible continuing growth in the urban centers of the western sunbelt.

The northeastern/midwestern regional caucus became increasingly effective during the 1970s. Several of its members joined committees traditionally dominated by westerners from reclamation states. The combination of OMB budget cutting with regionally motivated congressional action squeezed bureau budgets in the early and mid-1970s, forcing the western water industry to continually scale down its objectives.

Environmental opposition to corps policies and projects was at least equally intense and widespread as that directed toward the bureau. The Environmental Policy Center and the American Rivers Conservation Council, two of the more effective and insistent critics of the corps during the early 1970s, published at one point a detailed critique of corps and bureau policy based on ninety-five "theses" that were tacked on the door of the chief of engineers. These "theses" referred to flood control problems, phony cost-benefit analysis, and destruction of wildlife, including natural habitats, free-flowing streams, and especially wetlands, a key focus of much of the environmental opposition to the corps.

The wetlands issue had become by the early 1970s a major area of focus among environmental organizations. Post–World War II water development projects had caused a serious decline in this ecological resource. In twenty years, from the mid-1950s to the mid-1970s, almost ten million wetland acres had disappeared, nearly 10 percent of existing acreage. Since wetlands were often a rich and crucial source of sustenance for a variety of migratory birds and fish, their disappearance—up to two hundred thousand acres a year by some estimates—had become a significant environmental crisis. As a consequence, language protecting wetlands through a revised federal permiting process was included in the Clean Water Act Amendments of 1972.

The environmental groups had wanted the permiting to be administered by the newly established Environmental Protection Agency, which environmentalists then considered more accessible and open to their concerns. Congress, however, while acceding to the substance of regulation, placed the power in the hands of the army corps, which had previously been responsible for permits dating back to navigation law established in 1899. The corps, meanwhile, had begun to develop a facade of "responsiveness" around environmental issues in the swirl of events of the early 1970s.

Under the leadership of Colonel John "Jack" Morris, the corps established both an environmental unit and a public information program ostensibly designed to allow for greater public "accountability" and environmental sensitivity. In addition, the corps created an environmental advisory board consisting of leaders from several of the traditional conservationist groups. Though this board was established to advise the corps of its responsibilities under the National Environmental Policy Act, it had no formal veto power. The corps in fact disregarded the board's initial recommendations calling for an environmental restudy of two key corps projects, thus causing the board's chairman to resign. Congress nevertheless responded to the corps' gestures by rewarding the engineering body with what was potentially one of the broadest powers of any agency of government.

These powers were defined by Section 404 of the Clean Water Act legislation. They gave the corps the power to review any discharges that would "have an unacceptable adverse effect on municipal water supplies, shellfish beds and fishery areas (including spawning and breeding areas), wildlife or recreational areas." The corps, however, interpreted this language to limit its jurisdiction to only navigable rivers where the corps already maintained jurisdiction. Two environmental groups, the Natural Resources Defense Council and the National Wildlife Federation, took the corps to court and prevailed when a Federal District Court judge in 1975 defined the corps jurisdiction as encompassing all the waters of the U.S., including the disappearing wetlands.

During this period, the corps learned how to go through all the proper procedures in the environmental impact process, including public meetings and forums. A detailed study of these changes by the corps, however, noted how district engineers made

61

"an implicit distinction between the public involvement program and their 'normal' public duties such as attending luncheons given by local business or professional groups, meeting with local economic interests, coordinating with other governmental bodies and the like."

The Section 404 process only strengthened that dual interpretation of corps activity by its engineering staff. One chief of a permit section complained that "the permit activity of the corps can be an obstacle to further development." "Otherwise," he went on, "the agency is pro-development." The "real" activity of the corps was development; this environmental requirement was, in contrast, "negative" activity.

Shortly after the district court ruling in 1975, the corps also engaged in a more overt counterattack on its unwelcome regulatory power. At one point it issued a press release that absurdly broadened its expanded jurisdiction to include activities by individual farmers and ranchers, while talking about issuing twenty-five thousand dollar fines for offenders. Though the press release was successful in generating a storm of protests by farmers, it backfired as a scare tactic. Ultimately, the corps was forced to implement the 404 process as intended. While most corps reviews culminated in the granting of permits, the agency became savvy enough to claim credit for its "new look" whenever a permit was occasionally denied.

It was difficult for the water industry itself, however, to embrace that new look. Largely ignoring the admonitions of the National Water Commission, sympathetic to the problems of the federal water agencies and fierce in its hostility to the new environmental groups, the local water interests remained committed to a policy of continuing development through federal support. The programs advocated by the water interests were chiefly designed to benefit agriculture, still the leading participant in the water industry. But increasingly the major projects sought to include a place for urban and commercial/industrial interests as well. Though concerned about the delays in project construction and new authorizations, the water industry still perceived the Iron Triangle as basically intact.

HIT LIST

The first signs of trouble for the water industry emerged just prior to Jimmy Carter's inauguration in January 1977. Word began circulating that the new president would announce a new water policy. It would be based in part on the recommendations of a handful of advisors—several of them from environmental groups such as the Environmental Defense Fund and the Environmental Policy Center—who were critical of the big project/water development approach. Carter was interested in demonstrating his distance from traditional political approaches, symbolized in the water area by the Iron Triangle. From an initial list of more than eighty projects, Carter narrowed the attack to nineteen.

With great fanfare, the president announced his new policy a month after he assumed office. He stated that he would delete funds for these nineteen water projects from the current budget, while requesting overall project review on a case-by-case basis. In a press release announcing his action, the president justified it as "prudent and responsible use of the taxpayers' money and protection of the environment."

Carter's "hit list," as it came to be known, was timed more for its political and media effect as an early demonstration of his "outsider" status than as the culmination of a political process. Neither Carter nor his environmental advisors considered developing an educational and organizing effort and expanding opposition constituencies in project states as a way to combat long-standing biases about water development. Instead, his action effectively remobilized the water industry, which had been losing its ability to draw on those biases. Now the hastily developed hit list enabled the water industry to launch a state-by-state attack on the program, while revitalizing its own agenda.

The counterattack was based on the water industry's most potent weapons. It reasserted that water projects could claim a local consensus, suggesting that water project funding, as then-Utah-Governor Scott Matheson declared, "spelled the difference between

63

healthy economic growth and crippling stagnation." The press, particularly in much of the West and the South where the bureau and the army corps was most active, bitterly attacked the Carter policy in both its news and editorial pages, often using materials put together by water industry groups.

The water industry groups also took advantage of the hit list to strengthen their organizations and expand their coalitions. As relations between Congress and the president deteriorated (the president's attacks on the Iron Triangle contributing to the estrangement) the water industry was able to whittle away at Carter's overall water policy. Funding levels on the nineteen projects came to be restored, the policy review process was postponed, and other Carter initiatives were undercut, the most prominent of which was the idea of cost sharing.

Cost sharing was not a new idea. The National Water Commission, for one, had advocated that beneficiaries should pay a greater share of project costs. Carter's cost-sharing proposals were much more modest. Instead of tampering directly with project subsidies built into the beneficiaries' repayment contracts and the price of the water delivered, the administration proposals talked of the states assuming a small portion of project costs, 10 percent in this instance. Local interests, however, strongly resisted the idea, fearing an overhaul of a system they had nurtured and promoted for years.

Within a couple of years Carter had retreated on all fronts, from cost sharing to project review. The only significant contribution was the effort by Interior Secretary Cecil Andrus regarding the Central Arizona Project, one of the original nineteen on the hit list. Andrus used the threat of project suspensions for the CAP to force Arizona interests to address their groundwater overdraft problems before receiving CAP water. CAP was supposed to relieve the overdraft, but Andrus and CAP critics feared that without controls on groundwater pumping, the new CAP water would be used to stimulate further growth, thus exacerbating the overdraft. This in turn might create pressure for yet another project.

Aside from the CAP action, the Carter water initiatives had become a shambles. By the end of the 1970s, the water industry emerged feeling more secure than at the outset of the Environmental Decade. The election of Ronald Reagan strongly reinforced that self-confidence, masking the warning signs that conditions around water development had indeed changed. The hit list, ironically, had merely postponed that reckoning.

THE UNCERTAINTIES OF THE REAGAN YEARS

While it would be difficult to say at just what point the water industry began to grow concerned about the conflicting signals around water policy in the Reagan administration, it is clear that those doubts had already emerged within several months after Reagan assumed office. By the times James Watt delivered his talk at the NWRA fiftieth anniversary convention in October 1982, the water industry had come to recognize, rhetoric notwithstanding, that division and lack of clarity rather than consensus held sway in the administration's water policy debates.

For one, the Office of Management and Budget under David Stockman had once again become a major participant in shaping water policy. The OMB became a strong advocate of cost sharing, proposing a set of much higher figures than Carter's, including 35 percent for bureau projects and up to 100 percent for some army corps projects. OMB staff, moreover, often shared strategy with the water industry's number one nemesis: the environmental lobbying groups based in Washington. This unholy alliance, in the eyes of the water industry, had a substantial influence on congressional budgetary decisions. Bureau and corps budget requests were constantly whittled down throughout Reagan's first term to levels even lower than during the Carter years, if inflation is taken into account.

Though OMB advocacy of cost sharing might not have been surprising, the strong position taken by the new head of the army corps, longtime Reagan water advisor William Gianelli, confounded water industry groups. When Gianelli had been head of the California Department of Water Resources during Reagan's tenure as governor in the late 1960s and early 1970s, he was a forceful champion of the interests associated with the State Water Project. While

65

the state project was in some ways a California version of a federal reclamation project, for Gianelli the fact that it was conceived and paid for by California rather than the feds was significant in its own right.

When Gianelli came to Washington, he was quick to point to the California situation as a model for his conception of cost sharing. Gianelli was also placed in charge of an organization with its own institutional history, regional ties, and ways of operating that ultimately rubbed Gianelli the wrong way. "I found myself questioning many of the corps' projects and asking for details, which my predecessors may not have done," Gianelli declared in a 1984 "in-house" interview with a corps historian. The new corps head quickly discovered how the Iron Triangle functioned with respect to the corps, often bypassing the administration in favor of its ties with Congress. "Over the years," Gianelli complained, the corps "had been very used to considering itself almost as an arm of the Congress," and "did more toward working with the Congress sometimes, almost, than they did working with the executive branch of government."

Gianelli also tended to have run-ins with the corps's civilian staff, who had strong ties with both Congress and the regional interests, such as water industry groups up and down the Mississippi River. "I found it easier to work with the military guys than the civilians," Gianelli recalled in a 1986 interview, as he found himself in conflict with both his own staff in the corps and other figures in the Reagan administration.

Gianelli was by no means hostile to water development. His position on cost sharing and restructuring projects was based on an assessment that future water development could proceed only under these new ground rules. But others in the Reagan administration, most particularly the new head of the Bureau of Reclamation, Robert Broadbent, disagreed with that assessment.

A Nevada politician with few previous ties to the water industry, Broadbent quickly established himself as the industry's best champion in the White House. The new commissioner of reclamation not only argued against cost sharing, but he also constantly clashed with the OMB over the size of the bureau's budget and its reservations about completing the bureau's major projects, such as the CAP. And Broadbent disagreed with other officials in the Interior Department, most notably Garrey Carruthers. Carruthers, a New Mexico attorney with strong ties to energy interests in the West who later became governor of New Mexico, was assistant secretary of land and natural resources, which included jurisdiction over the bureau. Though not as adamant as Gianelli, Carruthers nevertheless argued that some form of cost sharing was appropriate.

Through these debates, James Watt and his successor, William Clark, were decidedly ambiguous as to their own position, particularly on cost sharing. Both refused to commit themselves to either a set of numbers or an overall approach. Watt's role in particular was crucial since he chaired the Cabinet Council on Natural Resources where both Gianelli and Broadbent had staff roles. Through Reagan's first term, water policy drifted without any clear strategic focus, with the OMB, in alliance with environmentalists and critical congressional figures, filling a partial void.

With the overall budget deficit creating additional pressures, the declining funding levels for projects pushed their construction schedules even further behind. Cost sharing, meanwhile, began to be debated on a program-by-program basis. Each new piece of legislation, such as a safety of dams bill that passed in 1984, established a new cost-sharing level. When states and local beneficiaries began to realize they might have to pay an increased share of the up-front costs for their projects, it began to diminish the attraction of those projects in economic terms. It also highlighted the importance of subsidies in keeping the price of the water low or at least manageable, particularly for agriculture. Some farm interests, in fact, seeing the new math applied to projects such as Animas–La Plata, began to complain that the federal water was becoming too expensive.

Part of the debate around cost sharing reflected a deeper readjustment taking place within the water industry and the federal agencies. By the 1980s, the historical dominance of agriculture was beginning to give way to the growing role of the urban interests who were fast becoming the largest users of new water supplies. By the end of Reagan's first term, this situation was compounded by the emerging crisis in agriculture, which was even affecting places like Arizona and California. As the price of farm commodities fell, the price of water began to rise. As a consequence, agricultural water use began to level off and even decline for the first time since the post–World War II boom in irrigated production. Meanwhile, the urban areas, increasingly aggressive in their own search for additional supplies, particularly in the arid West, began to entertain the notion that acquiring the water from the farmers might be a cheap source of new water.

This interest in water markets emerged rather tentatively during Reagan's first term. But it soon picked up momentum as the farm crisis deepened and funding for water projects became increasingly problematic. The OMB was especially interested in the water markets concept and the parallel notion of "privatization"—the idea of turning public projects and functions over to the private sector. OMB essentially hoped that by reducing the operations of the bureau and the corps, private sector companies, in part through the establishment of markets, would increase their participation. At one 1985 water conference, OMB staffer Edwin Dale noted that part of OMB's interest in cost sharing was designed to force the water interests, particularly agriculture, toward a "marketing" approach. "When their costs go up," Dale said of these interests, "selling the water begins to look more attractive."

By 1985, with the budget deficit as substantial as ever, the army corps, for one, recognized the crucial role that cost sharing would play in helping obtain authorization for new projects. For more than a decade, the traditional Iron Triangle method of securing funds through passage of an omnibus water-projects bill, with its bit of something for everyone, had either been stalled in Congress or faced a veto by the White House. The hurdles in passing such legislation had become substantial: the increasing costs of the projects, the problems of the overall budget, the growing clout of environmental lobbyists, and perhaps most importantly, the marginal nature, in cost-benefit terms, of many of the new projects. With

Gianelli and his successor Robert Dawson playing prominent roles, a new omnibus water development package with a substantial cost-sharing provision became the centerpiece of the new corps strategy. It came close to passage in both 1984 and 1985 and then finally made it in 1986. This legislation, HR 6, authorized new projects whose costs totaled an astounding $16 billion. These included 50 navigation projects, 115 flood-control projects, 61 development projects, 38 planning studies, and so on. The cost-sharing formulas provided that the feds come up with $11 billion while the initial nonfederal costs would be more than $4 billion.

At first glance, HR 6 resembled the omnibus water-development packages from the Iron Triangle days. Projects were spread out geographically, broadening the base of support for the legislation. Forty-seven states, Puerto Rico, Guam, and all the territories had a piece of the action. Unlike past legislation, however, much of HR 6 had to do with enlarging or modifying features of existing facilities rather than initiation of new projects, particularly massive ones like Tennessee-Tombigbee. Furthermore, some of the $16 billion was devoted to the planning and initial investigation of projects that were unlikely to be further advanced in the present climate of tight budgets and project criticism. Like the bureau, corps activities had already been shifting away from construction and toward operation and maintenance. At best, HR 6 only delayed that trend.

Yet corps officials were enthusiastic about their new omnibus bill, the first in ten years. "This creates a bright future for water resources development," exclaimed Robert Dawson a month after the bill was passed. According to Dawson, it could not have happened without cost sharing, and he contrasted the attitude of the corps under Gianelli and himself with the reluctance of the bureau to change its approach. "We saw the 'inevitabilities' coming sooner than they did," Dawson said of the two agencies. "They [the bureau] didn't believe it would happen. They clung longer to the feeling that the old methods would come back."

The bureau, however, had evolved its own strategy to cope with declining budgets and increased congressional scrutiny. In 1984, Robert Broadbent was elevated to Assistant Secretary of the

Interior, replacing Garrey Carruthers who returned to New Mexico. Despite his increased responsibilities, Broadbent was not able to prevail on James Watt's two successors at the Interior Department, William Clark and Donald Hodel, to appoint a new commissioner friendly to the water interests. For more than two years, the position of reclamation commissioner remained open, reinforcing the perception in Washington that the agency was vulnerable.

Those problems were heightened when California Congressman George Miller, a critic of bureau projects, became in 1985 the new head of the Subcommittee of Water and Power Resources of the crucial House Interior and Insular Affairs Committee. That position had been held over the years by strong champions of water development, and was central to the Iron Triangle system relating to the bureau. With Miller adding his critical voice to the now-formidable alliance of environmentalists, frostbelt congressmen, and OMB administration officials, the bureau, as a lead article in *Engineering News-Record* put it in 1985, was "in trouble."

During this period between commissioners, the bureau came under increasing review by Reagan administration officials, a process that was hastened when Hodel became secretary in 1984. Hodel, according to one of his assistants, "started talking about defining the parameters of a new bureau. Hodel would say," the aide went on, "that the circumstances of resource development have changed, but we haven't changed the bureau."

In the fall of 1986, a longtime Hodel acquaintance, C. Dale Duvall, was named commissioner of reclamation as part of the effort to reshape the bureau. Both Duvall and Hodel were particularly interested in shifting the bureau away from the multibillion-dollar agricultural-oriented projects that had characterized it in the past, but they hesitated around such issues as cost sharing and pricing. The new bureau tried to work around the conflict over cost-sharing figures that had dominated the debates during Reagan's first term by subscribing to a policy, first outlined in a 1984 letter from Reagan to Nevada Senator Paul Laxalt, that reviewed cost sharing on a project-by-project basis. In some instances—such as Arizona, where the water industry feared that without some financial contribution the Central Arizona Project would be continually delayed—that meant limited up-front financing of projects well under the projected 35 percent figure of OMB. Arizona, furthermore, tended to favor some form of cost sharing since it could also put the squeeze on other basin states, particularly Colorado, where there were already complaints about the price of the water being too high. If the Colorado projects did not come to pass, Arizona, according to the complex system of allocations for the Colorado River, would benefit as a downstream user. Bureau policy, however, allowed for certain exemptions from any form of cost sharing, such as the Garrison project in North Dakota, because, as Duvall put it in a 1987 interview, "they can't afford it."

Changes in pricing, the heart of the bureau's system of subsidies, were even less forthcoming. The protracted conflict over the pricing of water for the Westlands Water District, for example, ended with the bureau minimally raising the price to fifteen dollars an acre foot of water, well below the real cost of the water and far below the price advocated by bureau critics such as Congressman George Miller and environmental groups such as the Natural Resources Defense Council. The Westlands situation was even more striking because of the key role played by the Interior Department Solicitor Ralph Tarr. Tarr had previously been with a major Central Valley water industry–oriented law firm that had represented many of the water districts in the area, but nevertheless failed to disqualify himself from the proceedings despite strong objections from environmental groups.

The core to the new bureau strategy was unveiled in early 1987 with its annual budget request. Instead of asking for funding for a range of both unauthorized projects and those under partial construction, the bureau, under Duvall, decided to prioritize its funding requests. This involved a larger share for the Central Arizona Project and the Central Utah Project whose lengthy delays had come to represent the bureau's paralysis, alongside cutbacks or elimination of funding for new authorizations or projects just getting underway. With this strategy, the bureau risked undercutting whatever still remained of the old pork barrel system by narrowing the number

71

of projects (and presumably self-interested congressional supporters). The bureau leaders, however, given their unwillingness to push further for pricing reform or cost sharing, banked on this new, more "streamlined" version to carry it into the new era. "The water industry does have to change," Duvall remarked about his first year as commissioner. "The old coalitions are being eroded."

In late 1987, the Interior Department's new assistant secretary for water and science, James Ziglar, took the new bureau strategy a step further. Ziglar, a financial analyst with strong ties to urban water interests, had been a key private sector participant in the water industry. He replaced Robert Broadbent who had left the Interior Department just a few months earlier. Ziglar announced, to the surprise and consternation of some in the water industry, that the bureau was ready to formally change its mission from "an agency based on federally supported construction to one based on resource management." Such a shift would involve moving bureau headquarters from Washington to Denver and phasing out its planning function. The new policy would continue the emphasis on trying to centralize funds for the Central Arizona and Central Utah projects while seeking involvement in new areas such as groundwater protection, which was receiving far more attention in Congress than water supply projects.

The problems for Duvall and Ziglar, however, appeared even more intractable than those confronting the corps. While BuRec critics attacked the "new priorities" approach for its increased support of the old "dinosaurs" like CAP, traditional allies in Congress and the water industry attacked the elimination of their "marginal" projects. The proposed shift from construction to management outlined in Ziglar's plan, moreover, was seen as reflecting "more a fact of life than a real change," as longtime water lobbyist Robert Will put it. Furthermore, water industry allies within the Interior Department, such as Solicitor Tarr, were able to outmaneuver and isolate Duvall when it came to fundamental issues of pricing and project subsidies.

By the late 1980s, both the bureau and the corps, in recognition of the new realities, knew they were ultimately being forced to permanently shift away from construction. The old dreams that federally financed water development would, in the 1944 comment of a BuRec regional director, contribute to "the building of a great empire," were finally beginning to fade. Even the massive projects that had been completed, like Tennessee-Tombigbee or those partially completed like the Central Arizona Project, were or would be operating quite differently than originally anticipated. Tenn-Tom, for example, built to increase navigation, was operating at only 10 percent of intended capacity in its first couple of years. The notion that this vast new waterway system would stimulate all kinds of new regional economic activity, such as coal shipments for the export market, seemed at best a distant reality.

The old coalitions of the water industry, as Duvall had noted, were either losing their clout or unraveling in a variety of ways. Urban interests were beginning to clash with agricultural interests over the allocation and pricing of water supplies. At times, even regional coalitions failed to hold together, as local members of Congress decided that support for local projects was no longer an act of political necessity. The terms for water policy and governmental activity were now being set by the issues of water quality, pricing subsidies for surplus crops, falling commodity prices, and the overall decline of agriculture, and by the problem of the budget deficit. The notion of water markets and privatization, while intriguing to some in the water industry as well as the Reagan administration, didn't appear, initially at least, to offer a full-scale alternative to the old Iron Triangle system of public subsidies and private benefits.

"The old days, the pork barrel days where the Feds pay the bill, are now gone," stated Commissioner Duvall, citing what had in effect become a truism of the late 1980s. But the transition had been stretched out, and the changes were far from complete. The water industry had become a group at once resisting change and hoping for some new system to come along to preserve some old habits and objectives. New players had joined old players in the

73

debate, but solutions were not readily available. The two major players, urban development interests and agriculture, were redefining their roles and their position with respect to each other within the old water coalitions. With the feds passing from center stage, the water industry sought to find new ways to accomplish its central objectives of growth and expansion.

Chapter 3

Agricultural Empires:
The Farm-Water Connection

AGOREO'S RELUCTANT PORTFOLIO

When the phone rang in the hectic, cluttered offices of the California Institute for Rural Studies, no one, including the institute director, Don Villarejo, would have anticipated or even imagined the request that followed. The voice on the other end of the line identified herself as a representative of an obscure offshoot of the Bank of America—Agriculture and Other Real Estate Owned, or AgOreo.

AgOreo is the arm of B of A that handles land acquired by foreclosure, quitclaim deeds, and related transactions. By February 1986, when Villarejo was surreptitiously approached, and California's agricultural problems, including declining commodity prices and overproduction, were at their height, AgOreo could count in its reluctant portfolio upward of two hundred thousand acres of land in the Central Valley.

"We're having problems marketing some properties we've recently obtained," the AgOreo representative discreetly said, "and we need help in locating buyers. Would you be willing to see us?"

It was an unusual request for the activist-researcher. Villarejo and his associates were not, by any means, considered friends of

California's large landowning interests and their financiers. Through their institute and a parallel activist organization, the California Action Network, Villarejo and friends had scrutinized and exposed the structure and activities of California's biggest landholders. Yet it was Villarejo's substantial research skills and savvy about Central Valley agriculture that also attracted him to the AgOreo people. As Villarejo surmised from the phone conversation, the bankers seemed a bit frantic about their situation. The appointment was set for later that week.

On that day, Villarejo set out from the institute office in Davis, close by the University of California campus. He traveled past downtown Sacramento to a newly developed section of the city located on the banks of the American River. Set off in the woods near the river were a series of sleek office buildings, including the one with the address given over the phone.

Though Villarejo had a suite number, he noticed there was no mention of B of A or the AgOreo department on the directory in the lobby. When he got to the room, Suite 200, there wasn't any name on the door, just a buzzer and a deadbolt lock. He checked again the number of the suite he had jotted down in conversation. It was indeed Suite 200. He was about to ring the buzzer when the door opened and a man departed from the room, so Villarejo was able to let himself in and survey the scene. There was again no indication for what the suite of offices was being used. The scene was quite busy, however, with fifteen or twenty people working in a group of adjoining offices off the entrance. Villarejo walked over to the first desk he saw occupied—there was no apparent reception area—and mentioned his appointment. He was ushered to a modest couch off to the side that appeared to pass for a waiting area. In a minute an AgOreo representative appeared. It was the same person he had spoken to on the phone.

"You realize," she said almost in a whisper, "that absolute discretion is essential," referring to the location and the purpose of the meeting. Her supervisor, the manager of the AgOreo department, soon appeared. A large ring binder was brought out with a description of between one hundred and two hundred properties.

76

These properties were about to be put up for sale. The AgOreo people again repeated their admonition for discretion: If it became known how many properties and how much acreage was involved, their voices trailed off. . . .

It was an ironic moment for the bank and the fortunes of California agriculture. More than sixty years earlier, the active efforts of Giannini's Bank of America, with its lending policies and its thousands of acres of prime Central Valley land that it had either foreclosed on or purchased, had helped set in motion greater consolidation and concentration of agricultural land ownership. Since that time, B of A had been at the center of California agribusiness, promoting actively the big water projects in the state.

Then, beginning in the early 1980s, as California agriculture commenced its protracted decline, the bank's fortunes began to slip as well. Though it had withdrawn from purchase of land properties for a number of years, it suddenly found itself holding title to thousands of acres. These had come primarily from quitclaim actions, where landowners, rather than face foreclosure with its negative implications for credit, had simply quitclaimed their properties to the bank. The public, moreover, had no real way of knowing just how much land was being taken over. And the bank was extra cautious, as witnessed by the AgOreo location and admonitions, to keep that information out of the public eye.

Though the bank now held title to a huge amount of acreage, it was reluctant to get back into the farming business as it had been before the Depression. Instead, some of the land was being leased with managers hired to run the business. But the leasing business was also experiencing problems. A decision had therefore been made by the bank and the AgOreo people to sell or auction a number of properties. Though the bank knew quite a bit about the details of each piece of property—the number of trees, vines, or row crops that had been planted—surprisingly enough, they knew very little about the specifics of the market and the volatile changes taking place with California agriculture. Thus the call to Villarejo and the request for a meeting.

As the AgOreo people leafed through their binder they stopped at a page that described a fourteen-hundred-acre peach orchard in Merced County. "What can you tell us about this one?" they asked Villarejo, who gave out a chuckle. He immediately recognized the property as the original Del Monte orchard, the principal supplier for that company's canning operations. These operations had, at one time, been quite extensive in California.

The example was strongly symbolic of the situation facing the industry. Most of the peach canning operations in California were today shut down, reduced, or up for sale. At one point, when Del Monte was a major force in California, these operations were extensive and the peach orchards were profitable. Like many other farm commodities in post–World War II California, the peaches were produced primarily for foreign consumption, encouraged by government policies (including water development programs) that sought to expand foreign markets and production levels. In this case, 90 percent of the California peaches were exported to Western Europe. Then, beginning in the 1960s, the situation began to change. The European Common Market established tariffs on imported peach products to protect European producers, primarily from Italy. The tariffs made the California peaches less competitive, so Del Monte began to shift its production elsewhere, including Europe and South Africa with its cheaper labor force. By the mid-1970s Del Monte and others had phased out substantially in California. Then in the late 1970s, Del Monte sold its flagship orchard. The new owners didn't have much luck with it either and it eventually ended up in the hands of AgOreo.

Though the sequence of events around the Del Monte peach orchard had occurred during an earlier period than the current agricultural crisis, it was representative of many of the same problems: reliance on foreign markets and government subsidies, increased competition from abroad, the tendency to overproduce surplus crops, and declining commodity prices and profits. Then, when the price of water began to rise, as it did in the early and mid-1980s, it created chaos and confusion, and then restructuring, even for the powerful California landowners.

The B of A, its own policies having contributed historically to the problem, was as confused and troubled as the landowners who had quitclaimed their properties to AgOreo. After Villarejo finished his story about Del Monte and left the unmarked office by the woods and the river, he began to wonder whether the problem went even deeper than he had anticipated. It occurred to him that the bank people might well have trouble getting rid of properties they didn't want and didn't know quite what to do with.

Later that summer, the bank announced a series of auctions, first one in Fresno and then one in Sacramento. Portfolio descriptions were obtained by the institute and the auctions were monitored. The sales were indeed a flop. Less than 10 percent of the properties were sold. Soon after, the bank called off any further auctions for the immediate future.

The mood of chaos and confusion and the focus on restructuring had deepened. The entrenched power and economic clout of agribusiness in this state and elsewhere were still forces to contend with, though their influence and reach might have become a bit more problematic. Instead of the usual water industry talk about the inevitable expansion of irrigated acreage and more water development, one began to hear discussion of transferring rights, selling water, and bailing out. Though agribusiness still tried to call the shots in water policy, one now had to ask, for what purpose?

THE RISE OF IRRIGATION

The agricultural wing of the water industry has long maintained a special place in the politics of water. In the West it remains by far the largest single user of water supplies, averaging often over 85 or 90 percent of the total volume in any given state west of the 100th meridian. In the South and the Midwest, agriculture has often been the key beneficiary of water development projects, though it has increasingly lost overall market share to the irrigated farm interests of the West with the advent of large-scale water development.

These agricultural interests have dominated the lobbying and political organizations of the water industry. They have benefited from a special relationship not only with the Department of Agriculture, which implements a variety of crop subsidy programs, but the big federal water agencies as well. They have developed strong ties with key congressional leaders and influenced several of the committees that shape water policy.

Agriculture's greatest expansionary period was during the boom times of the 1970s, when the amount of land under production, particularly irrigated acreage, increased, the yield per acre was at its highest, land values had skyrocketed, and markets both foreign and domestic had grown substantially. Yet it was then that the agricultural industry also began to experience the conditions that led to its decline.

By the 1980s, the boom had largely turned to bust, and the issue of water was often at the center of that decline. A new competition emerged between agriculture and urban interests who began to covet the massive water supplies available to agriculture. The farm-water alliance, for so long at the center of the push for water development, witnessed a loss of influence, parallel to the changing fortunes of the big federal water agencies. Agriculture still remained a major force, but it could no longer claim the status of first among equals in a water industry seeking to contend with a changing agenda.

Control of water has long been associated with control of the land. This has been especially true in regions where irrigation has become the predominant mode of farming, and the amount and price of water available for irrigation correlated directly with the level of production, concentration of land ownership, and transformation of agriculture into an industrial activity.

The emergence of irrigation in the late nineteenth and early twentieth centuries coincided broadly with a new type of farming enterprise influenced by industrial changes and adopting business techniques, known today as agribusiness. The promotion of irrigation and land settlement, particularly in the West, had in its early years, however, a social dimension that tended at first to obscure the changing conditions for agriculture.

The land settlement policies of the Homestead Act of 1862, for example, were designed to help alleviate labor conditions in the North, including widespread unemployment and an underpaid army. This concept of making land available for agriculture as an outlet for social unrest became a primary justification for a number of land settlement advocates from Horace Greeley to George Maxwell, the founder of the National Irrigation Congress. In an article in *Irrigation Age* in 1899, Maxwell appealed to labor organizations to "use all their influence to open a channel through which all surplus labor can constantly return to the land. Arid America," Maxwell went on, "beckons to them with open arms."

This perspective was shared by farm and labor organizations through much of the late nineteenth century. It helped cast early water reclamation efforts as populist yearnings for a revival of the Jeffersonian yeoman farmer. Advocacy in favor of the small farmer contrasted with the western penchant for land monopoly and speculation that was already prevalent in this period, and in fact predated irrigation.

Prior to the Homestead Act, cattle ranching dominated the early use of the land. Huge estates, many of them taken over wholesale from Mexican ranchos, ringed the West and served to initially prevent the opening of lands for irrigation. But the emergence of rail shipping and expanding markets enabled wheat to displace the open range so that by the mid-1870s much of California's Central Valley, for example, appeared to be one huge wheat field.

The shift to wheat and later the emergence of irrigated agriculture was linked to widespread land speculation through the use of scrip, manipulation of government land distribution policies, and, with the advent of irrigation, the sale of water rights, among other practices. Huge land empires, especially in California, were literally created overnight, some as large as a million acres or more. The small farmers who backed irrigation and crop diversification were often locked in conflict with the massive wheat farmers who feared the irrigators could drive up property values and taxes, thus reducing their profits.

By the late 1880s, the momentum for irrigation was strong

enough to cause the California legislature to pass the Wright Act, the first major piece of legislation establishing irrigation districts. This legislation attempted in part to transform the giant wheat fields into small, intensively cultivated family farms. Supported by reform groups like the Grange, who looked to cooperative forms of marketing and purchasing, irrigation was seen as an extension of this cooperative mode, shielding small farmers from the caprices of nature. Irrigation, according to the much-used phrase of the time, would "make the desert bloom," while establishing a society of yeoman farmers. It was hoped it would recreate ideals lost in the wake of industrialization. Furthermore, these groups anticipated that irrigation would also stimulate new settlements and an expanding population, creating a kind of rural democratic force to counter the land speculators.

Instead, irrigation became, as one analyst put it, the "stepchild of land speculation." Water companies, many of which were little more than speculative ventures, were established to take advantage of the new interest in irrigation. Many of these companies subdivided large blocks of land adjoining canals that they or associated land companies owned. Controlled by promoters who were most interested in quick sales, the canal systems were often shoddily made and designed. Within a few years after enactment of the Wright Act, California's water supply had become a hodgepodge of uncoordinated systems. The economic downturn of the early and mid-1890s intensified the problems of irrigated agriculture and led to increased talk of intervention on the state and especially the federal level.

The call for federal intervention was heavily backed by the newly formed Irrigation Congresses of the 1890s. Strongly supported by the railroads, who perceived federal intervention as a prerequisite for expanding and stabilizing the development of irrigation, Irrigation Congress leaders kept up a concerted push for some sort of federal financing and construction of reservoirs and storage facilities in the West. The army corps was briefly enlisted in support of the cause, but the primary focus of the irrigators was the establishment of a new federal agency to underwrite and supervise the program.

When the Newlands Act was passed in 1902 creating the Reclamation Service, the concept of social reform and the Jeffersonian ideal dominated the legislative debate. Its final passage generated expectations similar to those created by the Wright Act.

The centerpiece for reform was the 160-acre limitation. This device of establishing acreage limitations for federal programs had been used through the latter part of the nineteenth century as a way to help establish small family farms in a region that did not easily lend itself to small units of farming. Reclamation advocates, however, were convinced that both the intervention of the federal government in financing large-scale projects and the social character of irrigation would enhance the ability of the small farm to survive. The 160-acre limitation in turn was designed to provide the legal framework in which the reclaimed water would be made available to enable the small farm to function effectively in an arid environment. The acreage limits were ultimately seen as the anchor for the overall philosophy of a democratically conceived, irrigation-centered society of flourishing small farms and rural communities.

The new law, however, was ambiguous from the outset about how to implement the acreage restrictions. Larger landholding units were not obliged to divest, since farmers could receive reclaimed water up to 160 acres while keeping their excess holdings intact. Furthermore, since the new act was designed to attract new settlers to the West (presumably unemployed or landless urban workers from the East), it established an incentive for existing landowners and canal-and-ditch company owners to speculate with their new source of water.

Until the 1920s, the Bureau of Reclamation's activities tended to be limited in their size and scope. The bureau never attempted to mobilize a broad public constituency in the West to provide support for small-scale irrigation. Instead, the new federal agency began centralizing decision-making power as to which projects to pursue and for what purpose. Though imbued with a philosophy and a social design, the bureau from the outset placed great emphasis on its technical/engineering expertise.

The bureau, even in this early period, never did provide an

effective counterweight to the tendencies toward land concentration and the industrialization of agriculture. The number of acres irrigated in California and the West increased in this period, but so did the size of the individual landholdings. Agricultural prices as well as the price of water also fluctuated substantially and there was a general inflation in the price of land and the tax on that land. Other factors, such as labor and machinery costs, were already creating negative pressures on small-scale farming. A handful of owners, particularly financial institutions such as Bank of America and the Trans-America Company, were becoming "factories in the field," to use writer Carey McWilliams's classic phrase, both in their use of labor and in the increasing corporate presence. Irrigation, once the dream of small farmer advocates, was becoming a distinct and relatively concentrated industry.

THE SUBSIDY AS KING

By World War II, agribusiness was poised for takeoff. In the West, the Bureau of Reclamation had begun to expand its programs. Its agricultural centerpiece, the Central Valley Project, was nearing completion of its first phase. The war had stimulated the introduction of new technologies, expanding markets, and the continuing shift toward mechanization. Throughout the country, with California and the West in the forefront, the labor-intensive family farm was giving way to a more capital-intensive, greater productive agricultural enterprise. The family was either becoming entrepreneurial or being displaced by a business organization, whether local or nationally based.

The focus on production was the key. The New Deal had devised a series of programs that had sought to link agriculture with industrial growth. The Bureau of Reclamation's western water programs, for example, were designed to create new urban and industrial centers, fueled in part by an expanding agriculture. New Deal programs such as rural electrification helped further the trend toward mechanization and the subsequent reduction of farm labor, which in turn augmented the labor supply for an expanding industrial base. New Deal initiatives such as price ceilings and limits for crops sought to reduce production levels and thus increase farm income. But they had the effect of creating incentives for higher yields in a smaller land base. The mechanized, capital-intensive farm, best exemplified by California's industrial agriculture, was becoming the primary mode for agriculture.

New farming techniques, especially the widespread introduction of pesticides in places like California, Texas, and Florida, helped further the emphasis on yields. New markets for U.S. farm products were expanding rapidly, as they became increasingly linked to U.S. foreign-policy objectives. Food for export programs, such as the PL 480 "Food for Peace" programs of the Eisenhower years, maintained the emphasis on production and were particularly instrumental in the expansion of California and western irrigated agriculture.

The availability of water, particularly inexpensive sources of new water supplies, was central to the postwar dynamic of agricultural expansion. New pumping technology combined with the postwar energy boom and relatively low electricity prices allowed water to be pumped at much greater depths to irrigate a larger number of acres. The Bureau of Reclamation oversaw a vast new set of projects, begun during the Depression years. These culminated in the Bureau's postwar adoption of a program of development that would make the Colorado River the most overbooked and overdeveloped river system in the country. As a consequence, land irrigated with bureau water jumped from 2.7 million acres in 1930 to more than 4 million acres after the war and nearly 7 million acres by 1960.

Entirely new cropping patterns were established, particularly in California's Central Valley where the longer growing season and the transformation of markets enabled the state to become the leading producer of cotton, grapes, and other commodities. The state's large landowners were adept at using federal programs to their benefit, whether in terms of reclamation programs, pricing mechanisms, or foreign-trade arrangements. In places like Fresno, Merced, and Kern counties the big farm operators were best able to afford the one-hundred- to two-hundred-thousand dollar wells, the high-volume production, and the increasing need for capital. "To have a farm out there," Congressman Bernie Sisk later recalled, "required having or borrowing a lot of money." The water programs, far from discouraging this concentration of ownership and emphasis on production, only contributed to it.

This was especially striking with respect to the Central Valley Project. From 1944 when Shasta Dam was first completed to 1982 when the agricultural boom had peaked, California's irrigated land nearly doubled from 4.9 million acres to 8.6 million acres. Most of this net increase—3.2 million acres or nearly 90 percent of the net additions statewide—took place in the Central Valley, by then considered the most productive agricultural valley in the world.

This was the period when the state's two enormous water systems, the CVP and the State Water Project, were constructed. In a little more than a couple of decades more new water supply capacity was added to the state's system than all previous capacity combined in the state's history. The availability of this supply made possible the expanding reach of California agriculture, which had far surpassed Iowa as the country's leading producer of farm products.

The postwar period also witnessed a rapid escalation of both the kinds of subsidies and the capital requirements involved in the big federal projects. Some of these subsidies were a result of provisions explicitly mandated by Congress, but others were either restructured, unintended, or even, according to some critics, illegal subsidies resulting from grower/BuRec collusion. These pricing policies, BuRec advocates countered, were never intended to be part of a "strictly business" approach to repayment methods. "A successful irrigation project," one longtime bureau employee argued, "becomes a generator of wealth for the community, state, and nation, and it must be accepted as worthwhile on faith."

Along these lines, the original Reclamation Act was conceived in part as a means to subsidize those who could either not afford the cost of building the capital facilities of paying for the delivery of the water for irrigation of the small farming units—the intended beneficiaries. The Act also established an "ability to pay" provision that allowed small farmers greater flexibility to deal with hard times. But the system as it evolved was essentially subverted by the bureau, which increasingly allied with larger growers, many of whom engaged in wholesale evasion of the 160-acre limitation through devices such as leasing. "Ability to pay" was also interpreted to mean that growers could pay less not only during "hard times," but also during more profitable periods. Instead of creating greater equity, bureau policies had eventually encouraged a greater concentration of ownership and income imbalance.

The CVP system became the most pronounced example of this abuse of the early intent of reclamation. The enormous expansion of irrigated acreage that resulted from the CVP essentially benefited some of the largest farming units in the state and the country. Far from limiting land concentration, the CVP only reinforced it. This involved not only large corporate entities, but also big "family" farms that were in actuality million-dollar operations. One study that compared landownership data in two California counties just prior to the CVP and forty years after its first unit was completed showed clearly that the ownership of irrigated land had become significantly more concentrated.

"Today," the study noted, "there are fewer owners holding more irrigated land." Average holdings of irrigated land had in fact increased by at least 50 percent.

The CVP system, furthermore, similar to other BuRec projects, was rife with subsidies. From the 1940s to the 1980s, a little less than a billion dollars was spent on CVP facilities by the feds. The amount of repayment, however, which should have been approaching 100 percent, amounted to no more than $50 million. Repayment periods for the CVP and other projects, originally mandated by Congress at fifty years, were extended on several occasions, thus stretching the length and terms of the pricing subsidies for the landowners. By the mid-1980s, the average price for CVP water was a little more than six dollars an acre foot. But that amounted to less than 10 percent of the actual cost—about seventy-three dollars an acre foot—involved in providing the water.

Ultimately, the system became something of a scandal. A series of audits and internal Interior Department reports during the late 1970s pointed to the fact that the rates for CVP, with their fixed and long-term contracts, were no longer sufficient to pay the operation and maintenance costs of the system, let alone the repayment costs for construction of the project. The system was sliding toward bankruptcy and the overall subsidies were extending far beyond the original intentions of the legislation.

The situation was further compounded by the fact that the availability of such inexpensive CVP water, combined with the strong tax and policy incentives in the 1970s to expand production especially for foreign markets, had created a production extravaganza in California. Crops like cotton, rice, and corn continued to be designated "surplus" crops, while at the same time bureau policies were encouraging the expansion of irrigated acreage. Some of this was happening on lands where there had been no previous history of irrigation.

As the surplus problem got worse, contributing to the protracted farm crisis of the early and mid-1980s, a whole new set of surplus-crop programs, such as the Payment in Kind and Set Aside programs, were put in place by the Reagan administration. These payment programs encouraged farm interests to produce less, or at least to produce on fewer numbers of acres. For California especially, but in other areas of the West as well, a kind of double-dipping effect was created. Some farm interests, through pricing subsidies, were encouraged to open new lands for irrigation, while other programs paid those same landowners to temporarily forgo such production.

The double-dipping effect was most revealing during the wet winter of 1983 in California. Rainfall throughout the state had been especially high, which had, ironically, created a set of problems as complex and extensive as the problems of the drought a few years earlier. In the Central Valley, the big landowners in and around the Tulare Lake Basin were hit particularly hard. The runoff from the rains, which usually settled in the lake, had spilled over, causing widespread flooding. As a result, thousands of acres were taken out of production.

Meanwhile, the Reagan administration had launched, earlier that year, its Payment in Kind program, designed to pay farmers to take those lands devoted to surplus crops out of production. In turn, the farmers would receive upward of 90 percent of that crop from the government's overflowing bins storing the surplus commodities. Once PIK was instituted, several Tulare farmers, including Boswell, immediately applied for the subsidy program. They offered to take their lands out of production, though many of those lands had already been flooded. Meanwhile, Boswell and others in the water industry continued to advocate Bureau of Reclamation pricing policies that served to encourage greater production, including production of surplus crops.

By the 1980s, the changes in agriculture that had been wrought from a combination of water development and subsidy programs, production incentives and tax initiatives, and the focus on technology and science to improve yields, had created a very different system than the one conceived of during the reclamation era and even the New Deal. The notion that agriculture represented a type of life-style, both a form of community and a set of values that anchored that community, had given way to a concept of agriculture as a business and a set of scientific techniques. Moreover, the rise of large-scale water development projects had increased the disparities between wealth and poverty in agriculturally oriented rural communities. In several of the areas where water deliveries had increased, such as the western San Joaquin Valley served by the California Central Valley Project, studies showed that the real income of those who farmed the land, especially farm workers, ultimately decreased. "Every farm structure correlate of increasing surface water supplies (i.e., increasing chemical use on farms, increasing dependence on new technologies, higher levels of absentee involvement, etc.) is associated with deteriorating conditions in the rural community," commented Dean MacCannell, the director of the Macrosocial Accounting Project at the University of California at Davis. California's irrigated agriculture, made possible by the large-scale deliveries of imported water underwritten by the federal and state governments, had in fact become the leading representative of this new form of agriculture, a model for other landowners not only in the West but increasingly throughout the country.

THE FARM-WATER LOBBY

The agricultural industry through much of the twentieth century has maintained an enormous level of political influence in Congress and at the statewide level. Its lobbyists have prowled the halls of state legislatures from Texas and Arizona to California and Nebraska. They have not only been able to maintain and expand pricing subsidies but have also sought to limit government intervention into other areas, such as pesticide contamination of local water supplies. In several regions, including the West, the South, the Mountain States, the Southwest, and the Plains States, agricultural-led coalitions have helped gerrymander legislatures, contain the political clout of the growing urban centers, and basically set the policy agendas.

Agriculture's influence has been especially pervasive in the water arena. Agriculture dominated the water industry, controlling its coalitions and lobbying organizations such as the National Water Resources Association. It had enormous influence within the Bureau of Reclamation, particularly after the postwar period. It was continually able to stymie initiatives outside the bureau, including those from higher-ups at the Interior Department. And several key legislators, many with tenure and occupying top committee posts, were an extension of agriculture's power.

When it came to water matters, the agriculture-influenced congressional figures of note were primarily from the West, especially from California and Texas, two of the more water-dependent states. For years, the most important water committees were locked up by the water industry's champions. The list of committee chairs— the Wayne Aspinall's (Dem., Colorado/House Interior & Insular Affairs), Carl Hayden's (Dem., Arizona/Senate Interior & Insular Affairs), Robert Pogue's (Dem., Texas/House Agriculture), and Claire Engle's (Dem., California/House—later Senate—Interior &

Insular Affairs)—reads like an honor roll of powerful water industry advocates.

Certain congressional districts, with their concentration of agricultural interests, became a special springboard for influence and power. The role of agriculture and money in California's fifteenth congressional district, which includes Fresno and Merced and much of the Westlands Water District, is especially noteworthy in this regard. From 1954 to 1978, the district was represented by Bernie Sisk, a conservative Democrat who unsuccessfully sought the position of House Majority Leader in 1972. Sisk, along with several neighboring Central Valley congressmen such as Bizz Johnson and John McFall, was extremely effective in obtaining authorization and funding for a continuing extension of the CVP. This included such controversial projects as the San Luis Drain, which became responsible for the fiasco at the Kesterson Wildlife Refuge. Sisk was also effective as a key member of the House Rules Committee in helping maintain the regional distribution of pork barrel–style expenditures. Part of Sisk's clout was his fundraising ability, not only frightening off potential challengers, but also demonstrating his access and reach.

Sisk aides were quickly trained in the skills of fundraising and influence peddling. One top aide, Gordon Nelson, later became a top farm-water lobbyist, bridging California interests with other regional players. But it was the hard-driving, ambitious young aide who took over from Nelson at the age of twenty-five and transformed the art of fundraising into a meteoric rise in politics, who literally and figuratively inherited Sisk's legacy.

It didn't take Tony Coelho long to eclipse his mentor. Coelho had already become influential in the halls of Congress, not just as Sisk's top aide and fundraiser, but also as a battle-scarred veteran with a sophisticated grasp of the inner workings of the House and his party. He had a substantial campaign war chest when he ran in 1978, and the groundwork had been so carefully laid through Sisk's endorsement and major support from the large landowners in the district, that Coelho ran, in effect, as an incumbent.

Coelho, described by House Speaker Jim Wright (D-Tex) as

"hyper as a hummingbird," was incredibly impatient, "always want-ing to move very rapidly," as Sisk declared. Not content to simply represent his powerful constituents, Coelho immediately seized his first opportunity to realize his ambitions. In 1981, he took over a relatively moribund Democratic Congressional Campaign Com-mittee, the main fundraising arm to help elect congressional Dem-ocrats. Coelho used his fundraising skill to parlay his already considerable base of agricultural and oil interests in the California fifteenth into a powerful money-gathering machine. His major con-stituency were the corporate PACs, with agriculture, oil, utilities, and financial institutions leading the way.

Coelho liked to tell his fellow Democrats that they were in the "business of politics." "The business I represent," he told one group of corporate executives in 1985, "is the Democratic Party. You should be more interested in my business, and by the way, if you are, I can take care of it." His propensity for mixing business and politics, fundraising and deal-making became his trademark. They occasionally led to some negative repercussions. Prior to the 1984 campaign, for example, the three largest political action committees representing the New York and Chicago commodity exchanges poured money into the DCCC's coffers and into Coelho's own campaign committee. This was happening at a time when Congress was considering a tax break favorable to the commodity traders, which Coelho supported. "If I were chairman of the [DCCC] or not," Coelho defended the PAC contributions in a 1985 interview, "I'd be involved with the commodity exchange. Why? They deal with agriculture. I am not going to turn my back on agriculture and water because I am chairman of the DCCC. That's my district. The difference between me and some others is that I don't run away from it."

To his colleagues, Coelho's success at fundraising easily offset the negative publicity that emerged from time to time. He was, for example, easily elected to the position of Majority Whip in 1987, the number-three position in the House hierarchy. It was Coelho that James Watt singled out in his 1982 speech to the NWRA suggesting that the water industry's support of this Democratic Party fundraiser was tantamount to "betrayal." Ironically, Coelho's enormous influence didn't always translate into effective lobbying for the water industry, his main constituents. "Tony is an extremely powerful man," one Washington, D.C., water industry lobbyist noted, "but we sometimes wish he could do a bit more for us." The lobbyist, of course, didn't want to be identified since "Tony never forgets."

This failure to come through for the water industry was particularly glaring in an October 1984 incident that came to be known among water industry pundits as the "Pleasant Valley Massacre." The thirty-five-thousand-acre Pleasant Valley Water District, located in southwestern Fresno County within Coelho's district, decided to try to hook up to the CVP in 1984 to obtain some of its cheap federal water. At stake was $37 million in interest-free loans from the feds to pay for a new distribution system for the CVP water.

One of the prime movers behind the scheme was the Chevron Corporation, which owned almost half of the land in the thirty-five-thousand-acre district. The big oil company, which leased this land, was also eager to arrange an exemption from the 960-acre limit imposed in the revised Reclamation Reform Act of a few years earlier.

Coelho tried to sneak through this Pleasant Valley/CVP connection by placing the matter along with other noncontroversial legislation usually voted on without discussion. A number of water industry critics got wind of what was going on and tipped off both the media and congressional opponents of bureau subsidies.

On the day of the vote, Coelho stood at the back of the chamber while his opponents, particularly Republicans smarting from his fundraising, had a field day blasting Coelho's "special interest" legislation. It was one of those rare instances where the issue of corporate/water industry favoritism was so blatant that nearly everyone, even some Central Valley Congressmen, lined up to defeat the bill. The vote was 402 to 19.

A more serious problem for the water industry was the selection of George Miller, a Democrat from Contra Costa County in Northern California, for the House Water and Power Resources Subcommittee, bypassing Coelho who was already head of the DCCC. Miller, along with James Watt and the Reagan administration, had been a chief architect of the compromise Reclamation Reform Act.

Miller's selection was an unhappy event for the water industry. The House Water and Power Resources Subcommittee as well as the overall Interior and Insular Affairs Committee had long been dominated by water industry advocates. In his new position, Miller continually railed at pricing subsidies and complained of the gross environmental "atrocities" such as Kesterson that he blamed on the bureau's collusion with the water industry. Though Miller and Dan Beard, his chief aide at the committee, were frequently characterized as "enemies" in private conversations at water industry gatherings, there were also limits to Miller's ability to restructure the relationship between the feds and the water industry, particularly agriculture. The farm-water alliance still carried weight in Congress and in the state legislatures, but many of its battles were defensive in nature. Issues like surplus crops, budget restrictions tied to fears around the deficit, the presence of someone like Miller in a coveted water-related chairmanship, and the relatively ineffective aid of a Tony Coelho, all served to eventually force the farm-water lobby to lower its expectations.

DESERT POLITICS

The agricultural wing of the water industry finds itself today increasingly on the defensive. Besides the political difficulties, a range of problems from declining export markets to lower commodity prices has created an economic dimension to agriculture's decline. By the mid-1980s, discussions at water meetings no longer focused simply on the ways to maintain subsidies and increase supplies. The once-scorned concepts of water transfers or reallocations of existing supplies from one group to another began to receive more attention. In this setting, the situation of California's Imperial Valley, one of the oldest and richest irrigated areas in the country, provided an early dramatic example of the politics of water transfers and the problems related to such arrangements.

For more than one hundred years, land speculators, visionaries, high-powered syndicates, and some of California's largest corporations, such as the Southern Pacific, have been active in this valley. Their focus has always been control of the Colorado. Seen as a cheap, abundant supply of water for irrigation, the river has also been an erratic source of flooding and drought.

One of the first parties to attempt to divert water from the Colorado was the California Development Corporation. The company used its diversion scheme to try to attract large numbers of settlers to the valley shortly after the turn of the century. CDC brochures promised cheap government land under the Desert Lands Act and cheap water through its diversion scheme. The company also created a complicated system of contracts, through water companies and sales of stock, that were designed to bypass the limitations of the Desert Lands Act.

The CDC diversion facilities were established without much thought to the Colorado's unpredictable ways, particularly the problem of high river flows. The company, at the same time, sought to keep the newly formed Reclamation Service from entering the valley and devising its own set of dams and storage facilities. Then, shortly after the company secured a loan from the Southern Pacific, a major flood in March 1905 broke through the CDC dam. Within a few months nearly half the entire flow of the Colorado River had entered the valley. The river continued to flow unchecked for the next two years, creating havoc to the irrigation system in the valley and rapidly filling a dry inland basin that came to be called the Salton Sea. The SP, which had taken over the company in order to secure its loan, and had earlier received more than sixty thousand acres in the Imperial Valley from federal land grants, soon began to pursue federal financial help. After receiving some federal support, the SP was further able to cut its losses through the sale of its decrepit malfunctioning waterworks system to the newly created Imperial Irrigation District.

The IID, created in 1911 by a vote of valley residents as a public agency to acquire property and sell bonds to raise money, quickly became the primary voice of the valley agricultural interests.

These interests focused primarily on further ways to control the Colorado, particularly through the construction of a facility near the U.S.–Mexican border called the All-American Canal.

The passage of the Boulder Canyon Act (which included the All-American Canal), was primarily engineered by the IID's first attorney and overall troubleshooter, Phil Swing. Swing, who also became the congressman for the area, had initially attempted to exempt Imperial in the legislation from the 160-acre limitation in the Reclamation law. When this failed, he helped orchestrate a last-minute maneuver for Imperial's exemption in the final days of the Hoover administration. This time he succeeded. Swing and other IID allies enlisted the aid of Assistant Secretary of the Interior Northcutt Ely, who had previously argued against the exemption. Ely, who would shortly be retained by IID, helped convince Hoover's Secretary of the Interior Ray Lyman Wilbur to issue the exemption in the form of a hastily composed letter less than a month before the Hoover team was to leave office. Ely, who would set up a water-related consulting business that included the city of Los Angeles as well as IID as clients, would eventually become, like Swing, one of the water industry's most colorful and powerful participants.

With the passage of the Boulder Canyon Act and the Wilbur letter, the Imperial Valley entered an era of federal subsidization and bail outs. In the immediate aftermath of the Wilbur letter both the IID and several of the valley's farmers faced bankruptcy. IID had become severely overextended from some of its payments to the Southern Pacific and from another deal with a Mexican land syndicate headed by the owner of the *Los Angeles Times*, Harry Chandler. It also confronted the problem of faulty irrigation works and the lack of any drainage system. Just before groundbreaking on construction of the All-American Canal in 1934, the IID, close to default on some of its bonds and obliged to sell its registered warrants at a discount, discovered that many of its bills were not and could not be paid by individual landowners. The district, teetering on the edge of bankruptcy, found itself holding title to thousands of acres of land.

Once the subsidies became available, however, with Hoover Dam on line in 1935 and the All-American Canal operational by 1941, the IID and valley farmers began to cash in on a variety of opportunities. The IID turned to federal and state agencies including the Reconstruction Finance Corporation and the Rural Electrification Agency to help underwrite the beginnings of a drainage program, retire the big debts, and, most of all, establish a substantial revenue base through power sales from the All-American Canal. Meanwhile, the tendencies in the valley toward a more concentrated form of absentee land ownership and industrial organization of farm operations were strengthened. Where the 1930s had witnessed a combination of bankruptcies and sharp conflict between farm labor and management, the 1940s and 1950s saw the flourishing of corporate farming, land speculation, and the opening of major new lands for irrigation.

The valley experienced a boom in both land sales and crop plantings, especially cotton, which vied with lettuce as the area's major crop. IID became an active player in land dealings, selling or leasing part of its tax-related holdings, including some land near the Salton Sea. IID, which had established itself as a major power within the valley, also became an active promoter of the recreational development of the area around the sea.

By the post–World War II period, the Salton Sea had become firmly established as the area's drainage basin. By the time the Colorado River made its way to the valley, the water was loaded with salts, a problem severely exacerbated by the poor irrigation and drainage practices of agriculture upstream. The valley lands, which were already highly alkaline, thus needed a great deal of water— two or even three times the amount ordinarily used in other areas in the Central Valley—to flush out the salts and maintain what the IID called a "positive salt balance." That made the problem of drainage crucial to valley agriculture. At the same time, the salt content of the Salton Sea increased dramatically, from a concentration of about 3,350 parts per million when the sea was created to more than 32,000 parts per million by 1954 when the drainage policy was firmly established. The salt concentrations continued to increase over the next several decades, ultimately reaching nearly 40,000 parts per million, which is 14 percent *higher* than the salt content of ocean water.

Through the 1960s and 1970s, IID policies actively supported the growth and consolidation of the area's agricultural interests. These, however, began to cause a set of problems that would soon come to haunt the local water industry. For one, the IID encouraged the expansion of irrigated lands, through both its land sale and its pricing policies. But with more land under irrigation and a drainage policy that allowed high runoff levels and minimized any conservation effort, the level of the Salton Sea continued to rise over time, eventually creating problems of flooding.

Consecutive years of heavy rainfall in the late 1970s brought this issue to a head. The flooding affected recreational and land development interests who had bought into seafront property, as well as farmers with lands adjacent to the sea. A series of court suits were filed against IID. Among the most significant ones was a civil action brought by two brothers, John and Stephen Elmore, who were among the biggest landowners in the valley.

The Elmores, besides filing a civil suit, also brought complaints before the California Department of Water Resources and the State Water Resources Control Board. They based their actions on a little-known and even less used provision of the state constitution that allowed individuals to bring action to determine whether water was being wasted through the lack of conservation.

The Elmores' actions touched off a chain of events that are still reverberating through the water industry. If water was being wasted, and the Elmores had a solid case on this issue, then a great deal of water, upward of four hundred thousand and even five hundred thousand acre feet according to the district's own later estimates, could be made available through conservation. These amounts were considerable, even greater than the additional supplies projected for urban Southern California from the Peripheral Canal. It didn't take long, then, for some canal opponents, such as the Environmental Defense Fund, to suggest that this one conservation-oriented source, cheaper and far more environmentally benign, could substitute for the other dam-and-ditch-type approach.

In 1981, while the Elmore suits and complaints were still being heard, EDF released a report entitled "Trading Conservation Investments for Credit." Its argument, which elaborated on the points raised already by the Elmores, was simple. IID had complained that many of the conservation measures, such as lining its canals in concrete, were far too expensive to undertake. The low water rates, furthermore, created disincentives for the landowners to improve their own irrigation practices. Therefore, the report suggested, why not have urban Southern California's Metropolitan Water District pay for the conservation and receive credits in the form of the conserved water. All this in turn would help lower the level of the sea and prevent future flooding. It was, as EDF's Tom Graff would later put it, "a win-win situation." It would involve a kind of ersatz market arrangement, cheaper and more efficient, to replace MET's expensive and environmentally problematic quest for Northern California water.

Aside from EDF, the Elmores had difficulty gaining any support from the water industry on their complaint. "Nobody, either within the valley or from the MET or San Diego, would touch it," recalled Elmore attorney David Osias. IID lined up support both from local public officials and various farm organizations who resented any "outside" evaluation of their system. It was an ironic position, given the valley's reliance on federal subsidies and the continuing, substantial role played by absentee owners and farm management operations.

MET itself quickly lined up behind the IID, as its top leaders extolled Imperial's existing conservation efforts as "the finest in the country." MET also denied that any water transfer, or SWAP, as it came to be called, was possible. Other members of the water industry, such as the Farm Bureau, lined up with IID and MET, pooh-poohing any talk of transfers or markets. "They were all scared of the Peripheral Canal comparison," John Elmore later complained, also pointing out the strength of the old-boy water industry network to rally support for one of their own.

99

The ties between urban Southern California and the agricultural Imperial Valley demonstrated in part the strengths of those networks. IID, for example, was legally represented by Paul Engstrand before the State Water Resources Control Board hearings that were held in 1983 on the issue. Engstrand's San Diego law firm was the longtime counsel for the San Diego County Water Authority, and Engstrand himself was the water authority's chief counsel. Prior to that, the attorney responsible for helping charter the water authority was none other than Phil Swing, who had also become a "special water counsel" for the City of San Diego after he had left Congress and the County water authority's first general counsel. The San Diego Water Authority was the largest and most powerful member agency of MET, pushing hardest for additional supplies like the Peripheral Canal.

There were other MET/Imperial ties. E. Thornton Ibbetson, a powerful MET board member from Los Angeles County who would become MET chairman from 1983 to 1987, was a major real estate developer in urban Southern California. Ibbetson's company, Union Development Corporation, had been active in Imperial since the 1950s and controlled several million dollars' worth of real estate in the valley at the time he was MET chairman. There were other MET directors who had land holdings in the valley, though the MET general counsel had ruled that such disclosures were not required under a state conflict-of-interest law providing for a statement of one's economic interests.

The ties were not simply limited to the MET board. The Irvine Company, a major participant in the water industry and a massive land developer in Orange County, was, at one time, the largest landowner in the Imperial Valley. Many of Imperial's absentee owners were based in urban Southern California, and many of Imperial's largest "local" landowners had homes in San Diego or up and down the coast.

By 1983, however, even the old-boy network couldn't resist the momentum for change. The Peripheral Canal had been badly defeated and the idea of an Imperial/MET SWAP seemed more compelling than ever. IID began to lose in the courts on the Salton

Sea Issue and was finally obliged to settle with the Elmores. Soon after, in early 1984, MET and IID cautiously entered negotiations on the SWAP.

By now, talk of water markets and "privatization" was in the air, both from academics and environmentalists and from "free market" conservatives and the Reagan administration, which was interested in the private sector assuming some of the functions of government. The situation was also ripe for "privatization" firms like the Southern California-based Parsons Corporation, which had already begun to explore participation in water quality and waste-water treatment projects with municipal utilities.

Encouraged by a Colorado-based privatization entrepreneur who worked out a consulting arrangement with Parsons, the IID began to see opportunity in the situation. "Parsons suggested to us that a market system for water was about to emerge and that we could get in on the ground floor," remarked IID board member John Benson. "They were telling us that we could become the market brokers of the Southwest." After a formal search to choose a firm, the IID board selected Parsons to come up with a conservation program, help with the MET negotiations, and ultimately figure out how to accomplish such a sale.

The Parsons-IID relationship was fraught with controversy from the outset. Parsons's contract with the district stated that the company would be paid by a percentage of the sale proceeds rather than a direct fee for service. That in turn created a set of built-in incentives for Parsons to sell as much water as possible rather than limit the transaction to a conservation-based transfer agreement.

The entry of Parsons into the SWAP proceedings also produced a strong outcry within the valley. Mistrust of the SWAP was already widespread in part because of fears of the urban behemoth to the West that had been orchestrated by IID and Imperial politicians prior to the SWAP negotiations. Now another outsider, a non-farming multinational corporation, had entered the picture and the mistrust exploded into anger. IID itself also became a target of the local opposition, which included residents from the towns of Imperial and Brawley (who were IID power consumers), some of the tenant farmers, and even some of the larger landowners who felt Parsons and MET were taking the valley for a ride.

After an initial agreement in 1985 was overturned by the IID board because of the strong local opposition, the MET/IID negotiations became jumbled. They were broken off by IID in the summer of 1986 shortly before the elections for IID board members, to resume again a year later though with both sides still far apart. Parsons was also removed after having handled some of the early negotiations. IID still spoke wistfully of a sale and looked to the possibility of dealing directly with San Diego, which had its own recent falling out with its MET parent. The San Diego Water Authority, though interested, kept its distance. The SWAP had become a political football with no clear conclusion in sight. The need for conservation, meanwhile, which had touched off the whole affair in the first place, had been transformed into dreams of a cash-rich sale of the water.

By the late 1980s, the Imperial/MET SWAP, despite the lengthy and inconclusive negotiations, was being widely touted within the water industry as a harbinger of future water markets and water sales, an increasingly attractive option for the agricultural wing of the water industry in light of its economic troubles. But lost in the talk about the SWAP were the valley's economically disadvantaged residents whose conditions had only deteriorated in recent years. These included the tenant farmers and small landowners who had begun to default or keep their lands idle.

By 1987, more than 15 percent of the valley lands had been taken out of production. Instead of benefiting from a SWAP, these farmers and landowners, to make up IID's deficits, were being taxed in the form of a water charge that especially penalized owners of idled lands. Further contributing to the decline in the valley was the heavy use of pesticides, which was no longer effective in fully controlling two key pests—the white fly and the weevil. This in turn contributed to reductions in lettuce and cotton plantings. Farm union activity, furthermore, which had a long and bitter history in the valley, had finally caused some growers to relocate their operations across state lines to Arizona or across the border to Mexico.

The valley also witnessed a number of landowners signing up for Agriculture Department programs that obliged them to take their lands out of production. At the same time, the largely agriculture-related unemployment in the valley reached as high as 30 percent, with per capita income the lowest in the state. In many ways, the valley had become a dual society—rich and poor, Anglo and Hispanic, large landowner and small or landless farmer.

As the SWAP talks dragged on, there was little talk within the water industry about the striking inequities among valley landowners and laborers. IID board members spoke of shaping the SWAP to primarily benefit the larger farmers, who, with the more concentrated the ownership, would receive the greater benefits. Water markets, transfers, and SWAPs, like the federal reclamation program before it, were not being designed to deal with the needs of the entire community or region, just those who dominate the water industry. In Imperial Valley, there have always been winners and losers, subsidies and inequities. The SWAP could well be just the latest version.

CENTER PIVOT CRISIS

On the east side of the Continental Divide, the agriculture/water issues of subsidies, inequities, and proper management have extended to the type of farming itself.

Stretching from the Great Plains and the western edge of the Corn Belt through the badlands of Oklahoma and the Texas High Plains to the Texas/New Mexico border region is the West's longest and most extensive underground body of water, the massive Ogallala aquifer. For years, the Ogallala areas supported a variety of rangeland, dryland farming, and limited irrigation. Then, after World War II, with new governmental policies and improved production techniques, the farming patterns related to the Ogallala began to change. From Texas to Nebraska, huge new lands were put into production through increased use of well water to the point that the Ogallala was being overdrafted at a dangerous rate.

By 1982, the situation had reached crisis proportions. Total

103

irrigated acreage had increased from 3.5 million to 15 million acres between 1950 and 1980, and during that same period the water pumped from the ground had increased from less than 7 million acre feet to more than 21 million acre feet. By the late 1970s, it had become apparent to even the region's biggest boosters that far more was being taken out of the ground than was being replaced, even during the wettest years. A range of problems, some severe, had been generated, from the groundwater depletion to soil erosion, dust storms, and air and groundwater quality hazards.

The situation was most critical for the Texas High Plains where the Ogallala was thinnest and the overdraft most severe. This is a semiarid region where average annual rainfall ranges between fourteen and twenty-one inches a year. Before 1945 much of the area was devoted to dryland farming. But that situation changed dramatically as more than five million acres, about half of all the cropland in the area, came to be irrigated in a few decades. The huge jump in irrigated farming after 1945 was related to many of the same reasons the agricultural industry flourished in the West in this same period: changes in pumping economics and technology, government production and pricing policies, tax laws, and the high rate of return for investors when the commodity prices were sufficiently high and the water costs sufficiently low.

Since the underground water was least plentiful at the southern end of the aquifer and recharge most minimal, the increase in irrigation began to have an almost immediate effect on the Texas high plains. More than one-fifth of the water available from the aquifer had been exhausted by 1980—much of that depletion brought about by irrigation of wheat, cotton, sorghum, and other crops, some of which were designated surplus commodities.

As the water tables declined, the Texas interests joined their counterparts in the high plains region to push for a variety of water importation schemes. These included plans to divert water from the Mississippi and Arkansas rivers. But transbasin transfer schemes, once the popular solution for the water industry for most water-deficient regions, were increasingly ruled out during the 1970s and

1980s as too costly and too controversial, with far too many environmental impacts to be successfully pursued.

The problem of overdraft in Texas was magnified by the irrigation practices in the water-rich part of the Ogallala in Nebraska. While the shift to irrigation in the south took place over a forty-year period, the change to irrigation in Nebraska exploded during the 1960s and 1970s. The state experienced a revolution caused by the widespread adoption of a new irrigation system, the center pivot. From 1970 to 1980, irrigated acreage in Nebraska nearly doubled to more than seven million acres, almost all as a result of the introduction of center pivots, which were used to produce perhaps the country's most overstocked commodity, corn.

If you fly over Nebraska on a clear day you can see vast numbers of green circles like checker pieces on a checkerboard. If you get closer to the land you might see a set of rotating sprinklers, consisting of a horizontal pipeline that moves on wheels and sprays its water, pumped from a well, through sprinkler nozzles. These center pivots, as they are called, usually extend about a quarter of a mile. Through their rotation, they irrigate a circle one-half mile in diameter. Most systems are designed for 160-acre plots, though they are available for different-sized operations as well.

The rise of the center-pivot system—particularly in such places as the Sand Hills region in the western part of the state, where the soil is sandy and the rainfall patterns more closely resemble the semiarid areas of the West—coincided with and in part influenced a range of economic and social factors that transformed Nebraska into a leading irrigation state, third only to California and Texas. Farmers in the state were initially skeptical of the system, but by the 1960s word had spread that the center pivots could make corn grow on dry, sandy soils and in some cases produce yields 50 percent higher than on dry land.

As the system began to catch on in certain counties in the late 1960s, more lands were put under irrigation, almost all of which were exclusively devoted to corn production. At the same time, the value of the land began to escalate rapidly. That, in turn, generated a lending spree, resulting from the policies of both the Production Credit Association and private banks and lenders who made it easier to borrow and thus encouraged the expansion of center-pivot irrigation.

As additional investment capital began to pour into the state, the boom of the late 1960s became the center-pivot revolution of the 1970s. Center-pivot technology was particularly attractive to the out-of-state investor primarily for two reasons. For one, center-pivot systems substantially reduced labor costs to the point that the labor itself was essentially reduced to a maintenance function. Even more importantly for some investors, acreage never before used for irrigation, such as the Sand Hills area, was not being transformed into a more profitable use of the land. The ability of the pivots to apply the water evenly created a degree of predictability for crop production, as in California. "It appeared to many people that the technology had prevailed," wrote a local analyst, "and represented the long-awaited solution to the risks inherent in farming the plains. This view of a new risk-free agriculture was shared by private developers and public experts alike, who contributed colorful rhetoric which further fueled irrigation development in the 1970s."

The investors were also motivated by a host of federal tax policies designed to encourage capital investment in agriculture, including some specifically designed for the Ogallala. The tax laws allowed the irrigation wells to be deducted as well as the entire cost of leveling the land and preparing it for irrigation. Investors had several options in buying the land and installing center pivots: They could speculate on land appreciation, hope for a profitable operation, use the investment as a tax shelter, or some combination of the above.

Through the 1970s, outside investors ranging from major corporations such as Prudential Life Insurance to tax-shelter entities based in Chicago, Minneapolis, or Denver entered the state. Their activities increased the speculative frenzy in land values and caused a jump in the use of the center pivot, even on some very marginal lands. A number of small farmers in the region were also attracted to center pivots. In the process, they changed their traditional farming practices and went increasingly into debt to meet the high capital expenditures involved in turning over the land.

By the 1980s, with the shift in the economics of irrigation and corn production in particular, the center-pivot revolution began to stall. The land speculation had highly inflated the value of the land and prices paid for center-pivot properties. This most affected the smaller farmer-operators, some of whom went out of business when the price of corn went down and the cost of pumping water went up. Others kept going only because of government subsidies from PIK and similar programs. Even the substantial tax advantages were reduced when the Tax Reform Act of 1986 eliminated a number of irrigation-related benefits such as accelerated depreciation and the capital gains exemption.

Ultimately, the center-pivot revolution, according to Ron Krupicka of the Center for Rural Affairs, an important Nebraska advocacy group for small farmers, "forced the farmer to abuse the land." The massive jump in center-pivot systems placed a major strain on the Ogallala, exacerbating the overdraft and accelerating the problems in the southern end of the aquifer. Increased irrigation, with its related heavy fertilizer and pesticide use, also brought problems of groundwater contamination to the fore, generating a major debate on the subject throughout the state by the mid-1980s. Finally, the introduction of the center-pivot system increased the problems of soil erosion and possible desertification of the land. This problem was of particular importance to the Sand Hills region where the shift from the sandy, cattle-grazing rangeland to the heavily irrigated and frequently overfertilized center-pivot croplands brought with it a host of unanticipated problems primarily related to weather-induced topsoil erosion.

Once the irrigated land was taken out of production, which began to happen to an increasing number of center-pivot plots by the mid-1980s, problems were magnified. When it rained, these former center-pivot cornfields turned into marshy areas overgrown with weeds. When it was dry and the winds picked up, dust storms kicked up throughout the area.

All was not lost for the center-pivot operators, however. As with their counterparts in California, agricultural decline and even retiring lands from production had some compensation in the form of new federal subsidies. This time the bailout came in the form of the Soil Conservation Service Conservation Reserve Program. This program paid farmers to idle land prone to erosion, an ironic feature of the center-pivot situation since the technology had increased the potential for erosion in the first place. During 1986, in the Sand Hills region alone, an estimated 365 pivots irrigating about 47,350 acres were placed in the reserve. In turn, center-pivot farmers were to be paid about $21.6 million over a ten-year period. And many of those participating in the program were the same absentee owners who had been so instrumental in generating the center-pivot revolution a little more than a decade earlier.

The center-pivot revolution of the 1960s and 1970s had turned into the center-pivot crisis of the 1980s. With declines in irrigated production from Nebraska to Texas, the anticipated severe overdraft of the Ogallala no longer seemed imminent. Instead of discussions of transbasin transfers, there was now talk of water markets. Some officials began to argue that water-surplus Nebraska, for example, should sell its water to water-scarce areas such as the urban Front Range cities in Colorado. The bureau and the corps, meanwhile, still harbored thoughts of transfer and importation schemes, but they remained largely in the background.

Ultimately, the Ogallala events have encouraged a form of restructuring of the region's agricultural industry. New technologies and new patterns of ownership were introduced, based on various pricing mechanisms and tax policies so central to the farm-water equation. Land speculation and intense irrigated farming quickly supplanted stable rural communities and traditional dryland farm activity. In this way, the turbulent history of the center-pivots came to reflect a Great Plains version of industrial agriculture's own rise and decline.

THE CONTINUING QUEST FOR CHEAP WATER

For the agricultural wing of the water industry, water policy has continued to evolve around the search for a cheap water supply and increased production. Once the price of water begins to approach its real cost, then the thoughts of the industry turn to water markets and bail outs.

During the Reagan years, the water industry was forced into a broad retreat on several fronts: surplus crop issues, construction of new facilities, water importation schemes, cost sharing, and even pricing matters as reflected in the "hammer clause" provision of the 1982 Reclamation Reform Act. Yet the water industry remained resilient and persistent. Even while its primary benefactor, the Bureau of Reclamation, was under attack and Interior Department officials spoke of a "change of mission," the federal agency was still able, for example, to complete the work and open a new extension of the California Central Valley Project, the San Felipe unit, twenty years after its original authorization. This federally subsidized project would provide perhaps the most expensive reclaimed water in the West for a few farmers to grow some vegetables.

The local water interests' access and influence with the bureau remained as extensive as ever, even as the bureau's role was changing. For example, the longtime California head of the bureau, Michael Catino, became, immediately after his retirement, the head of the California Central Valley Flood Control Association, a group that informally represented many of the Central Valley Project contractors. In the Westlands Water District situation, there were potential conflict-of-interest problems involving two key Interior Department officials, Solicitor Ralph Tarr and the department's top West Coast lawyer, David Lindgren. Tarr had helped negotiate a series of agreements with the Westlands Water District over pricing matters that caused many Westlands critics to cry foul. The critics objected to the fact that Tarr, prior to his appointment to the Interior Department, had been a senior attorney with one of the most powerful law firms in the Central Valley. This firm, in turn, represented a number of Westlands landowners. Lindgren was temporarily suspended from his job in 1987 because of allegations that he represented the government in legal negotiations with Westlands while he was discussing a possible job with the water district's law firm. As a consequence, several sources, including the Justice Department and the Office of Governmental Ethics, launched investigations. The Justice Department stated that Lindgren's case lacked "prosecutive merit," and Lindgren ultimately resigned in 1988 before the conclusion of the investigation by the Office of Governmental Ethics.

The bureau's claim to a new approach was most undercut when it issued its long-awaited regulations regarding the Reclamation Act's hammer clause in April 1987. When the Reclamation Reform Act was first passed in 1982, a number of western farm operations, especially those in California, restructured their form of ownership in anticipation of the provisions of the hammer clause. The intent of Congress, led by Water and Power Subcommittee Chair George Miller, had been clear: farm operations over 960 acres would be obliged to pay full cost for their water. The farm operators, however, had devised a number of ingenious methods to give the appearance that the large operations had been broken into farms of 960 acres or less, when, in fact, the divisions were made on paper only. These methods involved leasing, new ownership structures such as tenants-in-common, and "farm management arrangements" or "FMAs." But while the hammer clause regulations eliminated leasing, which had been widely used in earlier years to avoid the 160-acre limit, they failed to cover FMAs.

When the rules were announced, there were large numbers of corporate filings in farm-based rural counties, including a record number in Fresno County, California, in the heart of the Central Valley Project service area. Miller and other bureau critics vowed to go back to Congress to eliminate yet another loophole that had been created by the "new" bureau. Miller called BuRec's decision on FMAs a "fraud" that was caused by the political influence of a few large growers. "Flat defiance of the law," another critic said of the bureau, as the various players, from the water industry to its various antagonists, geared up for one more round of conflict. Even

Tony Coelho, who joined Miller in proposing amendments to eliminate the FMA loophole, worried that "the actions of a few farmers to circumvent the law [via FMAs] could eventually endanger subsidized water programs in general."

The hammer clause episode served to demonstrate both the continuing power of the agricultural wing of the water industry and its increasingly tentative posture. At water industry conferences and agency gatherings, the talk is defensive. The old-boy network of the farm/water alliance, though still in place, acts as if it is being displaced from the sources of decision-making. Its members speak at times bitterly of the present and nostalgically of the past, whether in terms of Congress, commodity prices, or the public acceptance of the farm-water connection. They worry about the future and the inexorable pressure toward higher water prices and reductions in subsidies. Agriculture, particularly western irrigated agriculture, is a creature of subsidies; the search for cheap water still shapes its agenda.

But, more and more, the agricultural industry has been forced to confront the restructuring that has taken place in times of both growth and decline. In the post–World War II boom years, when water use increased dramatically and the big federal projects reinforced the tendency toward concentration, agriculture came to be dominated by the large landowner and a technology and capital driven system. In the process, agriculture changed from a kind of life-style and a set of values—such as stewardship of the land and self-reliance—to a form of business enterprise and "science" of production guided by new technology-oriented "experts." Smaller farm owners, tenant farmers, and those remaining "family" farmers continued to be squeezed by the pressures of production and the costs of irrigation. When the revolution in production turned into a crisis of overproduction, with its falling commodity prices and farm income, the focus shifted to possible changes in water use, signaling perhaps a long-term decline in agriculture's role in water development. The new talk of agriculture selling its water rights corresponded with the discussion about the increasing needs of the potential buyers of those rights.

During the late 1970s, that process of buying and selling was first associated with the activities of energy companies who eagerly sought to purchase agricultural water rights in anticipation of increased energy developments, such as synthetic fuels, which required a great deal of water. Farmers in Colorado, Utah, and elsewhere began to sell or lease their water in what many presumed would be a dramatic reallocation of water, especially in the intermountain West. When the energy crisis faded in the early 1980s, the reallocations focus shifted to urban areas, which continued to seek additional sources of water.

Like irrigated agriculture before it, water-short cities have been constantly in search of water. As agriculture once grew, encouraged by a variety of policies that helped stimulate a revolution in production, the cities have also continued to grow, equally encouraged by policies that have taken expansion as a given. The common factor is water. Securing that water has become the means by which expansion is made possible. The water industry, once dominated by agriculture, has now become a wary coalition of development interests, a farm-city-water alliance, that threatens to unravel as the search for water becomes a competition for a more limited supply.

Chapter 4

The Urban-Development Complex: The Politics of Growth

MOON OVER HONEY SPRINGS

For the developers, everything seemed to be wired. They had hoped, when the plans for the Honey Springs complex were first laid out in the early 1980s, to touch all the necessary bases. Jack Felson— a former aide to the most "growth conscious" supervisor in San Diego County, Roger Hedgecock—was at the center of the effort. Felson had helped put together an interesting collection of architects, advisors, contractors, and consultants: people like Bill Press, a former Jerry Brown aide; Sim Van der Ryn, a former state architect who was part of Jerry Brown's alternative-technology circle; and Ralph "Mike" Graham, who had just been elected chairman of the San Diego County Water Authority and was one of the water authority's representatives to the Metropolitan Water District Board of Directors.

The Honey Springs plan, a proposed 2154-acre development located near the town of Jamul on the eastern outskirts of the San Diego metropolitan area, had much to overcome. There was, for example, plenty of opposition in the local community. Residents feared the development would bring about major changes and disruptions, including problems with the local groundwater supply.

There was the San Diego general plan, which restricted residential development to twenty-acre parcels in areas not served by imported MET water unless the developers could somehow demonstrate that adequate groundwater was available. And there was the growing constituency within San Diego itself that was wary of the consequences of the rapid growth taking place to the east and north of the city. They feared that San Diego could become a latter-day version of Los Angeles, with its sprawl, its smog, and powerful growth machine dictating the terms of development.

But the developer had so far succeeded in getting by hurdles at the San Diego Community Planning Board and the Board of Supervisors. Further, the local area had been annexed to the San Diego County Water Authority as the first step toward annexation to the MET system. Though the developer had scaled down the project to bypass those hurdles, the plan still involved the construction of 389 expensive model homes—"earth houses," as they were called—complete with solar panels, an alternative wastewater system to irrigate avocado and citrus fruit groves, a big lake in the center of the community, and its own fire, police, and education agencies. Like many projects in the Southwest, Honey Springs—situated at the edge of the Anza-Borrego desert—was designed to create a feeling of self-sufficiency in a mini-urban-oasis.

Self-sufficiency except for the water, that is. Groundwater supply was limited, but the developer had the good fortune of hiring CH_2M Hill, a major water-oriented engineering and construction firm. CH_2M Hill was to conduct a groundwater survey to see if there was enough local water to avoid any growth restriction. The contact with CH_2M Hill was made through Mike Graham, the company's business development director for the Southwest, who worked out of the company's San Diego office.

It was obviously the right choice. Graham was a key figure within the San Diego water industry. He had been with the city manager's office and became a major player within the city of San Diego's delegation to the San Diego County Water Authority. He had just recently become chairman of SDCWA and was one of San Diego's five representatives to the MET board.

The CH_2M Hill study, which claimed that a substantial source of local groundwater was available, appeared to get the developer past the most difficult obstacle. Local residents were furious with the study. They felt the groundwater source was tremendously overstated. A study conducted for the county by a San Diego State University professor agreed with that assessment and projected substantially different figures.

Ultimately, the developer settled on annexation to the San Diego County Water Authority and to MET as the best long-term solution. There was little discussion at the Water Authority board, which generally avoided any discussion of development issues when it came to annexation. The attitude at both CWA and MET was that the job of the agency was simply to provide water to whoever asked for it, regardless of circumstance. "We're not in the growth-regulating business," the directors argued, but they went about establishing annexation policies designed to encourage growth while avoiding any review of growth's consequences.

When the matter came before the MET board, most board members had no second thoughts about approval, despite possible variations involving MET's own procedures and potential political problems in providing several hundred acre feet of water for an artificial lake in the midst of the campaign for the Peripheral Canal. The directors, furthermore, had little idea of the local controversies at stake. As expected, the board, given its bias, voted overwhelmingly in favor of approval as a matter of routine.

Though the annexations had been approved, it was still not clear sailing for the Honey Springs project. A local San Diego newspaper got wind of Mike Graham's relationship with CH_2M Hill and that company's ties to the project. The ensuing controversy raised the question of the politics of annexation and the role of the water agencies in automatically providing imported water to new areas, no matter what the circumstance. Eventually a lawsuit was filed by local residents and the San Diego Sierra Club. The court suit in turn held up the development, which languished for a number of years. A fuller discussion inside the water agencies about annexation, however, never occurred.

Despite the solar panels, earth houses, conservation plans, and creative architecture, Honey Springs seemed, in terms of the water issues, representative of development schemes not just for San Diego but for the whole sunbelt. Water has become central to these plans of the urban-development complex. It is priced so that developments do not have to pay their way. It is made available from distant places so there is no mechanism to link development to what the resources of an area can support. And through its oversizing and dependence on increased sales, the water system has been structured so that growth follows the water.

Nearly ten years after the first plans were drawn up and more than five years after the final MET approval was completed, the Honey Springs development has still remained in limbo, a fading memory for the various players involved. Bill Press and Sim Van der Ryn are off into new careers, reestablishing their environmental credentials. Mike Graham left the water industry to retire to the Midwest. Meanwhile, local residents still live on the other side of large-scale development. And as the moon sets over a quiet and peaceful Jamul, where the lake, the avocado groves, and the earth houses were supposed to be, one awaits the next battle at the edge of the city, with water still likely to play a decisive role.

FROM PRIVATE TO PUBLIC

Water systems have influenced and reflected social organization. The history of our cities and farms has been bound up with the provision of water and with the organizations responsible for carrying out those activities. The emergence of the urban water industry broadly coincided with the patterns of rapid urbanization and industrial change that gave birth to the modern urban center. The systematic search for continuing sources of water supply was an activity that was deemed crucial to establishing an ongoing cycle of growth and development.

By the mid-twentieth century, the urban water industry had become a mature and important grouping of power in the urban community. Though often playing a secondary role to agriculture in the relationships and benefits provided by federal water development, the urban interests increasingly came to be recognized as representing the future of water development. The equation of increased water availability and urban expansion was particularly pronounced in the arid West, though water issues from wastewater to flood control to increased storage remained essential for urban/industrial growth interests throughout the country.

By the 1970s and 1980s, the prospects for new supply projects looked far bleaker than ever before in the history of the water industry. In order to continue expanding to accommodate new growth, urban water agencies sought new strategies while still pursuing the more traditional approach, the construction of additional storage and distribution facilities. Urban water interests began to tentatively explore ways to "stretch" and reallocate existing supplies instead of developing additional sources. Water reallocations, another way of talking about water markets or transfers from agricultural to urban users, became a new buzzword at water industry gatherings.

These new issues have placed the urban water industry at the center of the politics of water. Still loosely allied with agriculture on most occasions, urban-development interests have at times become competitive and ultimately clashed with their allies as their supply needs continue to expand. Urban water agencies remain growth-driven even as the means to accomplish its goals are modified. A product of the emergence of the forces of urbanization and industrialization, the urban water industry continues to be the meeting ground for an urban-development complex.

The issues of the urban water industry can be traced back to the rise of the American city. In the immediate aftermath of the Revolution of 1776, the newly emerging cities along the Atlantic seaboard needed to develop appropriate water systems to deal with the problems associated with the rise of urbanism. Through much of the eighteenth century, the leadership of the new urban communities had been reluctant to provide the capital resources and create the organizational structures to keep up with increased water needs.

The public wells were limited in number, frequently dwarfed by the burgeoning number of private wells serving the wealthier parts of the community. Public water service was essentially reduced to a fire-service function and was often inadequate to deal with the changing and growing patterns of urban development.

By the 1790s, population growth and economic expansion had far outstripped the chaotic and unregulated system of private and public wells and pumps that dotted many of the larger communities in the new country. Meeting the expanding demands for domestic use, fire service, sanitation, and overall public health invariably meant a search for new sources and construction of new facilities, including distribution networks and hookups. The political leadership of cities such as Boston, New York, and Baltimore were reluctant to press for a "public utility" concept around water services since that meant large initial outlays of capital and substantial operational expenditures. Instead, these leaders turned to newly chartered private water companies.

The rise of the private water companies at the turn of the century only compounded the problems of growth. The interest of the new companies was less in public service and more in the possibility of controlling a source of capital, much in the way of a bank holding company. Such interest was widespread: one-tenth of all new corporations in the young country—twenty-nine all told—were created for water-related purposes between 1791 and 1800.

Many of these private companies exacerbated the problems of adequate service by a reluctance to pursue new sources of supply (which would have tied up their capital) and an unwillingness to upgrade the cities' distribution systems. Even in a city like Baltimore, where the private companies were considered fair and competent, the pressure for new supplies quickly outstripped the capabilities and financial resources of the private sector groups. Where those companies functioned more explicitly as capital pools than as water utilities, service problems reached crisis dimensions.

Nowhere was that as striking as the takeover of New York City's water supply system at the turn of the century by a high-powered ersatz banking combine whose main players included at one time or another Alexander Hamilton, Aaron Burr, and DeWitt Clinton. During the late 1790s, New York actively began to explore alternative sources of water, including the Bronx River and the Croton River watershed upstate. In the midst of these discussions, the state legislature, in March 1799, passed an "Act for supplying the City of New York with pure and wholesome water." The act included a clause that allowed the company named in the bill to use its surplus capital in transactions other than those related to its water activities. This firm, known as the Manhattan Company, opened its offices on a Wall Street site five months after the legislation was signed and immediately established a full-scale bank operation.

The Manhattan Company episode became as thorough a scandal as can be found in the annals of the water industry. Steered through the legislature by Assemblyman Aaron Burr, who, along with Hamilton, was an early partner in the undertaking, the maneuver was clearly designed to escape the regulations around bank charters. The Manhattan Company charter instead had no safeguards. It was not required to put the city's streets back in satisfactory condition after it laid pipes, which it frequently didn't. There was no provision for the free use of water in firefighting activities, nor were there any limitations on how the rates were to be set. The only real restriction was the provision that a water supply had to be created—in ten years' time.

Instead the new company jealously guarded its "surplus" capital by minimizing its water-related activities, even to the point of violating its own service requirements. Time and again, through the first decades of the nineteenth century, the company argued that its minimum engineering operations met the "supply in ten years" guarantee. Meanwhile, customer complaints increased in scale and intensity while the deteriorating quality of the water in the city's wells contributed to a supply crisis. In the 1820s, with the city facing its most serious crisis to date, the Manhattan Company led the attacks against suggestions that the Croton watershed be tapped. The company was joined in the attacks by a number of small entrepreneurs—water-cart owners—who took advantage of the city's chaotic supply-and-delivery system by tapping pump sites at natural springs

119

and then reselling the water by the bucketful at twenty times the original cost.

By 1830, the crisis had come to a head. A major fire two years earlier had destroyed a substantial amount of property, mobilizing business and political interests to seek a new supply. The public was totally disenchanted with the Manhattan Company, with two-thirds of the city dependent on the foul-smelling, polluted wells. The streets were also filled with sewage and drainage that created a stench detectable as far as two or three miles away. By 1834, the state legislature had established a Board of Water Commissioners for the city to lay the groundwork for the creation of the Croton Aqueduct and a municipally owned water system. The Manhattan Company, pleased to be rid of its water business, went on to become a major Wall Street financial powerhouse, known today as the Chase Manhattan Bank.

Through the early part of the nineteenth century, several cities experienced supply shortages or anticipated shortages similar to those in New York. This was largely a result of rapid population and industrial growth as well as changing patterns of both residential and industrial use. The water closet, for example, patented in the 1830s and used widely after the Civil War, led to a huge jump in per capita use.

During the period of rapid industrialization and urbanization following the Civil War, most large cities had been forced to turn to new, large-volume water supplies, often imported far from the city limits, to meet the phenomenal growth in water use. Per capita water consumption had increased in some areas from two or three gallons a day to between fifty and one hundred gallons. And while both per capita use and overall use were increasing—often geometrically—the private water companies were becoming ever more reluctant to expand to meet the increased demand. Furthermore, both the private companies and the public utilities that replaced them had a strong class bias. Pipes were laid through districts that promised the greatest return on such investment. That frequently left the poorer or more remote districts without a supply except from the most contaminated sources. As the cities grew larger, the lag in providing adequate service became more serious.

By the turn of the century, most municipal business and political leaders began to advocate public ownership of the water system. The shift from private to public was considered crucial for mobilizing the necessary capital resources to allow for urban and industrial expansion by providing a continuing water supply. New York went first to the Croton, then the Catskills, and eventually to the Delaware River; Boston, after a protracted political debate, went to Long Pond, later named Lake Cochituate; Philadelphia, with the most modern and best-run system (though also class biased), tapped the Schuylkill River, and so on. These patterns were also repeated in the West, as major metropolises like Los Angeles, San Francisco, and Denver based their patterns of growth on the availability of imported water supplies from distant watersheds, with the system shifting from private to publicly run operations at the moment of expansion.

In the process, a new powerful interest group emerged, led by engineers but including a range of political and business figures who recognized the crucial role of water in the development of the new urban and industrial forms of organization. This group had no name or even explicit identity—the concept of an urban "water industry" emerged in the twentieth century—but they had begun to make a mark on the events happening around them. Preeminently local in character, these water leaders would soon be joined by various national interests, both governmental and corporate, who would take over the task of building bigger and more far-reaching projects.

For the budding water industry, the link between water availability and urban expansion became the motivating factor behind the search for new supplies and construction of new capital facilities. A great deal of the expansion was taking place in the West, where new cities were being created almost overnight. Expansion, however, was not limited to the western sunbelt. Cities in the East and Midwest, particularly commercial centers like New York and Chicago, as well as the new industrial centers such as Cleveland and Pittsburgh, were either improvising on old sources or devising major new systems.

In New York, the annexation of Brooklyn, the rapid growth of the boroughs, and the commercial boom in Manhattan created pressure by the 1930s for the city's water leaders to find another distant water source. A project on the Delaware River, similar to the earlier developments in the Catskills, was designed with the expectation that growth was continuous, that per capita use would continue to rise, and that supply-side planning merited the city's exclusive attention rather than a more conservation-oriented approach.

The city of Chicago, like many of the Atlantic seaboard cities, experienced the shift from private to public ownership of the waterworks system as a way to meet growing demand. Unlike cities such as New York or Boston, Chicago had a vast supply of potable water at its doorstep in Lake Michigan. But it was the problem of quality rather than supply that began to place a strain on Chicago's system.

During the late nineteenth century, industries had located along the banks of the Chicago River, which ran out to the lake, and sewers had been constructed to empty into the river. "As a result," an internal history of the Chicago Water Department noted, "the Chicago River was turned into a veritable cesspool by the sewage that was poured into it in addition to the wastes from the slaughter houses and distilleries." Eventually the pollution reached the lake, and the city's supply was severely contaminated.

The local water industry's supply-side solution was ingenious: reverse the flow of the Chicago River. Instead of emptying out into the lake, the river was redirected, along with the wastes discharged into it. At first, a canal was built to help redirect the river, but by the 1890s, as the volume of sewage increased substantially, a larger system was created. The sewage from the Chicago River was redirected to the Des Plaines River, a small stream that emptied into the Illinois River and eventually to the Mississippi. The relatively secure Lake Michigan supply could now be tapped for both the expansion within the Chicago city limits as well as the growing suburbs to the north, while the sewage flowed south, away from the lake. Downstream users, such as the city of St. Louis, were unhappy with the arrangement, and a series of court actions were filed over the years that only modified but didn't fundamentally alter the arrangement.

Water supply as an instrument for urban expansion was also characteristic of dozens of small, medium-sized, and major metropolitan areas throughout the West. The rise of irrigated agriculture, also heavily dependent on water development, served the growing urban markets of the West in the early twentieth century and established a link between the two systems. By the 1930s, the Bureau of Reclamation began to incorporate municipal and industrial uses as part of its development plans. Urban water-industry lobbyists such as the ubiquitous Northcutt Ely were also becoming instrumental in putting together water-development packages.

By World War II, urban expansion in such places as Phoenix, Denver, Houston, and Dallas had become an industry in its own right. Many of the key interests responsible for the policies of expansion came to dominate the politics and decision-making of their communities. Those interests overlapped with an emergent water industry, which was busily devising projects bent on establishing continuing sources of supply and pricing mechanisms designed to encourage growth.

THE GROWTH MACHINE

The urbanization of vast stretches of land in the South Coast Basin from San Diego in the south to Ventura and Riverside counties northwest and east of Los Angeles is perhaps the most striking example in the country of the emergence of an urban-development complex. Los Angeles was always a rather arbitrary hub in this development, from its selection as a southern terminal point by the Southern Pacific to the frenzied and often chaotic boom-and-bust cycles that have lasted more than seventy-five years. The center city lacked many of the essential prerequisites of growth, but the expansionary policies of its elite overcame obstacles in order to "fulfill [for Los Angeles] its magnificent and manifest destiny," as the elite's leading organ, the *Los Angeles Times*, put it.

The foremost obstacles were the limitations imposed by the relative lack of rainfall (an average of about thirteen inches a year) and the extent to which local sources could sustain the expectation of rapid and continuing expansion. As early as the turn of the century, with the transition from private water companies to the public Los Angeles Water Department, local development interests were already assuming that "the future development and prosperity [of the area] will be measured largely by the available water supply," as the city's consultant and troubleshooter, J. B. Lippincott, put it.

The search for new sources of water also had a political dimension that was instrumental in defining the shape of the city for years to come. Shortly after Los Angeles voters approved the bonds to finance an aqueduct from the Owens Valley in Inyo County, opposition forces in the city, led by the local Socialist party, began to question the assumptions behind the project. The conflict of interest of the aqueduct promoters both inside and outside the Board of Water Commissioners, a core water-industry group, became a rallying cry of the Socialists and other aqueduct critics. These promoters also had extensive land holdings in the San Fernando Valley to the north of the city and had structured the project so that the additional water would make possible urban subdivision of these undeveloped lands, with big profits for the subdividers.

Perhaps more than in any other city, the early water industry in Los Angeles directly overlapped with the forces of urban development. The land syndicates that subdivided huge tracts in the San Fernando Valley were busy subdividing throughout the Basin. In each case, they employed essentially the same strategy. The bankers and financial interests provided the startup capital; the railroad and interurban streetcar interests provided the transportation links; the electric utilities provided new hookups; the water commission and other government agencies provided the water and other essential services; and the newspaper owners promoted the projects and stimulated interest in the subdivisions. The land syndicate, meanwhile—represented by each of those interests—bought up the undeveloped land in large tracts, organized campaigns to encourage settlement, linked the feasibility of the project to water availability, and launched the land rush.

To succeed, the water industry-cum-land syndicaters devised a strategy based on several related factors: a large imported water supply, a major, inexpensive source of energy, a large supply of cheap labor made possible in part by continuing population growth, and the attraction of new industries to the region.

At the moment the water arrived from the Owens Valley to the intake gates at Sylmar in the northern end of the San Fernando Valley in 1913, the shape of the city began to be altered radically. Over the next fifteen years, the city dramatically increased its land area, almost entirely through a policy of annexation. Both developed and undeveloped areas, incorporated cities and unincorporated territory, were faced with a kind of water blackmail. They could annex and receive the imported water, or face the limits of growth imposed by the lack of water since the aqueduct water could not be sold outside the city limits. Some communities, such as Pasadena, Santa Monica, and Beverly Hills, had functioning wells to provide an adequate supply and were able to resist. But other areas, from the seacoast community of Venice to the Watts area to nearly the entire San Fernando Valley, were forced to annex. The city of Los Angeles became the largest municipal land mass in the country, surpassing New York at the height of the push for annexation.

By the early 1920s, the annexation battles had become particularly bitter. Scare campaigns were commonplace, compounded by a sequence of dry winters that heightened tensions over future supplies. As the urban expansion proceeded beyond even the new city limits, development interests throughout the basin finally sought a truce. All agreed that an additional source of imported water would allow the growth to continue without the need to extend the city's boundaries. That source this time would be the Colorado River. The organization created for the purpose of securing that supply, the Metropolitan Water District, was seen as representing urban-development interests both inside and outside the city.

Once MET was organized and Hoover Dam and the Colorado

River aqueduct were authorized, however, the presumptions about continuing growth were soon called into question. The Depression of the 1930s dramatically slowed down the rate of immigration, despite the arrival of poor and bankrupt farmers from Oklahoma, Texas, Arkansas, and elsewhere. Opposition to the water industry's plans surfaced within the city of Los Angeles itself, as some local politicians began to realize the city had little immediate need of any Colorado River water. Meanwhile, the financing arrangements were structured so the city would provide the giant share of the district-wide tax revenues needed to build the aqueduct and finance the operations and maintenance costs once the water arrived.

Though the city of Los Angeles's representatives dominated the new MET board and management, they immediately established policies that were favorable to newly developing areas rather than the city itself. They did so in part as developers in their own right, and as participants and leaders in the urban-development complex that transcended the boundaries of particular municipalities. These policies were designed to draw on the tax base of the developed areas while creating pricing incentives for water use and development of the new areas. Once again, the key to such policies was annexation, this time not to the city, but to the water district.

After Colorado River water arrived in the Basin in 1941, so much surplus water was available at first that MET practically offered to give it away for free in order to establish a more substantial revenue base. Annexation charges, amortized interest free at first, were just a pittance of the real costs of providing the water and building the facilities. Developers were able to receive subsidies on a scale that resembled the pricing policies of the Bureau of Reclamation for its agricultural constituents.

By the end of World War II, MET, led by a new aggressive chairman from the city of Los Angeles, Joseph Jensen, embarked on a rapid-fire series of annexations even more impressive than the reworking of the Los Angeles city boundaries between 1913 and 1928. The patterns of new urban subdivision in Orange, Riverside, and San Diego counties as well as the growth patterns within Los Angeles County followed the lines of annexation to the MET.

Jensen, an oil industry executive and a key figure within the various water committees of the Chamber of Commerce before assuming his position at MET, was a vigorous advocate of the link between annexation and growth. The top leaders at MET were often themselves directly involved in the growth business. E. Thornton Ibbetson, for example, a MET director from the Los Angeles County Central Basin Water District and a major developer with holdings from the Imperial Valley to the Long Beach and Lakewood areas within the Basin, traced his involvement in the water industry to the recognition that without the water he couldn't subdivide his land or build his shopping centers. "So I joined the water board," he recalled, "to get the water."

By the 1950s, certain tensions related to the annexation policy began to surface. Several areas within the Basin, such as the Pomona and Chino communities, which straddled Los Angeles and Riverside counties, were still largely agricultural but showed signs of the shift toward urbanization. These areas opted for annexation to MET to secure future water supplies. Some on the MET board resisted, since the district charter explicitly specified just municipal and industrial use for the MET supply. But the agricultural areas threatened to sign a separate contract with the State of California's Department of Water Resources to eventually receive water from a potential new project designed to bring water south from Northern California. Though this State Water Project was still just an idea at the time, MET directors went along with the annexation for fear of losing their monopoly on imported water sources.

As a consequence, the MET board established its new policy, known as the Laguna Declaration. The basis for annexation was expanded and the district stipulated it would seek out a permanent supply of water for the region. Water would be provided, according to the policy, to anyone who requested it, whether an urban or agricultural user, in any area within the South Coast Basin. This MET territory now included six counties, stretching from Ventura County in the north to the Mexican border. The water system, already supportive of the phenomenal postwar growth in the Basin, had institutionalized a continuing basis for expansion.

127

For the next twenty-five years, the Southern California water industry, armed with the Laguna Declaration, consolidated its preeminent position within the urban-development complex. Major annexations continued during the 1950s and 1960s, stimulated in part by the authorization of the State Water Project from Northern California. The trend toward urbanization continued uninterrupted, with farmlands and undeveloped land giving way to suburban housing tracts, mini-malls, and instant communities such as Diamond Bar to the east, Thousand Oaks to the west, and Irvine to the south. The wildest and most speculative claims of its boosters—that the entire South Coast Basin would be transformed into a giant megalopolis—no longer seemed exaggerated. Continuing growth and continuing water supplies seemed always within reach.

But conditions changed, first with the drought of 1976–77, then with the protracted and ultimately losing battle to build a Peripheral Canal. The water industry became more visible and occasionally divided as the pursuit of growth came to represent a more costly and complicated objective. Within the MET system, the focus turned to San Diego, where the battleground over growth was most severe. It was there, just north of the Mexican border, that the water industry seemed strongest, and the future of the urban-development complex seemed ready to play itself out.

END OF THE PIPELINE

Among MET member agencies, the San Diego County Water Authority has been the system's largest and fastest growing user and its most consistent and insistent advocate of growth. At the same time, San Diego has sometimes seemed to be a passive participant, more a team player than an aggressive advocate. This posture related to San Diego's long-standing fears about its location in the system and its growing water needs. More than any of the other twenty-six agencies belonging to MET, the San Diego water interests saw themselves at the end of the pipeline, dependent on factors outside their control.

"We were more MET than MET," as the San Diego Water Authority's former general manager characterized his agency's attitude of support for the larger district's central role in promoting development. Similar to MET and other water agencies in Southern California and the West, the San Diego County Water Authority, designed to secure an imported water supply, was conceived as a necessary adjunct to the forces of urban development. With limited local sources placing potential constraints on future growth, San Diego development interests became interested in the Colorado River as that outside water source as far back as the 1920s. During the mid-1930s, the Water Committee of the San Diego Chamber of Commerce began sponsoring meetings to explore the possibility of San Diego building its own aqueduct to the Colorado via the Imperial Valley. This was an idea that was favored by the city of San Diego's water advisor Phil Swing. The meetings were dominated by real estate and land interests who saw "a big opportunity to make some money and to develop the interior area of the county," as one of the participants put it.

It was the U.S. Navy, however, rather than the San Diego water interests, which made the first move on the Colorado. Unlike the water industry, which was less concerned about shortage than future development, the Department of Defense sought an assured supply in the immediate term. During World War II, the Defense Department had decided to extend its naval operations in the San Diego region as part of its thrust toward the Pacific. Concerned about even the slightest threat of shortage for their bases, the Navy pushed for San Diego to hook up with the MWD system and build an extension of the Colorado Aqueduct to San Diego.

At the Navy's insistence, the local water industry created the San Diego County Water Authority in 1944 in order to join MET and tap the Colorado. The CWA was structured in roughly the same manner as the MET system and for basically the same reasons. In both cases, the leaders of the new water agencies came for the two big cities in the system—San Diego and Los Angeles—which were essentially underwriting their agencies' initial water development projects. At the same time, these leaders wanted to explore development possibilities both inside and outside their city limits. Both CWA and MET became coalitions between the central "inner city," and the outlying areas. And both agencies went through a rapid series of annexations that altered their structure while encouraging growth in the perimeter areas.

Those expansionary moves did meet some resistance. One of the old elite, San Diego's Arthur Marston, objected to the new arrangement on the grounds that the newly annexing areas had no local source of water themselves and were therefore developing "a very risky type of economy," as CWA's general counsel William Jennings characterized it. Thus, these areas would be completely dependent on the imported water from MET. That, in turn, would change CWA's function from being a source of *supplemental* water to becoming the area's *primary* source. The Laguna Declaration, which was also a response to San Diego's request for additional water, ultimately symbolized both agencies' emphasis on imported water for their regions.

By the 1960s and 1970s, growth in San Diego, along with Orange and Riverside counties, became the focus of the urban-development complex. These were the years of phenomenal growth and urbanization throughout Southern California. Huge new tracts were subdivided, dwarfing the promotional schemes of the Owens Valley period when the land syndicates made their fortunes. These were also the years when the problems of development—air quality, transportation, waste disposal, and, by the end of the 1970s, water supply and water quality—became pervasive.

The push for the Peripheral Canal culminated this period of development. When the referendum battle took place, San Diego was at the forefront of the MET effort. The local San Diego water industry undertook a systematic campaign, with massive advertising, a major push by public officials and business interests, and unequivocal, passionate support from the media. "We are dependent on 90 percent of our water from the MET system," the San Diego water leaders emphasized, an exaggerated but effective claim in the heat of the battle. "Our very future is at stake," these water interests implored. "Without the water this area will revert back to desert."

More than in any other area in Southern California, the San Diego water industry's arguments worked. But despite the fact that 73 percent of the voters in San Diego County backed the canal in the 1982 election, support in the rest of Southern California was less substantial, with the outcome determined by the huge majorities in the north. When the water industry failed again two years later to get another water development package out of the legislature, the San Diego water industry, which had argued so forcefully about imminent crisis, began to realize that its arguments were leading to trouble.

Several businesses, including a couple of high-tech companies from Japan, were at the time toying with the possibility of locating in San Diego. The area, in fact, was hoping to become a new center for the high-tech industry. Playing off different communities, one Japanese firm in particular decided to settle in Oregon, suggesting that, among other reasons, it was concerned about the anticipated future shortfall in water supplies. This decision generated substantial discomfort within the local business community. As a result, several business leaders from the San Diego Chamber of Commerce passed the word to the water authority to reduce the rhetoric and quiet down the talk about imminent crisis. The newspapers were also disturbed about the crisis talk and wanted to know what CWA was now going to do. If the Peripheral Canal was dead, what did the future really hold in store?

The situation was ripe for a fast-talking Louisiana speculator-entrepreneur named Doyle Galloway Berry. During the late 1970s, Berry and his associates, incorporated as the Galloway Group, had gone around buying water rights on the upper Colorado in anticipation of a synthetic fuels boom in the West. When the synfuels boom collapsed in the early 1980s, energy companies dropped out of the water rights market, leaving Galloway with its unsold water. The Galloway Group then began to seek out other buyers. They pursued the idea of building a dam on the free-flowing and scenic Yampa River, a Colorado tributary, to establish rights to the water, and then pay off upper and lower basin states in the Colorado River system for use of their entitlements to the water. At that point,

Galloway would seek out a buyer downstream. The obvious candidate—the agency at the end of the Colorado River system—was San Diego.

The San Diego water industry, in the wake of their manufactured crisis, was eagerly seeking some demonstrative way to put forth a post–Peripheral Canal strategy. The Galloway Group moved fast. They sent out their attorney, a young baby-faced lawyer named John Musick who had cut his teeth on water market sales in Colorado. Musick spoke to the water authority staff and then flew out several directors to the Yampa. He wowed them with Galloway's plans and heady talk of changing the sixty-year system of rights and allocations on the Colorado River collectively known as the "Law of the River." The CWA directors went back to San Diego convinced they had found their solution, describing Galloway to the press as an "enterprising group with an interesting and unique concept."

The San Diego water leaders, particularly a new generation of business and politically oriented directors who were at the center of the region's urban-development complex, were enthusiastic about the deal for several reasons. It would demonstrate that the water authority was indeed "doing something" to secure an additional supply of water to allow growth in the region to continue. At the same time, the San Diego agency would be participating in a "market" arrangement that appealed to its leaders' business orientation and entrepreneurial self-image. This group was especially conscious of appearing "forward-looking" within an industry whose traditional approaches were under increasing attack.

The key player within this group was Mike Madigan, widely regarded as one of the most powerful figures in San Diego political and business circles. Madigan had become influential during the 1970s as a top aide to Pete Wilson, when the San Diego Republican served as mayor prior to his election to the Senate in 1982. Madigan, with effective political and PR skills, had helped develop Wilson's image as a growth-conscious politician while still maintaining close ties to the urban-development complex, who were among his key backers. When Madigan decided to go into the private sector as a public spokesperson and vice-president of one of San Diego's largest developers, Wilson asked him if there was any appointment he wanted. Madigan, to Wilson's surprise, chose the San Diego County Water Authority. "I saw CWA as fundamental to San Diego," Madigan later recalled, "and there was not a lot of appreciation of its importance."

With Madigan and others in the "power caucus," as this new leadership group came to be known, the CWA decided to pay a ten thousand dollar option on the Galloway deal. Much to CWA's surprise, all hell broke loose when the Galloway plan was made public. MET staff were livid at the idea, since, according to them, it violated the Law of the River, and by extension the careful accumulation of deals and distributive arrangements between the different players in the Colorado River system. MET staff provided a barrage of materials attacking and even belittling the Galloway plan and San Diego's role in it. MET general manager Carl Boronkay told the *San Diego Union* that he wondered whether CWA directors "actually smoke [controlled substances] before meetings." "Do they look woozy in public," he jokingly asked the reporter, a comment for which he would later apologize. MET also helped mobilize water industry and political figures in Colorado, Arizona, Utah, and elsewhere to blast the plan. Even Bruce Babbitt—a "malevolent leader," according to Musick—who otherwise talked of "markets" and "new arrangements," attacked Galloway for usurping Arizona's rights. And those environmentalists who were also touting "markets" were aghast at the idea of damming the Yampa and constructing another storage facility when the Colorado River system was already overbooked with dams.

The CWA was unprepared for the initial reaction, especially the attack from MET. After having dominated the growth-oriented district during the 1970s with support for new annexations and for aggressive pursuit of new sources of supply in the State Water Project, the CWA directors were now being belittled and marginalized within the MET system for pursuing what was being called a project of dubious merit. Yet, after some initial thoughts about abandoning the idea altogether, CWA leaders decided to tough it out. The San Diego media and business and political establishment, after all, were lauding the water authority for indeed "doing something," albeit a controversial option. "You have to take risks," Madigan said about the period. "You have to be a player in the game."

The enormous press attention that Galloway received also created an impression within the water industry that CWA was at the forefront of the new push for "market"-type deals. The Imperial Irrigation District, for example, wondered whether they could bypass MET and deal directly with their closer neighbor, San Diego, on the water transfer–related SWAP. In 1987 IID directors actually tried to entice San Diego to enter negotiations, to no avail. Some of the big farmers in Kern County also trooped down to San Diego to try and cut some deals. Though the CWA took a position that all arrangements first had to be negotiated through MET, it appeared to many in the water industry that San Diego, which had for so long proclaimed its dependence on MET with its end-of-the-pipe-line rhetoric, might be in the business of securing its *own* supply to maintain its continuing growth.

Much of that focus for growth was in the northern part of the county, where the urban-development complex was most active and where resistance to growth was most substantial. The water authority was also involved in a major battle with local environmental and community groups over the construction of the Pamo Dam storage facility in an undeveloped valley in this North County area. While the CWA argued that the dam was necessary for emergency storage in case of an earthquake, it was also clear that the facility would allow rapid development in the area. The arguments by the environmentalists, meanwhile, were largely adopted by the EPA and the Fish and Wildlife Service, who took opposing sides from the Army Corps of Engineers, which favored the Pamo project. It was another classic example of a problematic supply-side strategy that continued to preoccupy the water industry even in the midst of changing conditions.

By the late 1980s, the battle lines for the water authority had been drawn along two fronts. On the one hand, the growth issue, which had long figured prominently in San Diego politics, had once again come to the fore with the passage of a growth management initiative and the emergence of a "slow growth" movement with concerns about water supply and water quality as well as transportation, housing, and other issues tied to the dynamics of urban growth. On the other hand, the CWA had developed an unwarranted reputation as an innovator. Primarily because of the publicity around the Galloway proposal, the water authority quickly became, by the mid-1980s, a magnet attracting a host of possible market arrangements. The CWA neither initiated nor pursued any of these, becoming at best an interested observer rather than an active buyer. Yet the water authority, being at the right place at the right time, was receiving recognition for leading the way in exploring new options for the water industry.

Similar to San Diego, MET had also been besieged with market deals, beginning in 1985, as the declining conditions in agriculture sent farm communities south to look for deals. MET also responded cautiously, confining their approach to possible transfer or exchange agreements, such as a landowner being paid to keep lands idle in a dry year to thus free up the water, rather than through an outright "sale" of water rights. Meanwhile, both MET and San Diego still actively supported the supply-side option of new dams and new facilities. The interest in markets was, for both agencies, part of the search for new water supplies. And conflicts between San Diego and MET were in the end more a territorial issue over jurisdiction and control of water than a strategic distinction over whether to pursue "markets" as a means to an assured water supply.

The emergence of a MET/San Diego rivalry, then, didn't call into question the framework of growth politics. Both agencies remain instrumental in continuing to shape and influence the urban-development complex in Southern California. Both still subscribe to the fundamental notion underlying the Laguna Declaration, which defines the water industry's activity as making possible the next increment of growth in the region. The new items on the agenda relate to the mechanisms of supply rather than the management of demand. In this light, water markets become just another form of the politics of expansion.

URBAN-SUBURBAN RIVALRIES

Despite the supply-side orientation of the water industry in urban growth areas, the construction of new facilities to import water from distant places had become, by the 1970s and 1980s, increasingly difficult to accomplish. Big projects were in trouble not only with the corps and the bureau, but on the regional level as well. Local agencies that had developed the financial capability and political clout to build large-scale facilities on their own were also finding that such projects were becoming too costly, too controversial, and too complex to handle compared to the past. As a result, new tension points in the system emerged, as in the Denver metropolitan area.

Since its organization in 1918, the Denver Water Department has played a kind of water-development gamesmanship with its surrounding suburban neighbors as well as the more rural, agricultural, and undeveloped areas on the western slope of the Continental Divide. Much of the maneuvering has centered on securing new water supplies for both the city and adjoining areas that became dependent on the expanding Denver system. Eventually the water issue came to symbolize, beyond the issues of growth, the urban/suburban rivalries that continue to influence the patterns of future development.

The city of Denver, founded at the point where Cherry Creek and the South Platte River come together, has always been conscious of the role of water in defining how the city might grow. The eastern slope of the Divide, where Denver, Boulder, Colorado Springs, and other Front Range cities are situated, is a relatively arid region. Rainfall averages between thirteen and fifteen inches a year, nearly identical to the Los Angeles area. The western side of the Divide has both the rainfall (several times the amount of the Front Range) and most importantly the sources of water—the main stem and the tributaries of the Colorado.

As with other expanding urban areas, Denver's water development became part of its cycle of expansion. The creation of the municipally owned Denver Water Department in 1918 was undertaken as a prelude to the search for new supplies and new facilities. The new department immediately began to purchase additional water rights on the South Platte River outside the city limits to help promote further expansion of the city. It also began to explore the acquisition of Colorado River rights and development of facilities on the western slope, where more than 70 percent of the state's water flowed.

The water department's first major project was the leasing, enlarging, and lining of a portion of the Moffat Railroad Tunnel. This tunnel, completed in the 1930s and originally authorized by the state legislature as part of an alternative transcontinental railroad route, became the first large-scale transmountain water-diversion project in the region. A major treatment plant and reservoir were added within a year after the water first flowed under the mountains.

During the late 1940s and 1950s, the Denver region experienced substantial growth, similar to the boom conditions in several other western metropolitan areas. Prior to this period, the Denver Water Department, with its expanding infrastructure, had been able to accommodate growth both within the city and for the suburbs. Many of the suburbs had become heavily dependent on purchasing "surplus water" from Denver. Some of the surplus water went to unincorporated territory outside the city limits, partly in anticipation of annexation to the city.

After the war, the Denver Water Board, which had developed close ties to land-speculation and housing-development interests in the region, began to embark on another ambitious round of water development. In 1946, construction began on a new tunnel under the Continental Divide that would eventually be completed in 1962. This project, the Roberts Tunnel, was at the time the longest underground water tunnel in the world. While construction plans were underway, however, the water board decided to place a moratorium on the use of its water supply by the suburbs. In 1951, the water department established what it called a Blue Line, beyond which water would not be delivered. This position threw the urban-suburban relationship into turmoil.

The Blue Line policy had a curious mix of motivations. The unanticipated boom of the postwar years had increased the city of

Denver's own water needs, as well as those of the suburban areas, many of which were now resisting the push for annexation. A drought in the early 1950s had further exacerbated the situation around existing supply and demand. The Blue Line policy allowed the city to stretch out the construction of facilities and thus postpone the bond elections necessary to raise additional revenues. The city's water interests, meanwhile, still hoped to promote and channel the growth within the city's boundaries. By putting pressure on the suburbs, however, it also forced the suburban interests to more actively support the water department's long-term goal of system expansion.

The suburbs, for their part, were left with little choice. Most simply accepted the Blue Line strategy and waited hat-in-hand for the new facilities to be built and the water to be made available. Others, like the city of Aurora to the south of Denver, eventually developed their own supplies.

When the city charter was changed in 1959 and the Blue Line subsequently lifted to allow more extensive service to the suburbs, the Denver water system continued to expand. Its large infrastructure was now more and more oriented toward delivery to the suburbs. Both the city and the outlying areas continued to boom during the 1960s and early 1970s, with much of the growth concentrated in the suburban areas. With the two tunnels under the Continental Divide, and water rights locked up on both the South Platte and the Western Slope, the Denver Water Board had much of the regional water infrastructure centralized within its system. The water board had become the water industry's most powerful body, envied, feared, and mistrusted not only by the suburbs and the Western Slope, but even increasingly within the city limits.

In the early 1970s, the water board attempted to further strengthen that infrastructure with construction of a major treatment plant. Despite an impressive array of developer and water industry–related support, it took two elections before the water board could muster enough votes in the city to obtain the bonds for construction. Part of the problem related to the suspicions of city residents, bolstered by statements of water officials, that while the city had plenty of water, the suburbs did not. The water board, despite substantial funds for lobbying, also had its problems with the state legislature and members of the congressional delegation. By the 1970s it had come to symbolize Denver's "arrogance," as Congresswoman Pat Schroeder put it, toward the other regional players.

The political relations between the city and the suburbs came to a head in the early 1970s when the legislature, responding primarily to racial and class antagonism toward "inner city" Denver—primarily fear of busing for integrated schools—passed the Poundstone Amendment, named after suburban activist Freda Poundstone, who later became the mayor of one of Denver's suburbs. The amendment, which froze in place the Denver city limits and prevented further annexations, directly affected the water board. With its massive infrastructure and continuing ambitious plans for expansion that related directly and explicitly to suburban growth, the water board faced the anomalous situation of becoming the de facto planning agency and provider for areas outside its legal boundaries. No longer able to control and channel its instrument for growth, the water board was left with the classic power of an expansionist water industry, but with no real institutional relationship to the areas and constituencies for whom that power was being exercised.

In the immediate aftermath of the Poundstone Amendment, the water board undertook a calculated retreat from its expansionary designs. The Two Forks Dam and Reservoir, a major new supply project on the South Platte designed to serve system expansion needs—primarily for the suburbs—was temporarily put on the shelf. One water board member resigned, suggesting that with the Poundstone there was no future for the water board. Charles Jordan, a prominent local political figure who would later become a water board member and then special advisor to the water department, recalled the period as one where anger and resentment within the city were widespread. "Something had been done to the city," Jordan remarked, "and the Water Board was now thumbing it back at the suburbs by saying, 'You can damn well find your own water.' "

By the late 1970s, the initial shock over Poundstone had given way to the beginnings of a new Denver Water Board approach. We can put the system expansion plans back on the drawing boards, the water board suggested to the suburbs, if a quid pro quo is established. To strengthen its bargaining position, the water board in 1979 proposed a moratorium that would prevent expansion of the service area beyond those suburbs that had historically been provided with Denver's surplus water. At a future point in time, on December 31, 1986, a date the suburbs came to characterize as "Black Wednesday," Denver would impose a tap moratorium on deliveries to these areas.

The response of the suburbs varied widely. When the 1979 moratorium policy was announced, many of the new developments, particularly those to the south and east of Denver, turned toward their limited groundwater supplies and started pumping furiously to meet their own anticipated development boom. Without any effective state or regional regulatory jurisdiction over the use of groundwater, some overdraft problems quickly emerged. The well water, however, continued to figure in the developers' plans.

Several other suburbs, most notably Thornton to the north of the city, followed the example of Aurora and began to search for their own source of water, particularly through purchase of agricultural water rights. Most of the suburbs, however, still attempted to play Denver's game. During the early 1980s, they worked out a series of agreements with the water board designed to address the new Denver strategy. These agreements were signed by the city and forty-seven suburbs and water purveyors who called themselves the Metropolitan Water Providers. They provided for the suburbs to pay a share at the front end of any future purchase of water rights and development projects, such as those for Two Forks.

By the mid-1980s, Two Forks had become the centerpiece of the maneuvering and debate involving the city, the suburbs, and water industry critics. For environmentalists and many Denver residents, the Two Forks project was an unnecessary outrage, destroying twenty miles of virgin trout stream and flooding a rugged river canyon that had become one of the South Platte's last and most cherished recreational attractions after eighty years of water development. For the suburbs, particularly those most dependent on Denver's water, Two Forks was a savior, ineluctably laying the groundwork for future growth and development. For the Denver Water Department, Two Forks represented a continuation of its historic policy that had become Denver's equivalent of the Laguna Declaration: providing water for all who request it. And for the Denver Water Board—the governing body for the water department, and more politically oriented since its members were appointed by the mayor—Two Forks represented a bargaining chip to force the suburbs to deal with the city on the city's terms. This meant not only sharing the costs of system expansion, but also procuring additional funds to address the inequities of Poundstone.

This quid pro quo concept had been around since the passage of Poundstone. Soon after Poundstone took effect, city officials had entertained the idea of the suburbs paying for a kind of trust fund for Denver to help finance the city's museums, symphony, libraries, hospital, and other facilities used by suburbanites. Though suburban residents benefited from these institutions, they didn't pay for the services, either through taxes or by other means. When Two Forks began to be a matter of negotiations between the city and the suburbs a few years later, this quid pro quo notion reemerged as well. It was this time raised by a local public official and power broker named Monte Pascoe, who had been appointed to the water board in 1984. "The old order in delivering water is ending," Pascoe told the *Denver Post*. "A new era must begin. Water should be considered a part of other metropolitan concerns and not isolated from these concerns." Pascoe wanted to create a Metropolitan Water Authority, a metropolitan-wide agency of both the city and the suburbs, which would control the infrastructure, allocate resources, and coordinate the entire Denver water system. The suburbs would fund much of the system expansion including Two Forks and some Denver facilities such as the museums and hospitals. In turn, they would get to participate and have a decision-making role in the new urban-suburban, Greater Denver water system.

Among the suburbs and the western slope interests, however, the mistrust of the Denver Water Department and especially the water board was substantial. It made difficult any attempt at resolution. "The perception of the Denver Water Department," one county commissioner told the *Denver Post*, "is that of an arrogant, domineering, and inconsiderate bully, with vast resources and cavalier attorneys capable of manipulating people, situations, and the law to gain whatever their objective is." Ultimately, the suburbs divided into several groups, each with a different perspective on just such an urban-suburban deal. Those dependent on Denver tended to look favorably on the plan. Those who had pursued groundwater were more skeptical. And those, like Thornton and Aurora, who sought water independence, were not fully inclined to merge interests.

For critics of the Denver water industry, the urban-suburban maneuvering tended to deflect from their main issues. For one, it removed the focus on the water system's substantial inefficiencies, including Denver's high per capita use of water and the lack of metering for the majority of Denver residences. Most of the critics, particularly mainline environmental groups, were most concerned with Two Forks and other plans to import water from the South Platte or the western slope, which they saw as potentially violating some important scenic resources. Their efficiency criticisms were less an argument about growth than the ways to accommodate growth. Critics advocated such measures as pricing reforms and stretching existing supplies rather than the traditional water industry strategy of overdevelopment through the construction of big facilities such as Two Forks.

The growth issue, then, had come full circle. Instead of critics complaining about how water development created the basis for new growth, it was the water industry, led by the suburban areas, who proudly proclaimed the relationship. We need the water, the suburbs said of Two Forks, because we need the growth. That argument had become more compelling to public officials like Colorado's Governor Roy Romer, who became an advocate for increasing the water supply in the state.

By the late 1980s, the debate in Denver had turned into an argument about how to best make the system work. The Denver Water Board and the Water Department were keyed toward the issue of control—using and expanding the massive infrastructure.

The suburbs were focused on system expansion as a precondition for continuing urban growth, an assumption that still prevailed within the water industry. And the environmentalists, new players in the water policy debates, talked of making the system more efficient, the better to save some wild flowing streams and rivers. To expand by building new facilities, restructuring urban-suburban relationships, or by concentrating on system efficiency had become the question, not whether or why the cities should grow.

BEAT THE PEAK

The relationship of water development and urban growth is no longer, in this era of change, exclusively linked to the construction of large, usually oversized facilities. The interest in new approaches, such as water markets, appears to underline the water industry's desire to redirect its singular preoccupation with dams and ditches. Water agency managers now like to say that agencies are no longer just run by engineers but include those versed in legal issues, politics, and public relations.

Yet this shift is hardly a revolution. As in the Denver case, major new facilities play a significant role. And in the case of Arizona, and particularly the city of Tucson, the big project emphasis—the push for the Central Arizona Project—has coincided with less traditional approaches. These include the purchase of agricultural water rights and, most especially, the adoption of a conservation and efficiency strategy that became a necessary precondition for accommodating the city's anticipated growth.

Arizona water politics has, over the years, been framed by the massive CAP. Though other projects have played a significant role in water development in the state, most especially the Salt River Project that was first authorized in 1903, the Arizona water industry has always defined the construction of the CAP as its central objective. The project was looked upon as the state's birthright, a project associated with the long-standing competition with California over the Colorado River as well as the solution to a fifty-year-old groundwater overdraft problem.

Most importantly, the CAP was the water industry's link to the politics of growth. When the project was still an idea, first introduced in the U.S. Senate by Carl Hayden during the 1940s, the CAP became the state's frontline of defense against concerns in the eastern financial community and suggestions by the out-of-state press that the region would not be able to grow, bound by its scarce resources and its desert environment. Then, as the state boomed and its two urban areas, Phoenix and Tucson, mushroomed, the CAP changed focus, becoming specifically an urban rather than an agriculturally oriented project.

Physically, the project remained the same. Authorized by Congress in 1968 as the centerpiece of the last of the big water development packages, the CAP was designed to carry Colorado River water from Lake Havasu at the California border through the desert lands south of the canyons in the central part of the state. Phase one of the project would provide water for the Phoenix area; Phase two would serve the area immediately to its east and south in Maricopa and Pinal counties; and Phase three would terminate in Tucson while passing through the cotton-growing areas of Pinal County. What changed over time was both the emphasis on project beneficiaries and the project costs, which escalated dramatically. By 1987, the CAP had become the BuRec's most expensive project, its final costs estimated at $4.1 billion, up from the initial estimate of $823 million when authorized in 1968.

As phase one to Phoenix neared completion in the mid-1980s, Arizona agriculture, the longtime advocate of the CAP and its original intended beneficiary, had begun to realize that CAP water would be far more expensive than existing sources such as groundwater, as the project's critics had long argued. Agriculture in Arizona, like elsewhere, was in general economic decline. Most farmers in the state, according to University of Arizona economists William Martin and David Bush, were going to "find themselves worse off with the CAP than they would without it for many years to come."

For the urban interests, the CAP represented an insurance policy for future development. The cities in the Phoenix area defined their water needs more in terms of future growth than present-day needs. The Salt River Project still provided a substantial source of water for urban users, particularly the city of Phoenix. Thus, initial phase one CAP sales, particularly to the cities, were far lower than the potential amounts of water available.

Meanwhile, the water industry in Tucson nervously awaited the completion of phase three. The completion date is still projected for the early 1990s, though that date could be pushed back because of reduced budget authorizations. Tucson, unlike the Phoenix metropolitan area, has nearly always been dependent on its groundwater, a scarce resource that has looked increasingly finite to the city's urban development interests as the construction of the CAP moves ever so slowly.

As in Phoenix, water availability in Tucson has been inextricably linked to growth. The concern has been that the lack of an existing supply or delays in obtaining it can interrupt future patterns of growth. It became important, then, for the Tucson water industry to demonstrate that it had little fear of water shortage and that water was available without any limits imposed on its use. Thus, there could be found artificial lakes (more lakes per capita than any other state); rapid increases in water hookups to new urban subdivisions; low water rates, which further decreased with higher levels of consumption and thus acted as a disincentive for conservation; and an increasing and relatively high per capita water use that peaked at slightly over two hundred gallons per day in the early 1970s.

By 1974 this approach in Tucson had run into serious trouble. The CAP, designed to help meet Tucson's long-term water needs, was proceeding quite slowly during the Nixon years in the face of a hostile OMB and a president who defined the project as "pure pork." During the spring and summer of 1974 an exceptionally hot dry spell hit the city. For several days the city's pumps were unable to meet the afternoon peak demand. It had become clear that the city's water policy needed to shift gears, especially if the rapid growth in the city was to continue.

The Tucson Water Department had already begun to explore such a change in policy when a series of political events intervened and brought the water issue to the fore. In elections for the Tucson

City Council in 1975, a group of candidates, known as the New Democrats, had successfully challenged the traditional pro-development coalitions. As the new majority on the city council, these incumbents were eager to select an area of policy to translate their campaign positions into specific programs. The transition in water policy seemed to afford just the right opportunity.

In ways that partially resembled the approach associated with the Carter hit list, the New Democrats initiated a new set of policies within a short period of time. These were based on restructuring the water rates as a device to promote conservation and manage and possibly limit the growth patterns that had gotten out of hand. Meanwhile, in response to its developing supply crisis, the Tucson Water Department had also begun to redo its rate structure and increase residential rates when the New Democrats seized the issue. Like the Carter hit list approach, the New Democrat council members, against the advice of one of their senior figures, a member of the County Board of Supervisors, plunged ahead. In the process, they failed to work closely with community and neighborhood groups and establish the constituency for reform.

The water department had recognized that the city's rapid growth had outstripped the system's capacities to finance the additional distribution facilities and the new hookups now required to keep up with the growth. Costs were increasing far more rapidly than revenues based on the old rates. The department shrewdly appealed to the New Democrats to institute a series of new and higher water rates, system development charges, and policies aimed at reducing the highest or "peak" use during the summer months. These would be based on a price structure that *should*, as a department memo advised, "discourage peripheral growth and encourage the development of vacant land within the metropolitan area where supporting public services already exist or are much cheaper to provide than in the fringe areas."

The water department objectives, however, were still linked to system expansion and continuing growth requirements. The additional revenues to be raised from the revised rates were to be directly used to finance land purchases from agriculture in the nearby Avra

146

Valley in order to obtain the right to use the water and finance a delivery system to Tucson. While the New Democrats saw growth management and conservation implications in the new rates, the water department saw additional revenues that would help develop new water sources and maintain the conditions for rapid growth.

When the council majority passed the new rate structure, it created an immediate backlash. The peaking policies and a newly instituted "lift charge" to partially offset the costly pumping of water to the wealthier developments in the foothills were most responsible for the various increases in water bills. They became the focus of a successful recall effort against the new council members, which was encouraged by a media hostile to the New Democrats and a wary water industry that had never trusted the group's motivations and objectives. However, the new "pro-growth," anti-rate-hike candidates who took over, thanks to the recall, immediately backed away from tampering with the water department initiatives. With the exception of the "lift charges," the one rate initiative most directly linked to equity considerations, the water department convinced the pro-growth council that a return to the pre-rate-hike status quo would have disastrous implications for growth.

Instead, the council and the water department devised an educational campaign to gain public acceptance of the new rates, particularly summer-use "peak" rates. In meetings with policy leaders, the electronic and print media, and various other groups, a "Beat the Peak" campaign was launched in the summer of 1977. Calling the effort "the single most important educational undertaking that we have had, certainly within the last fifteen years, if not in the history of the city," pro-growth, anti–New Democrat mayor Lew Murphy enthusiastically led the political, business, and media establishment in support of Beat the Peak. Each year, from June 1 to August 31, the air waves and newspaper columns became filled with spot announcements, newspaper stories, and television weather forecast reminders about Beat the Peak; there were also water bill inserts, tent cards for restaurants, fliers in grocery bags, and postage-metering ads. All of this was designed to drum up support and establish a community-wide consensus.

Beat the Peak helped to link the concepts of conservation and growth for the water industry and the larger business and political establishment of Tucson. To their delight, per capita water use and summer peak use at first declined, to help defer what was still seen as a potential supply crisis related to the long delays in the much anticipated Central Arizona Project. These declines occurred in the midst of continuing population growth, thus enabling the water department to create new hookups without placing an undue strain on the system. Even when per capita use began to increase several years after Beat the Peak was instituted, water industry groups still applauded the relative success of the campaign, arguing that future growth had not been constrained. Conservation had become the instrument for sustaining rapid and what some hoped would be permanent growth.

Beat the Peak also created a political model for the water industry. Instead of dismissing conservation, efficiency measures, and water marketing initiatives, water industry groups such as the Southern Arizona Water Resources Association (SAWARA) linked their growth and expansionary policies directly to those approaches. Furthermore, water industry and business groups, in reviewing the lessons of the rise and fall of the New Democrat insurgency, saw fit to incorporate both the language of conservation and the participation of environmentalists in their coalitions. Beat the Peak became the cornerstone of a Tucson water industry policy based on the three pillars of Conservation, Growth, and the Central Arizona Project.

What Beat the Peak did not address, however, were the equity issues as they related to the patterns of growth. Instead of addressing the allocation of costs for new growth and development, Beat the Peak in fact helped shift the focus away from those costs. To have priced CAP water at its actual cost in real dollars per unit of water, for example, would have priced it out of the market. Yet such prices would have more accurately reflected the additional costs required to accommodate new growth in this desert city.

By the mid- and late 1980s, a new "slow growth" movement concerned with the consequences of development began to emerge in Tucson. Ten years after the New Democrats had failed to develop a sufficient community base for their plans, a grassroots movement, largely based on neighborhood associations, had emerged. This movement sought to address the implications of growth and over-development, particularly in the area of transportation policy. But with the CAP still several years away from completion and water policy debated once again largely outside the public arena, the neighborhood groups only indirectly touched on water supply questions, though they were becoming increasingly concerned with questions of water quality. Their appearance placed the water industry on notice, suggesting that growth as an issue was still central to the dynamics of urban politics in the arid West.

NEW APPROACHES, OLD OBJECTIVES

By the late 1980s, the urban water industry had emerged as a more dominant player in water politics. At the same time, urban water interests began to realize that the traditional strategies of expansion needed to be complemented with nontraditional approaches: developing a buyer's and seller's market, implementing peaking and other "efficiency" measures, and establishing increasingly centralized organizations uniting new and old growth areas, cities and suburbs and fringe agricultural areas. The old approach—the big development project or "structural" solution—still remained crucial, though it was no longer the exclusive route to system expansion. Both new and old approaches, however, were designed with the same objectives in mind: how to develop policies that allowed for new growth, even the extraordinary rapid growth characteristic of the recent history of the arid West; and how to establish a consensus in an era of increased conflict over water development.

The search for a new consensus has produced some tentative efforts to expand the base of the old water industry coalition or at least welcome some new players to the table. On the national level, that search has been linked to a greater acceptance by urban interests of limited forms of cost sharing, water markets, privatization and a reduced role of government, and greater system efficiency by such agencies as the Bureau of Reclamation and Army Corps of Engineers. But the search for consensus suffers from the fact that most of these agencies are still wedded to a water development scenario and seek ways to accomplish such an approach, despite the changing economic and political dynamics.

On the regional and local level, where the water industry has always been strongest, the urban water agencies have gradually staked out an independent posture separate from agriculture that has continued to depend on large-scale importation schemes and heavily subsidized pricing programs. Though not directly challenging these programs, such as subsidized water for surplus crops, the urban agencies have increasingly found themselves on the other side of the negotiating table, particularly in the area of water markets. And while growth has been the central objective of urban agencies since the days of the Manhattan Company, the scale of expansion, varying methods of securing or "stretching" supplies, and the emergence of urban agency behemoths such as Southern California's Metropolitan Water District and the Denver Water Department have come to characterize the pursuit of that objective.

The traditional opposition to water development, led by environmental groups concerned with scenic resources and instream use, has, especially since the 1970s, been successful in limiting large-scale projects. Most have encouraged the pursuit of markets, conservation programs, and the "efficiency" motif that has brought certain environmentalists into occasional coalition with the urban water industry. But what has largely been absent from their discussions and debates are the equity considerations of growth: who pays, who benefits, and its consequences.

While the established environmental groups have increased their clout and found a place for themselves in water policy decision-making, another kind of opposition has emerged. While not always focusing on questions of water development, this new opposition is most concerned with "quality of life" politics. Growth and over-development are central to these movements as are the issues of the contamination and quality of the water supply.

By the early 1980s, water quality had emerged as a national

issue, affecting both groundwater and surface water, wastewater and treated water. From a concern over contamination of lakes and rivers, water quality came to focus on issues of drinking water and public health. The new constituencies that emerged to address these issues were outside the mainstream environmental organizations. They were largely locally based, located in both urban and rural settings. A new politics had come to the fore. And the urban water industry, which had matured on the politics of growth, joined forces once again with its agricultural counterparts. Together they sought to ward off this most recent and most serious challenge to the water industry's sense of purpose, its priorities, and its objectives.

PART THREE

New Issues, Changing Faces

Chapter 5

The Water Quality Battleground: Entering the Age of Trace Organics

IMAGE DEVELOPMENT AND
BEHAVIOR MODIFICATION

For the old-timers who attend these water conventions, the topic at this session of the Municipal Caucus of the National Water Resources Association was a relatively new one, different from the usual dams and ditches and reservoirs. The issue of water quality had forced its way onto the agenda of groups like NWRA in just a few short years. By the time the organization's December 1986 annual meeting came to order, the importance of quality had clearly supplanted that of quantity for the public at large, even in the arid West.

This fact preoccupied many of the speakers, including one of the newer faces at NWRA, the city of Phoenix's water and environmental resources manager, a one-time Bruce Babbitt advisor named George Britton. Britton's delivery was fast-paced and quick to the point. He perked up his audience, even though many of the delegates were already beginning to drift off to get ready for the cocktail hour. Britton was a new breed water industry participant, schooled more in the art of politics and public relations than the details of engineering and water development.

"As we enter an era of uncertainty," Britton told his audience, "we find we are dealing with a very concerned public." Turning to his charts, Britton described what he considered some alarming statistics gathered from a public attitude survey. Forty-five percent of the Phoenix residents surveyed drank bottled water or used a water treatment device; 59 percent felt they didn't receive enough information about the quality of their drinking water; 57 percent were very or somewhat concerned about health risks from tap water "that will be responsible for their death," as the survey had phrased it; 45 percent said they would be willing to pay to remove known or suspected carcinogens that present a one-in-one-million to one-in-ten-million excess cancer risk; and 58 percent said the media was their main source of information on water quality compared to 15 percent who primarily received their information from the Phoenix Water Department. And while only 31 percent felt the media were the most accurate source of information, a bare 8 percent looked to the city water department. "Obviously," Britton declared to a sea of nodding heads, "we have a major public perception problem to deal with."

The problem, as Britton and most water industry participants saw it, had to do with the public, the press, and the regulators and elected officials who were increasingly responsive to public pressure. The trace elements of the potentially carcinogenic compounds that had entered the drinking water supply were dismissed as insignificant risk: "a drop of vermouth in a sea of gin," as one Southern California water official put it.

"The media coverage of the drinking water issues," Britton continued, "often causes or exacerbates the public perception problem and resultant political consequences." Exaggerated coverage, he pointed out, meant articles about the detection in wells of these potential carcinogens, "even if the detected level is well below an existing or proposed drinking water standard." This complaint, shared by many water managers, said more about water industry skepticism about the problem than a headline-seeking press.

The City of Los Angeles Department of Water and Power, for example, similar to many other water agencies, often complained of articles about TCE (trichloroethylene) contamination of its wells in the North Hollywood area of the city. TCE, a potentially carcinogenic industrial solvent widely used in the 1950s and 1960s and still used today, had received a fair amount of attention throughout the country after being detected in numerous groundwater wells. DWP officials would express outrage whenever press coverage mentioned wells that recorded trace levels below regulatory standards, at say three or four parts per billion (ppb). This was "well below the standard," DWP officials would exclaim, although the California health advisory standard (later adopted by the EPA) was just five ppb. Yet when the press focused on wells with levels at seven or eight ppb—or more to the point at two hundred, two thousand, or even twenty thousand ppb, all of which had been detected at several well sites—DWP officials, like their counterparts in Phoenix and elsewhere, did not of course insist that the press describe such wells as "well above the standard," or suggest that such levels called for heightened media coverage.

Britton, however, had some suggestions on how to handle the press, the public, and ultimately the policy makers. Phoenix's new approach, Britton declared, "is based on the assumption that 'credibility is currency'; the more you have, the more options you have." This program of "institutional confidence building" would include more effective use of the media. It would attempt to portray the water agencies as more "accessible," to make both the public and the media more confident in the water industry.

Specifically, the water department wanted to host a conference for journalists on the water quality issue. Such an event would be a major undertaking, Britton later commented. Dow Chemical had already pledged twenty-five thousand dollars to underwrite this effort, but the city would look for some additional backers, "so the Dow sponsorship would not be obvious."

Britton's suggestions were in line with what other water agencies and water industry participants were already exploring. At meetings of NWRA or at other water industry gatherings, more and more workshops and general sessions were being devoted to "image building" and other ways to establish "credibility." Water quality had

157

become the driving force in transforming this period into "an era of transition, and thus an era of uncertainty," as Britton put it.

"The public is concerned and emotional, and the media is very attentive," the Phoenix official warned his audience as his speech drew to a close. No longer should the water industry see itself in its traditional roles. "We must grow into new areas," Britton concluded, "involving public education, image development, public perception, and behavior modification."

I left the meeting intrigued by those remarks. I was particularly struck by the use of the concept of "behavior modification." As water quality rose to the top of the agenda, the water industry frantically began to seek ways to alter the thinking of the public. By modifying the public's behavior, the water industry was hoping the issue might ultimately be forced to go away. Perhaps then this beleaguered group could be left to its real business of providing water and building empires.

THE SEARCH FOR SAFE WATER

For the water industry, water quality has always been an issue whose importance has been judged in relation to its primary mission: the supply of water to its various constituencies. Despite public preoccupation with matters of public health, water agencies have defined themselves as purveyors rather than public utilities. This strategic choice has been reflected in organizational emphasis, funding priorities, and politically related decisions concerning the definition of the problem and the ways to treat it.

Through much of the nineteenth and twentieth centuries, this country experienced a significant and protracted water quality crisis. Rivers and streams were heavily polluted and drinking water supplies were seriously contaminated. The water industry, however, came to focus exclusively on the safety of drinking water supplies. The discovery, early in the twentieth century, of new and viable forms of treatment, especially chlorination, appeared to eliminate drinking water quality as a problem. It also allowed water agencies to disregard the equally troublesome problem of dealing directly with industrial, municipal, and agricultural forms of discharge and contamination. For more than fifty years after the discovery of chlorination, the growing pollution of lakes, rivers, and streams continued to be disregarded by the water industry, preoccupied as it was with serving an expanding agricultural, urban, and industrial set of interests— the very parties responsible for the contamination problems.

By the 1970s, the issues of water pollution and drinking water quality had once again become linked. The new concern with *chemical* contamination expanded the focus beyond biological and bacterial contaminants, raising once again the specter of the safety of the drinking water. The water industry reacted defensively, alarmed that this renewed preoccupation with public health challenged the very basis of water industry activity. A new set of conflicts emerged, calling into question the water industry's old agendas, new approaches, and long-standing objectives.

Water quality has always preoccupied our society. The search for additional water supplies in the early days of the republic was also a search for a safe water source. Many of the wells inside the city limits of places like Boston and Philadelphia were contaminated from the poor and rapidly declining sanitary conditions in the new urban centers. These conditions were thought (accurately in part, it turned out) to be the cause of a series of epidemics, primarily yellow fever, that devastated a number of cities in the early and mid-1790s. Philadelphia was particularly hard hit, with more than seventeen thousand people—greater than 10 percent of the population—contracting the disease in 1793. For the public, health considerations emerged as the driving force in improving water systems. To have water "pure and plenty in great cities," a Boston newspaper declared in 1796, "must be of the highest consequence to prevent putrid and pestilential fevers and other fatal diseases."

Additional water supplies, it was felt, would provide alternative, presumably uncontaminated sources to substitute for or at least supplement existing sources. Additional water, furthermore, could be used to more thoroughly hose down streets, settle the dust, and make main thoroughfares and back alleys less a breeding ground for disease. The yellow fever epidemic provided the impetus for Philadelphia's launching of the country's first major public water-works program.

Philadelphia's system, designed in the late 1790s, contributed to the overall program of public health that became associated with that city's water system. Its success—the number of epidemic-related diseases did decline—reinforced the notion within Philadelphia that water service was a public-utility function. This in turn generated support for continued improvements and expansion of the system as well as a framework for long-term planning in the public interest.

The Philadelphia example, however, was limited in scope and never effectively became a model for the development of other water systems. During the early nineteenth century, the relationship be-tween water quality and public health was not firmly established. Services within cities were not evenly distributed and the poorer neighborhoods were often left with the most severely contaminated sources and unreliable deliveries. The number of epidemics de-clined overall, but major outbreaks of yellow fever, cholera, typhoid, and amoebic dysentery remained a serious problem through much of the nineteenth century.

The first clear indication that water supplies could be a source of infection and disease came from epidemiological studies by Dr. John Snow in London in 1854. In the midst of a serious cholera epidemic, Snow was able to show that the highest incidences of the disease were linked to the use of a particular well in the center of the city.

The problem of drinking water contamination was exacerbated by the industrial boom in the post–Civil War period and the growing number of wastes and industrial discharges that found their way into drinking water sources. Most water agencies and municipalities had either a limited or nonexistent filtering system. It continued to be common practice, well after the Snow discoveries, for water to be taken directly from creeks, rivers, and wells without prior treatment.

With the discovery of bacteriology and the germ theory of disease during the 1880s, the scientific basis was laid for a new approach to the treatment of the water supply. Water agencies, however, were relatively slow to respond to the problem and major plagues continued to beset cities in this country and in Europe. In the industrial belt along the Merrimack River in eastern Massachusetts, for example, communities like Lawrence and Lowell were subject to typhoid plagues of crisis proportions.

By the 1890s, a social movement had emerged that linked the concerns around sanitation, public health, water quality, and industrial activity. "Public sanitarians" pushed strongly for more treatment facilities, including filtration, and a greater focus on the overall purification of the supply. Their cause won a growing number of adherents because of the persistence of large-scale epidemics traceable in part to a lack of filtration. In Philadelphia, for example, the annual typhoid rate during the 1880s and 1890s never fell below thirty-five deaths per one hundred thousand people and often ranged around seventy deaths. But once a filtration system was developed after the turn of the century, the rate dropped significantly.

The Philadelphia experience and similar situations with several other communities served as warning signs for water agencies. Filtration eventually came to be adopted during the first decade of the new century. Chemical purification methods also began to be employed, with liquid chlorine introduced in 1908. The striking results of chlorination and filtration combined with the social pressures around community health standards created a powerful momentum for the development of a new approach to the treatment of drinking water. After 1914, when the first set of standards specifying maximum permissible limits of bacteriological impurities was adopted, municipal water departments and other water utilities moved quickly to embrace the new approach. The attempt to control the bacteriological agents that had plagued U.S. cities with a range of epidemics dating back to the yellow fever crises of the eighteenth century appeared to be successful, at least in terms of public drinking water supplies.

THE INDUSTRIAL FACTOR

The battle over water quality, however, had only just begun. Through the mid- and late nineteenth century, the by-products of industrialization emerged as a new and often overwhelming source of contamination. Public officials were often reluctant to challenge the practices of dumping sewage and industrial wastes into streams and rivers, some of which served as drinking water sources. In 1861, for example, the Philadelphia chief engineer argued that it would be importune to "interfere with the large manufacturing interests which add so greatly to our permanent prosperity," and that any restrictions on dumping be done "without putting manufacturers to large expense or great inconvenience."

By the 1870s and 1880s, industrial-based pollution had created serious environmental hazards. In areas such as Pennsylvania's Monongahela Valley, rivers and streams were contaminated beyond recognition and the waters became unfit to swim and fish, let alone be used as a supply source. Dumping had become so widespread that traffic on the rivers and other waterways was being seriously undermined.

The first tentative regulations regarding dumping, in fact, reflected the concerns of navigational interests rather than the development of water quality standards. In 1886, Congress first addressed the issue by prohibiting the dumping of refuse into New York Harbor. In 1899, legislation was extended to the national level with the passage of the Refuse Act, which banned the dumping of solid materials impeding waterway commerce and gave jurisdiction to the Army Corps of Engineers to implement the legislation.

The U.S. Public Health Service was created in 1912 in part to investigate the range of water pollution problems, including the health effects of pollution in navigable lakes and streams. The PHS, however, was not granted specific enforcement powers. Instead, it established voluntary nationwide standards. Furthermore, bacteriological but not chemical or physical standards were developed.

The widespread introduction of chlorination and the setting of biological standards, while vastly improving drinking water quality, had the unintended consequence of further reducing the pressure on industry and municipalities to more effectively handle and treat their wastes. Even prior to chlorination, a clear distinction was being made between "drinking water" and "discharge" issues. In 1899, for example, largely from pressure by industrial interests, the city of Newark abandoned the Passaic River as a drinking water source and instead contracted with a private supplier to develop an upland tributary. As a consequence, the condition of the Passaic so deteriorated that within five years it had "all the characteristics of an open sewer," as one historian commented.

By the 1920s, the problem of contamination of both inland and coastal waters had significantly increased despite the apparent success of the new drinking-water treatment methods. The Izaac Walton League, a Midwest-based group of hunting and fishing interests, became the champion of the clean water movement that arose during this period. In one report, prepared in the late 1920s at the request of the Coolidge administration, the league reported that 85 percent of the nation's inland waterways were polluted and that only 30 percent of the country's municipalities treated their wastes, many inadequately.

Though some limited legislation and standard setting occurred during the twenties and thirties, the problems of water contamination increased in scope and intensity. The problems were heightened by the resistance of industrial interests such as the American Petroleum Institute, the Manufacturing Chemists Association, and the American Iron and Steel Institute. These groups insisted that the dumping of industrial wastes presented no environmental hazard. They were encouraged by key legislators in Congress who borrowed liberally from the multiple-use conservationist ethic to assert that "streams are nature's sewers." Waterways could be used for different purposes, including industrial discharges, it was argued, an approach that came to be accepted even by the water industry. As late as the mid-1960s, an Illinois water official would comment that "regardless of how one may feel about the discharge of waste products into surface waters, it is accepted as a universal practice and one which in Illinois is considered a legitimate use of stream waters."

Accelerated industrial activities during World War II worsened the pollution problem in many of the inland waterway systems throughout the country, particularly those adjacent to municipalities and industrial sites. The municipally based water agencies remained passive in spite of the increased volume of industrial contaminants and dumping of wastes. They rested secure in their improved treatment methods and the widespread use of chlorination, which had successfully eliminated bacteriological contaminants from the drinking water supply nearly everywhere. The municipalities were themselves contributing to the problem by failing to adequately address their own waste disposal and sewage dumping.

Furthermore, many water agencies had become closely linked with industrial interests. Industrial executives had established themselves, in the communities where the industries were located, as participants in various leadership groups, including those associated with the local water industry. Water rates, designed to encourage growth and development, were also often structured to favor the largest users. These were predominantly the locally based industrial plants. Similar to electrical rates, these declining block rates (the larger the amount of water used, the lower the rate) provided a public subsidy for such operations and a disincentive to use the water efficiently. And the water discharged from some plants—almost always untreated—contributed to the wastewater load in the region.

As a consequence, the water industry, despite its reliance on heavily polluted lakes and rivers for its source waters, tended to ally more with industry than antipollution activists. Water agencies were reluctant to support efforts to pass legislation to either regulate discharges or enforce more substantial treatment of wastes. The early legislation that passed in the 1940s and 1950s provided only limited federal support for local agencies to treat wastes and undertake sewer construction. Clean water issues tended to be addressed as conservation rather than public health matters, with water utilities continuing to emphasize that water quality issues, defined in terms of the success of chlorination, had been fully resolved.

Such attitudes, however, began to change over the next decade. In 1958, the Interstate Sanitation Commission reported that a giant 6.4-mile mass of polluted matter was "moving to and fro with the ebb and flood of the tide" in the Arthur Kill area, a narrow eleven-mile stretch of salty water dividing New Jersey from Staten Island. The pollution "blob," according to the commission, was trapped like a "monster in some hideous primeval fan."

Four years later, Rachel Carson's *Silent Spring* was published, first as a series of articles in the *New Yorker* and subsequently as a national best-seller. The chemical industry bitterly attacked Carson's research, particularly her key contention that chemical contamination from a range of pesticides and other petrochemical products was capable of serious groundwater and surface water pollution. The publication of *Silent Spring* was a pivotal moment in the growing public concern over water quality. While it focused primarily on a group of pesticides known as chlorinated hydrocarbons, which include the potent DDT, it raised the specter of chemical and industrial contamination of human as well as natural and wildlife environments.

A few in the water industry began to recognize the seriousness of the new contamination for drinking water supplies. A seminal article around this time in the *Journal of the American Water Works Association*, the water utility trade publication, pointed to the increasing concerns about these new forms of pollution. "Today the new challenge facing the water supply profession," the AWWA article noted, "is the control and removal of the hazardous nonliving contaminants—the chemicals and isotopes which are being produced in a bewildering array of new compounds. . . . Unfortunately, very little is known about the extent of the pollution of the nation's water supplies by these new chemicals which include many commercial poisons."

While public recognition and concern grew rapidly during the 1960s, legislative, regulatory, and administrative efforts to respond were slow and uncertain. The rapid growth of the petrochemical industry and its wide array of industrial and consumer products compounded the problem, with industry officials belittling the extent and seriousness of the contamination.

Industry groups were also effective in refining "economic blackmail" tactics employed since before the turn of the century. When state legislatures, responding to increasing public pressure, toyed with the possibility of instituting discharge standards or other regulatory approaches, industries threatened to relocate to other states with less restrictive water quality regulations. This threat became, according to a report prepared for the National Water Commission, "one of the major deterrents to energetic state enforcement."

By the mid-1960s, however, the momentum for a new round of water quality initiatives had become too strong to resist. Increased water contamination resulting from discharges began to receive greater media attention. One of the more visible and widespread of these problems in the postwar period related to the use of synthetic laundry detergents, a key postwar petrochemical product. At first, public attention focused on the sudsing agent in detergents, linked to the petrochemical alkyl benzene sulfonate (ABS), which was extremely slow to decompose in water. Often, huge mounds of detergent foam would appear, even in rivers and streams located in remote areas. The foam also began to appear in tap water, since drinking water sources were similarly affected. As outraged citizen groups began to push Congress to create strict standards for decomposing, the industry, which had earlier claimed unsurmountable problems regarding cost and consumer acceptance, quickly shifted gears by converting to biodegradable products before legislation could be passed. Soon thereafter, however, it became known that a far more serious problem was associated with phosphates, another petrochemical ingredient in synthetic detergents. These were responsible for a range of serious contamination problems, including those experienced at the time by Lake Erie. But instead of pushing for regulations banning phosphates, the Public Health Service, the lead federal agency at the time, called for secondary treatment for the sewage discharged into the lake and other waterways, to ensure

166

the removal of phosphates. The water industry was largely absent from these debates.

The late 1960s became a dramatic period in the developing confrontation over clean water. In 1969, the Cuyahoga River, which flowed through the state of Ohio and into Lake Erie, became so polluted with oil and other wastes that it caught fire in a neighborhood in Cleveland ringed with factories. The river had become an extraordinary cesspool of discharges from the wastes of steel mills, chemical plants, and other industries. Earlier that year the blowout at Platform A in the Santa Barbara Channel imprinted on the minds of Americans the sight of birds and ducks dying on shore, their wings coated with oil, and pushed to the fore the problem of coastal contamination. Dozens of rivers, from the Hudson to the lower Mississippi, became battlegrounds between industrial interests and water quality advocates, with municipalities and water agencies often caught in between. Many of the water utilities had expanded their operations to include secondary treatment plants, relying on federal funds that had become available during the sixties. While the agencies, mindful of their municipalities' own problems with waste discharges and of the economic link to industrial interests, tended to oppose and resist discharge regulations, they were nonetheless being forced to deal with the pressures around clean water.

With the passage of the Clean Water Act in 1972, the water quality debates took on a new dimension. Most of the provisions of this legislation fell under the purview of a new federal agency, the Environmental Protection Agency (EPA). The tough language of the Clean Water Act (strengthening a no-discharge provision and setting deadlines to meet a range of clean water standards) placed EPA at the center of the water quality battleground. And while the water industry played only a secondary and often ambiguous role in the conflicts over clean water, it would become the center of controversy when regulatory efforts shifted to the question of drinking water.

THE DISINFECTION QUANDARY

In 1971, the American Water Works Association published an updated handbook called *Water Quality and Treatment*. When the text had first been published twenty-three years earlier, there was widespread agreement among water agencies that water quality had become a nonproblem, limited to maintaining and refining existing treatment and disinfection methods. That attitude still prevailed in the 1971 edition, though in the chapter on water quality, a passing warning was made. "Although it is generally accepted that present drinking water standards establish satisfactory control of microbiological quality," the authors noted, "the possible health hazard associated with chemical pollutants is a matter of increasing concern."

By 1971, concern and anger related to water pollution and the discharge issues began to be linked to the question of drinking water. Through the 1960s, a series of accidental spills into source waters for drinking water supplies brought increasing recognition that even routine discharges were creating serious problems. The Public Health Service intervened in a number of instances, often by requiring more advance-treatment methods, as in the case of a Nitro, West Virginia, water utility.

Nitro's water source at the time was the Kanawha River, which eventually flows into the Ohio and ultimately the Mississippi. During the postwar period, the Kanawha came to be used as a dumping ground for a number of industries that had mushroomed in the area, including petrochemical companies. Local boosters liked to call the Kanawha Valley the "chemical center of the world."

By the mid-1960s, the Kanawha had become a foul smelling, highly polluted river, containing numerous organic compounds, including those known as volatile or synthetic organic compounds (VOCs or SOCs). The Public Health Service intervened primarily because of "taste and odor" problems at Nitro, though there were also increasing concerns that public health issues were at stake as well. The PHS insisted that the local water utility switch its treatment method to include granular activated carbon (GAC), a more potent and expensive treatment method that dated back to the 1920s.

The Nitro problem, it turned out, was not unique. Through the late 1960s and early 1970s a series of studies of water systems by the PHS, the newly organized EPA, and the General Accounting Office of Congress, all pointed to possible problems with organic compounds in the water supply. These studies focused on surface waters such as the Mississippi and the Ohio that were widely used for industrial and agricultural discharge. One of the more widely publicized cases took place in Minnesota and involved the dumping policies of Reserve Mining Company into Lake Superior. For eighteen years, Reserve Mining had been processing taconite, a low-grade iron ore, on the lakeshore sixty miles northeast of Duluth and dumping the tailings into the lake. Though the company denied any environmental hazard, the strong intervention of a local anti-pollution group, the Save Lake Superior Association, helped focus attention on the fact that the tailings contained a form of asbestos. Studies by the EPA and the state of Minnesota subsequently confirmed that the citizens of Duluth were indeed drinking water heavily laden with asbestos fibers. A resulting court trial, which began in 1973, created widespread interest in the Reserve Mining case, and heightened the recognition that discharge and drinking water issues were connected.

Despite these controversies, legislation introduced as early as 1971 dealing with this form of contamination was having difficulty getting through Congress. The clean water battles had generated a more substantial public outcry than these initial drinking water matters. The visible form of the pollution—oil slicked beaches, viscous substances in lakes and rivers, dying fish and wildlife—provided dramatic evidence of the problem. The chemical contamination of the drinking water, on the other hand, measured in minute parts not visible to the human eye, seemed less evident. The focus on cancer, furthermore, served to blur rather than heighten the issue, given cancer's sometimes lengthy gestation period and the inconclusive health studies at the time.

Despite the uncertainties, antipollution consumer and citizen groups, led by consumer advocate Ralph Nader's network, were convinced that a more rigorous approach to drinking water standards had to be developed. In the summer of 1972, Nader, worried that Congress would not move on the issue unless confronted with new evidence, brought together some researchers to survey the possible problems with the water supplies of twelve different cities. A couple of those cities, including New Orleans and Cincinnati, had already received a modest amount of public scrutiny, though the water industry had dismissed the criticisms as coming from alternative "fringe" groups and publications.

The lead researcher in the group, a Naderite with a sanitation-engineering background named Robert Harris, was convinced, as he later recalled, that this would be "the dullest issue he could possibly research." Like others in his field, Harris felt that "there were no more important public health issues with drinking water." Still, the young engineer, aware of the PHS review and other studies just then surfacing, wondered whether some serious issues might emerge as a result of the study.

Harris's main contribution was to focus on the issue of the organics, whose significance neither he nor Nader had yet understood. He soon discovered that various organics were present in the water supplies of each of the cities under review. Furthermore, the research pointed out that the allegations about contamination by organics in some key cities like New Orleans were more extensive than anticipated. Armed with their findings, Harris and coresearcher Edward Brecher produced a three-part series for *Consumer Reports*. The first article ran as the cover story for the June 1974 issue.

Soon after the *Consumer Reports* articles hit the stands, water officials from the city of New Orleans and the state of Louisiana requested that EPA do a sample test to determine "the identities and the quantitative concentrations of trace organic compounds that might be present in the finished water of New Orleans and other surrounding communities." The lower Mississippi River, in the 150-mile area between Baton Rouge and New Orleans, was the site of more than one hundred chemical plants and refineries. It would

170

eventually become known as the "petrochemical corridor," given the large number of hazardous chemicals that were produced, transported, and spilled into the river each year.

This New Orleans corridor had also been a primary focus of the *Consumer Reports* articles. Public officials, including water industry leaders, had been quick to condemn the series as poor research and sensationalist in nature. The EPA study, they hoped, would lay to rest the issue. Instead, five months later, EPA identified eighty-six organic compounds in the water, twenty more than previous tests. This was due, the EPA explained, to "improvements in analytic techniques." At the same time that EPA issued its findings, the Environmental Defense Fund released a report, later criticized and attacked, which suggested that persons drinking Mississippi River water, including New Orleans residents, had a greater chance of developing cancer than nearby residents who relied on local groundwater sources.

The focus on drinking water now began to extend into the mass media. A CBS documentary and an NBC "Nightly News Report" brought further attention to the situation in New Orleans and also in Cincinnati, where an unpublished study by the Public Health Service pointed to a substantial presence of organics in the water supply. When the head of the Cincinnati utility was confronted with the study, he dismissed it, explaining that if a serious problem did indeed exist, he would have been told about it.

Even more worrisome for the water utilities was the preliminary research just then surfacing regarding another class of organic compounds in the treated drinking water. These compounds were identified as "disinfection by-products" because of their link to the chlorination process. Much of the initial research on one key group of organics, trihalomethanes (THMs), had been performed by a former brewery chemist in the Netherlands. He had discovered that when chlorine was used for disinfection, it combined with organic material present in the water to form the THMs. This created an entirely new kind of problem for the utilities. Unlike the volatiles or synthetics that were present in the source waters and related to the question of industrial discharges, the THMs were formed as a consequence of the use of the chemicals in the treatment process. This was indeed new and difficult information for the water industry to absorb. Chlorination, long considered the very reason for creating high-quality, "safe" drinking water, was now being held partially responsible for making the water *less safe* to drink.

On the very same day that the EPA issued its first report on the organics in the New Orleans water, it announced a nationwide study of eighty cities to determine the extent of the THM problem in the U.S. The combination of the media coverage, publication of various studies, and the emergence of an entirely new and potentially ubiquitous problem, finally pushed Congress to pass its first drinking water legislation. The Safe Drinking Water Act was signed into law by President Gerald Ford on December 16, 1974, and it immediately set in motion a chain of events that would mobilize much of the urban side of the water industry. In the process, most water utilities would drop their more passive and ambivalent posture and become forceful critics of the growing public concerns. They would also become strong opponents of the move toward new and more stringent water quality regulations.

Though much of the water utility industry mobilized against the implementation of the new law, there were some important initial exceptions. The incoming president of AWWA during 1974–75, Robert Hilbert, said in his introductory remarks (prior to passage of the Safe Drinking Water Act) that the increased media coverage and newly developing water quality problems, had "serious implications for the water supply industry." "As public awareness grows," Hilbert declared, "we may be sure that we will be called upon, as keepers and dispensers of the nation's waters, to offer solutions. How the public will view the water-supply industry will depend largely upon actions now. We could be looked upon, with some indignation, as the custodians of antiquated water systems. . . . On the other hand, we could be looked upon as visionary, progressive leaders who anticipated these problems and requested and obtained timely and appropriate measures of correction."

The experience of the Cincinnati water utility demonstrated one route for the water industry. Cincinnati drew its drinking water supply from the Ohio River. Its problems were not only found along the Ohio, but included the Kanawha River (that had so polluted Nitro, West Virginia), which fed into the Ohio. Steel plants from Pittsburgh, petrochemical plants from West Virginia and thirty million annual tons of cargo designated as hazardous were all sources of possible discharges into the river.

After the spate of publicity in 1974, the Cincinnati utility dug in its heels, skeptical both about test results and the potential health consequences related to the organics. The utility was particularly concerned about being forced to increase rates. This, they argued, would lead to an industry exodus from Cincinnati since several industrial plants were the largest users of water in the system. Furthermore, both utility leaders and local elected officials were convinced that the public responded to narrow-pocketbook rather than water-quality considerations.

Despite the resistance of the local utility, the EPA pushed for more information on the nature of the local water supply. A series of events, were, in fact, bringing the matter to a head. A major spill of carbon tetrachloride, a compound already identified as a serious potential carcinogen, had entered the Ohio River from the spill site on the Kanawha and contaminated the Cincinnati water supply in February 1977. This all occurred before the company responsible for the spill, the FMC corporation, released the information publicly. FMC, it turned out, had been discharging two to four thousand pounds a day of carbon tetrachloride into the Kanawha for nearly two years prior to EPA's discovery—quite by accident—that Cincinnati residents had been drinking water with carbon tetrachloride levels nearly one hundred times the national average. A few months later, partly as a result of the public outcry from the FMC spill, EPA provided a sizable grant to the Cincinnati Water Department to look into the possibility of the utility converting to a GAC system. At the same time, the utility, which had recently installed a more advanced measuring system to detect trace levels of organics in the Ohio, decided to find out for themselves what was actually in the river.

"When we set out to do the research," Cincinnati utility head

173

Richard Miller recalled, "I originally wanted to prove that we didn't need the GAC." Miller, who had become head of the utility shortly before the carbon tetrachloride spill and the EPA grant, was convinced that the findings would be insignificant and that public opposition to the costs of GAC would outweigh any concerns. He eventually found out he was wrong on both counts. After four years of research, the utility discovered that more than two hundred organics were present in the water system in varying amounts. Although the EPA had yet to regulate these organics, which included such toxic compounds as benzene and tuolene, the utility knew it had to somehow respond. "We had to answer a question that couldn't be answered," Miller declared. Namely, "what do all these contaminants do together when combined?"

The following year, the EPA-funded Cincinnati utility study on GAC was completed. The costs would be considerable, with capital costs for a prototype plant as high as $50 million, and annual operation and maintenance costs as much as $8.5 million. The average annual rate increase would come to $25, high for an industry that had long sought to keep rates low, especially for its largest users, but substantially lower than the cost of bottled water, much of which was simply GAC treated.

Over the next several months, Miller and other utility officials undertook an extensive outreach effort. They appeared on radio and television and talked to community and neighborhood groups, explaining the trade-off between the additional costs versus the new treatment. "There was hardly any public opposition," Miller recalled. To his surprise, in January 1983, the Cincinnati City Council decided, despite their earlier fears about an economic-related backlash, to go along on the first design stage of the system. Completion of the plant was delayed by a rate-structure dispute between the city and the county, but the overall experience made a believer out of Miller and his utility.

While the Cincinnati utility sought to confront its water quality problems, the water industry continued to head in a diametrically opposite direction. Water agencies were most concerned with EPA's implementation of the new Safe Drinking Water Act. EPA's eighty-city survey discovered that the THM problem was indeed ubiquitous. Every city had THM levels substantially higher than the amounts projected to cause one cancer death per million population, the guideline most widely used in assessing health risks. More advanced detection methods also pointed to the widespread presence of organics in many of the surface water systems. A congressional report in 1974 had already warned that more than twelve thousand chemical compounds were being used commercially, with five hundred compounds added each year. To start the process of regulating the organics, the EPA established a rule-making procedure to determine what standards to set and what treatment methods to require.

The water industry responded on both those counts. Under the leadership of utility heads from Louisville; Indianapolis; Elizabethtown, New Jersey; and elsewhere—particularly heads of privately owned utilities from the Northeast—a water industry–created Coalition for Safe Drinking Water was established to contest and ultimately influence the EPA rule-making process. The opposition of the new coalition to regulation and new treatment was based on its general disbelief that any serious problem did in fact exist. One of the leaders of the coalition, Louisville utility head Foster Burba, recalled the period as one dominated by "pseudo-science," a "stampeded" Congress and EPA, and "unworkable" requirements. Burba felt the problem had in part been *invented* due to the more advanced detection techniques. "The idea that if contaminants can be measured, then they should be removed is not proper science," Burba exclaimed. "It's like the dog chasing his tail. We have to measure the health effects first." If the organics had not been measured by the new instruments in the first place, Burba concluded, stating a position widely shared throughout the water industry, then there would not have been a problem at all. "The best solution," AWWA executive director Eric Johnson said of the recent detections of THMs by the new sophisticated lab equipment, "is to get rid of that lab equipment and we wouldn't have a problem."

Through 1978 and 1979, the Coalition for Safe Drinking Water led the fight against a dwindling and ultimately outgunned group of consumer and environmental advocates. Many of the mainline environmental groups had failed to get involved in the drinking water fight. They concentrated instead on what they considered their bread-and-butter agenda, such as the protection of scenic and natural resources. Although Ralph Nader and a handful of environmental experts, such as Harris and then Environmental Defense Fund attorney Jacqueline Warren, continued to press EPA for implementation and to ward off the water industry's counterattacks, the debate, as Warren recalled, "took place outside the public eye." Even local community and neighborhood groups, who would later so prominently take up groundwater issues, were absent from these debates that appeared to focus on obscure scientific arguments with no immediate and visible consequence.

The water industry coalition, meanwhile, gathered strength by mobilizing utilities and backing EPA into a corner. Their counterattack was primarily based on economic arguments, suggesting, for example, that GAC could "bankrupt the treasury" as one water agency official would later put it. Furthermore, the coalition hammered away at the "inexact" science theme, dismissing the significance of contamination by organics. They argued that regulations should be developed only after all the evidence was in, a position some critics defined as the "falling bodies" approach.

The debate between the water industry and its opponents was fierce at times, despite its low public visibility. Many of the water industry officials were indignant that such problems as trace organics or disinfection by-products were being raised in the first place. To suggest that chlorinated water might be contaminated was taken as a personal affront. New health studies were dismissed as scientifically inconclusive, and GAC technology was disparaged as untested despite its long use. "Their position," Jacqueline Warren would later lament, "turned out to be quite effective. But then the public, thanks to the increased attention around hazardous wastes and groundwater contamination, finally got more involved."

The coalition counterattack was at first largely successful. The water industry group convinced EPA in 1979 to set a THM standard four hundred times higher than the usual one-cancer-death-per-

176

million guideline. Most utilities in the country, with some important exceptions, such as Southern California's Metropolitan Water District, met those liberal guidelines. But even those water agencies—in Detroit, Portland, Chicago, Denver, and Seattle, to name just a few cities—still had THM readings at levels more than one hundred to two hundred times the one-cancer-death-per-million figure. The EPA decision was ultimately influenced by the economic argument of the coalition that the water agencies would be able to meet the more stringent standard only by switching its treatment method to GAC, which was far too expensive.

The water industry forces were even more successful with the overall organics issue, beyond the question of the THMs. Though the water industry groups were unsuccessful in their attempts to gut the Safe Drinking Water Act, they were able to help slow down the regulatory process along with unanticipated allies from the Office of Management and Budget. Ten years after passage of the act, EPA had succeeded in establishing standards for only two compounds—THMs and radronucleides. In the battle over contaminants in surface waters, the water industry had gained some early victories. It would soon discover, however, as the conflict shifted terrain, that in doing so, it had become more vulnerable than ever.

GROUNDWATER CRISIS

The safe drinking water battles of the seventies had focused on the contamination of surface waters, both from industrial and agricultural discharges and the chlorination process. More than 80 percent of the country's water systems, however, were *groundwater* based, derived from waters stored in underground aquifers. Groundwater accounted for 90 percent of the country's freshwater supplies and more than 50 percent of its drinking water. This water had long been considered better protected than surface waters since it was felt the ground would always act as a natural filter in removing impurities, even with the ever-increasing volume of discharges into the ground through landfills and by other means.

But these discharges, it eventually became apparent, were also creating significant contamination problems, with greater long-term impacts than the pollution of surface waters. During the mid- and late 1970s, dumps and landfills, brewing grounds for a vast array of hazardous substances, received public attention and legislative and regulatory review. The discovery of underground seepage and groundwater contamination in places like Love Canal (in New York), Stringfellow (in California), and Times Beach (in Missouri) had an enormous impact on public attitudes and quickly placed toxics at the top of state and federal legislative agendas.

At first, the Love Canals and Stringfellows were presumed by the water industry to have only localized impacts, no matter how severe the situation, given that groundwater moves slowly, often only as much as ten to twenty feet a year. Then, in December 1979, the Aerojet Corporation, which had a plant based in the San Gabriel Valley, a collection of bedroom suburbs to the north and east of downtown Los Angeles, discovered quite by accident that one of the wells in the area had very high levels—eighteen hundred parts per billion—of trichlorethylene (TCE).

TCE is a solvent used in aerospace and other industries as a degreaser. It has also been widely used in septic tanks and cesspools as a cleaning agent. During the 1950s and 1960s, TCE had largely replaced carbon tetrachloride as a primary solvent for these industries after studies had shown that carbon tetrachloride was a potential carcinogen. During the mid- and late 1960s, TCE use increased even more from heavy aerospace and military demand during the Vietnam War, largely as a degreasing solvent for military equipment. Production peaked at 277,000 metric tons in 1970.

During this same period, TCE production began to face major constraints. In 1968, Los Angeles County adopted Rule 66, which limited TCE emissions into the air because of its contributions to photochemical smog. Later tests highlighted the potential for TCE to cause serious water quality problems as well. (About 90 percent of the TCE used in production becomes a hazardous waste.) This led to a long and politically charged regulatory process that finally culminated in 1987, when EPA established for TCE a five parts per billion maximum contaminant level for drinking water supplies.

The 1979 discovery of TCE in the San Gabriel Valley led to a series of tests for groundwater contamination throughout the country. The results were astounding. Hundreds of wells were shut down in Maine, New York, New Jersey, Connecticut, Massachusetts, Tennessee, Michigan, Wisconsin, California, and elsewhere, after high levels of TCE as well as several other suspected carcinogens including perchlorethylene (PCE) and tetrachloroethylene (TCAA) were discovered.

Through the early 1980s, news stories about groundwater contamination appeared almost daily. It seemed that each community discovered it too had a groundwater problem, particularly those with some kind of industrial activity that relied on organic chemical compounds. While drinking water quality had tended to be a relatively obscure issue debated among "experts" when limited to surface water problems, it suddenly became a major public concern when related to groundwater contamination. This form of contamination appeared more tangible, generating a more visceral reaction from the public, a stronger feeling of violation.

There was, as it turned out, considerable reason for concern. Though the groundwater moves slowly, the contaminants themselves move in unpredictable ways in what are called underground plumes. These plumes are difficult and expensive to measure and even more difficult to treat. To shut down a well, which many water agencies did in the aftermath of the test results, only postponed dealing with the problems and often made it worse. Frequently such delays simply spread the contamination to other well sites, depending on how and where the plume moved. The best method of dealing with the contamination required the water to be pumped out of the well and as much of it as possible treated before being returned to the ground. That raised the same issues that emerged during the EPA rule-making process during the late 1970s, since the best treatment method available to reduce the levels of the contaminants, granular activated carbon or GAC, was also the most costly.

With each new discovery of a contaminated well, public pressure increased for the water industry to provide greater information about the extent of the contamination, the nature of the health

179

problems involved, and a plan of action to clean up the groundwater and prevent future contamination. More systematic testing and analysis failed to lessen the concerns. In most instances, in fact, the problem was shown to be more widespread than ever.

In California, the Department of Health Services was directed through legislation in 1983 to conduct an extensive statewide survey of groundwater wells. Three years later, the results were in. Of the more than twenty-five hundred wells tested in the state, 18 percent had contaminant levels above the federal or state standards or guidelines. Even more striking was the fact that the contamination was prevalent throughout the state, from rural areas with their heavy pesticide-related contamination, to the inner cities and the suburbs. Areas where industrial activity was extensive, such as Silicon Valley, were most affected. The groundwater problem cut across class and geographic boundaries, affecting the water supplies of both lower- and middle-class communities. As with the controversy over hazardous wastes, the focus on groundwater quality was shifting from a local to a regional and national level.

The California survey was not an exception. Similar studies in other states and communities were analyzed by various bodies such as the General Accounting Office, the Office of Technology Assessment, and the Academy of Natural Sciences. Their reports suggested that groundwater contamination, while its full extent was still not known, had nevertheless become, in the words of the GAO study, "a significant and widespread problem."

The recognition of the seriousness of the problem and the rapid rise in public interest transformed the debate that had begun during the seventies over implementation of the Safe Drinking Water Act. For a time, during the late 1970s and early 1980s, the public focused more on the inaction of the regulatory agencies and various state and local health departments than on water industry recalcitrance. EPA, in particular, was of special interest because of the politicization and counteroffensive that took place during the first term of the Reagan administration. This was the period when Ann Gorsuch ran the EPA and her assistant Rita Lavelle, who ultimately went to jail for perjury, was in charge of the groundwater program. Their policies seriously undermined groundwater clean-up programs, including those established through the hazardous wastes "Superfund" legislation just before Reagan assumed office.

The Reagan administration's OMB also became, during the early 1980s, the foremost advocate of industry's position concerning environmental regulations, including those related to organics and chemical contamination. The OMB, in turn, pressured Gorsuch's EPA to even further relax or modify its procedures, as the environmental agency made special efforts to alert industry that it was no longer considered an adversary in regulatory proceedings.

Lavelle, for one, was directly involved in attempting to influence the scientific debate about TCE health risks and cancer-risk policy in general. The pressure to change these policies originated early on in the Reagan administration. It began with the White House–sponsored regulatory reform task force chaired by Vice-President George Bush. This group developed its own "hit list" of undesirable regulations. These were then sent out to the new federal administrators appointed by Reagan, including Gorsuch at EPA. The task force had served "as a complaint center for industries dissatisfied with government regulation," as a *Science* magazine article put it, and cancer policy, particularly with respect to water quality regulations, was high on the list.

Lavelle, along with several other high EPA officials, moved quickly on these issues. An October 5, 1982, memo from Lavelle, who had been a top executive with the Aerojet Corporation, a major TCE polluter, to the number-two figure at EPA, John Hernandez, spelled out a suggested change of EPA policy on TCE. The key to the change was the revision of EPA's approach on assessing TCE's toxicity. This approach, Lavelle wrote, was the first step in "an expeditious, well-conceived, planned, and executed communication to the scientific and regulated communities of our plans for application of 'good science.' "

"Good science," suggested Lavelle, meant rejecting those studies that indicated that TCE was a carcinogen. Such an approach, furthermore, called for the establishment of greater and lesser risk categories, with its implications for a much narrower basis for regulation. Lavelle's "good science" approach, however, never came to be implemented, thanks in part to the series of political exposés during 1983 and 1984 that sent her to jail and forced Gorsuch to resign. But the attempt to restructure the way the cancer risks of various organics such as TCE were assessed, became, even after the departure of Lavelle and Gorsuch, a major objective for the water industry.

Water agency leaders continuously denigrated various cancer risk studies used as the basis for regulations and pooh-poohed the low thresholds associated with such evaluations. The trace amounts of organics in the water supply were constantly likened to that "drop of vermouth in a sea of gin" metaphor that came to be widely adopted by water industry leaders. One prominent water industry figure, Howard Hawkins, from the San Gabriel Valley in California, liked to boast about how he confronted community groups concerned with the contamination issue. These groups were particularly anxious about water quality, since the San Gabriel Valley was the location of a major Superfund site because of the extensive groundwater contamination, including TCE, in four separate areas of the valley.

Hawkins is a former chairman of the Metropolitan Water District and active water industry participant, as well as the head of a local chemical fertilizer company. To the meetings he would bring a dropper that he said contained small amounts of TCE. He would put some drops in a glass of water and drink the water. He would then proclaim that he had swallowed the equivalent of the five parts per billion TCE that the state of California and the EPA had established as their guidelines. This amount, Hawkins declared to the San Gabriel Valley residents, was supposed to result in one additional cancer death per million population after the water had been ingested over a seventy-year period of time. "And see," Hawkins told his audience, "I haven't died."

In a similar vein, water industry groups were quick to embrace the position of a UC Berkeley biochemist Bruce Ames. Ames had become involved in attempts to establish a hierarchy of risks and provide a comparison of the relative degrees of toxicity by contrasting what he called "natural" and man-made carcinogens. In earlier years, Ames had researched the cancer-causing properties found in tris, a synthetic fiber used in children's clothing, and had as a result locked horns with government agencies in attempting to ban the product. By the early and mid-1980s, however, Ames had shifted his focus to attack what he considered public "chemophobia." Ames's transition came about, in part—according to one colleague who had worked directly with the UC scientist—because of his growing dislike of government regulation and his embrace of the promarket, antigovernment libertarianism of economist Milton Friedman.

Ames's argument was based on two key points: that "natural" carcinogens, such as the aflatoxin mold in peanut butter and corn oil, provided a greater risk than industrial chemicals such as TCE, and that attempts to regulate such chemicals in drinking water or food products detracted from the "few really serious hazards," such as tobacco. Ames indicated that he considered products such as the pesticide EDB or industrial solvents such as TCE superior industrial products that contributed to "the national wealth." This attitude, moreover, framed his discussion of comparative risk.

Ames himself had warned on occasion that information about the cancer-causing potential of natural carcinogens was scant. It had not, furthermore, been subject to rigorous scientific review, and was controversial within the scientific community. The carcinogenicity of the aflatoxin mold Ames used as a prime example was linked moreover to a man-made practice, namely the length and condition of storage of the peanuts. This in turn related to marketing and distribution factors, not a naturally occurring condition.

Nonetheless, the water industry quickly adopted Ames's argument as their major refutation of the need for regulations related to chemical contamination. Ames became a favorite speaker on the water industry circuit and his speeches and commentaries in newspapers were widely reprinted by water industry groups. By the late 1980s, Bruce Ames had become the water industry's (and the petrochemical industry's) chief advocate. Following Ames's lead, the

183

water industry, adopting what came to be called the "peanut butter refutation," lashed out at advocates of regulation, dismissing water quality concerns by suggesting the health risks were nonexistent.

The debate in fact had become a classic encounter between two diametrically opposed points of view with respect to the question of risk. Consumer, environmental, and neighborhood groups insisted that where studies demonstrated the possibility of carcinogenicity or other serious health hazards, as EPA scientists had indicated for TCE and THMs for example, regulations were obviously warranted. In many instances, however, as with the introduction of new pesticides or other petrochemical products, there were few studies to draw on, due primarily to the snail's pace at which industry made information available on its products. Several groups argued that even in these situations it would be better to err on the side of caution and take an exclusive public health posture in devising initial regulations.

Along these lines, community groups such as the Silicon Valley Toxics Coalition in California insisted that the mechanisms regarding burden of proof had to be changed. Since scientific uncertainty surrounded much of the risk assessment debate, the key public policy question remained: "Who should bear the burden of that uncertainty?" "Up to now," the group argued, "it has been the innocent victim of toxic poisoning that has had to overcome these uncertainties in trying to establish cause and effect." That situation, the group declared, had to be reversed. The burden needed to shift to the potential polluter who had to demonstrate that the particular product at stake did not result in any degree of toxicity or contaminate the water supply.

The water industry, on the other hand, based its approach on economic considerations (it would cost too much), comparative risk factors (eating peanut butter sandwiches or driving a car produced more risk), and a more absolute notion of scientific evidence (we have to see the dead bodies first). All of these conditions argued against regulations. In the process, the water agencies de-emphasized—and even rejected in certain instances—being defined as *public health institutions*. Instead, they emphasized they were part of an *industry* that had economic objectives, with direct and indirect ties to other industries. In the case of drinking water standards, the water industry in fact entered into coalition with the petrochemical industry and related industrial groups that had the most at stake in this debate.

As the debate sharpened, it also extended into the public arena in a number of ways. The issue of TCE toxicity, for example, became a key factor in a well-publicized trial in Woburn, Massachusetts, a city of thirty-five thousand people twelve miles north of Boston. A suit by several residents in the community against the W.R. Grace & Co charged the company with substantially contributing to the contamination of two municipal wells with TCE and another compound, tetrachloroethylene. The contamination had been responsible for a significant "cluster" of cancer cases, including the leukemia deaths of at least five children and one adult since 1978 and cardiac and neurological problems for twenty-five other people.

For several years, local residents had been told that the burden was on them to "prove" a connection between their health problems and the contaminated site. State and local agencies were initially "adversaries in this battle to prove that we had a problem," as one local activist testified at a U.S. Senate hearing. Finally, a study by the Harvard School of Public Health and a subsequent Massachusetts Department of Health study were able to back up the residents' "falling bodies" contention. After the release of these studies, the Grace company, in a 1986 out-of-court settlement, agreed to pay more than $8 million to the eight families who had filed the suit.

The Woburn suit, combined with dozens of similar suits nationwide and the continuing discovery of groundwater contamination in nearly every state, had placed much of the water industry on the defensive, despite the peanut butter arguments and their earlier success in influencing EPA. During legislative debates in 1985 and 1986 over amending the Safe Drinking Water Act, for example, the water industry was far less effective in limiting the legislation by conjuring up its various arguments. By 1986, the momentum around safe drinking water had clearly shifted. The legislation passed Congress by extraordinarily high margins (no recorded opposition in the Senate; 382–21 in the House) and was reluctantly signed into law by President Reagan in November 1986. Furthermore, EPA, already under the gun from the criticisms dating back to the Gorsuch period and with a new detailed mandate from Congress, indicated to the water industry that it too might take a more restrictive approach. This was particularly true in terms of chlorination by-products, with new research suggesting that several other compounds besides THMs were cause for concern.

Despite the strong message from the public and Congress, the water industry as a whole seemed reluctant to reevaluate its position. Cincinnati utility head Miller, for example, often found himself snubbed at water industry gatherings because of his utility's willingness to pay for more expensive, community-supported treatment methods. Several research polls, including those commissioned by water industry participants, found that large majorities of the public, as in the Cincinnati situation, would in fact "support additional controls on chemicals in their drinking water, even if it might cause considerable costs to business and to consumers." This caused one Northern California utility head, John DeVito, to suggest at one water conference that the water industry was "overreacting" about the issue of the cost of treatment. DeVito's remarks, however, were not popular with other water agency managers.

While a few water leaders warned of the public's impatience with the pace of addressing the contamination problems, most water industry leaders continued to argue resistance. New water industry coalitions, similar to those of the 1970s, sprang up to influence the latest EPA rule-making procedures in the wake of the revised Safe Drinking Water Act.

As the water industry dug in its heels, it discovered a new kind of affinity between its urban and agricultural wings. Water quality was clearly an agricultural as well as an urban problem. The products of the petrochemical industry, the leading cause of the new forms of contamination, had a wide reach and numerous applications. And it was perhaps the petrochemical industry's most successful product—agricultural industrial chemicals or pesticides—that had come to absorb the public's attention as much as any other would-be set of contaminants.

THE LEACHING FIELDS

In March 1985, the California Assembly Office of Research issued a major report on agricultural-related contamination of water supplies in the state. Entitled *The Leaching Fields*, the report revealed that agricultural "non-point source" contamination problems primarily in rural areas were as widespread and serious as the urban-based "point source" problems related to specific and identifiable industrial or municipal waste discharges. One year later, the California Department of Health Services, in response to a legislative directive, released the findings of its extensive testing of groundwater wells throughout the state. Once again, the contamination in rural areas due to agricultural activity was found to be far more extensive than anticipated. Furthermore, even in newly urbanized areas—such as the Chino Valley in Southern California, east of downtown Los Angeles—there was serious contamination of wells from the highly toxic DBCP, despite the fact that this pesticide *had been banned from use eight years earlier.*

Rural communities also had their share of water quality–linked crises, equivalent to the Woburns and the Stringfellows. During the summer of 1985, residents in the two small farming towns of McFarland and Fowler discovered clusters of cancer cases and other health problems in their communities. Aside from the cancer cases, there were also high numbers of miscarriages, fetal deaths, and low-birth-weight babies. The contamination in McFarland, a farming town of 6,400 people in Kern County that liked to call itself "The Heartbeat of Agriculture," was suspected to be the high level of nitrates in the wells. Nitrate contamination, which has been primarily though not exclusively linked to the use of nitrogen fertilizers in agricultural areas, can cause methemoglobinemia, a blood disorder also known as "blue baby syndrome." Blue baby syndrome is not a problem specific to California. Several cases resulting in death have occurred throughout the country, particularly in the Midwest, where nitrate contamination is a serious problem in Nebraska, Kansas, and elsewhere. Nitrates have also been linked to stomach cancer.

But in McFarland and especially in Fowler, an even smaller community of 3,000 in Fresno County, there were concerns that the problem was also linked to the widespread use of pesticides. Fowler, like other areas in the state and especially Fresno County, had discovered DBCP in its water supply. An epidemiological study in the county, conducted by the California Department of Health Services, indicated a significant increase in the incidence of leukemia and stomach cancer where DBCP had been detected in the groundwater.

The McFarland and Fowler situations, which had received limited publicity outside the area only because of hearings in their community by a sympathetic state legislator, were not isolated events. The key to agricultural-related pollution, it was becoming clear, was directly related to the intensive—and increasing—use of pesticides. Pesticide contamination was showing up in wells and surface waters in every county and every state where pesticides were being used extensively. Yet, for the agricultural wing of the water industry, pesticides, like subsidized water supplies, have become part of its way of doing business.

The growing use of pesticides has coincided with increases in irrigated acreage. Both, in turn, have contributed to the dramatic increase in the levels of agricultural production after World War II. California has been the country's pesticide leader (as well as the leader in the number of irrigated acres), with Florida and Texas, the country's other leading agribusiness states, following suit. In places like Nebraska, where irrigation increased substantially with the introduction of the center-pivot system, pesticide use has also increased. In most irrigated plots, the center-pivot spray frequently includes a mix of the groundwater and the pesticides, creating a practice that has been called "chemigation."

Since the 1950s, most of agriculture, particularly irrigated agriculture, has developed a kind of pesticide culture. This shift, along with irrigation, has changed the shape and structure of agriculture.

The growing use of pesticides, which presents an additional capital burden for the farmer, creates a new kind of relationship between crops and pests. Pests who have been sprayed, and who were thought to have been brought under control, start to develop their own resistance to the chemicals. (This key factor had already been pointed out by Rachel Carson in *Silent Spring*.) The resistance factor has in turn generated the need for more potent pesticides used at higher and higher levels, which increases the volume of use. As a result, overall pesticide use, since its large-scale introduction in the 1950s, has increased dramatically throughout the country. "It's got to a point where we can't farm without them," Sacramento Valley farmer Jack Grimmer told some researchers from the California Agrarian Action Project. "Cut my pesticides off and I'd be dead next year," Grimmer lamented. "Kind of like a dope addict, we're hooked on pesticides."

Already by the 1950s, when Rachel Carson had begun her research, pesticides were suspected as a possible source of health problems for people as well as the birds and wildlife that were the focus of Carson's research. Contamination of water supplies was also feared, although agricultural interests, who had by then developed a strong allegiance to pesticide use, were quick to dismiss such fears and attack the motivation of those raising the issues.

By the 1960s and 1970s, however, it had become increasingly clear that certain pesticides were an obvious public health hazard. The most serious problems were faced by farmworkers who handled the pesticides directly, inhaled the chemicals as they were sprayed, and tended to live near the fields where they were applied. Production workers at chemical factories where the pesticides were made were also at risk. The banning of DBCP for example came about after it was discovered that a surprising number of male workers at a Lathrop, California, plant producing the pesticide were completely or partially sterile.

Residents, particularly in rural communities, have been exposed to pesticides both through the foods they eat and the water they drink, since it has been contaminated by the pesticide-laden runoff reaching the surface waters or groundwater. Frequently, it has only been after a dramatic event—such as the Lathrop situation or the July 4th, 1985, poisoning of hundreds of people who ate watermelons contaminated with the acutely toxic insecticide aldicarb—that testing or regulatory action has taken place. Pesticide-related legislation, particularly the 1972 Federal Insecticide, Fungicide, and Rodenticide Act (FIFRA), which requires registration of pesticides, has been limited by the fact that regulators have had to work with terribly inadequate or even fraudulent health and safety data. Both EPA and the Food and Drug Administration (FDA) have largely relied on information from manufacturers to set their regulations, information that has been extraordinarily slow in coming. In 1976, FDA investigators accidentally discovered that Industrial Bio-Test Laboratories (IBT), the largest testing lab in the country dealing with pesticides and used extensively by the industry, had for years been producing seriously fraudulent data. IBT data was responsible for EPA registering numerous pesticides, many of them thought to be highly toxic, including DBCP. Three IBT executives went to prison as a result of the fraud. Yet EPA let stand the registration of some two hundred pesticides even though they were partially based on the fraudulent IBT data.

Agricultural interests within the water industry have largely remained loyal to the pesticide manufacturers, despite the growing evidence of health hazards. Water lobbying groups have joined with the chemical industry to block new legislation and stronger regulatory efforts. The resistance has been primarily based on long-standing biases regarding intervention and regulation of the production process. While the agricultural wing of the water industry helped shape government policies concerning water development and pricing subsidies, it has fiercely resisted regulation related to a range of water quality problems stemming from runoff and drainage issues, including those directly related to pesticides.

In states as diverse as Hawaii and Kansas, pesticide contamination has become a major issue, pitting the agricultural water interests, allied with the chemical industry, against water quality advocates in both urban and rural areas. In Hawaii, trace levels of such pesticides as EDB and DBCP forced the Honolulu Board of

Water Supply to reluctantly close down nine wells during the summer of 1983. In the Midwest, the growing recognition of pesticide contamination has come about through new information about the extent of the pollution. In Iowa, for example, the state Geological Survey Bureau reported that of some five hundred wells surveyed, 39 percent were contaminated by pesticides, and a quarter of those showed levels of nitrates above federal standards. A U.S. Geological Survey study in 1984 reported nitrate problems on a national level in nearly every agriculturally oriented state. Other forms of pesticide contamination were also showing up in places like Nebraska and Kansas, creating significant support even within rural communities to explore possible controls on certain pesticides.

Despite these growing concerns in rural communities, the water industry has continued to mobilize to prevent any outside interference with the business of farming. This was particularly striking in the sequence of events surrounding a groundwater pollutant study in Kern County in California. Originally put together by the Kern County Health Department, the study traced the extent of contamination, primarily agricultural-related, in the area, and offered a range of recommendations, including restrictions on pumping and the establishment of an Agricultural Chemical Use Council to initiate guidelines for the use of chemicals.

When the report came out, the Kern County Water Agency, the key water industry body in the county, as well as other local agricultural water districts, immediately mobilized to attack it. They attended hearings, pressured the Kern County Board of Supervisors and other politicians, and kept up a drumbeat of criticism. They suggested that the recommendations would stifle the Kern economy, place unwanted government regulation on the agricultural industry, and create an intrusion on private property rights. In response the county supervisors immediately withdrew the report and turned it over to a rewrite committee dominated by KCWA—"a committee of advocates rather than experts," as one participant noted. The rewrite shifted the text and eliminated the more controversial recommendations.

The new report, released in 1982, became the official Ground-

191

water Quality Report. The earlier report became a collector's item. Pulled from circulation, it became nearly impossible to find, its information no longer in the public domain. Though the press had generally ignored the controversy, it appeared to policymakers and various participants in the two studies that "the whole lesson of what happened," as one KCWA former staff member noted, "was to reinforce what people here always say, that 'you can't fight the agency.' " The water industry, even in this instance, remained the key power broker in the county.

Yet the water quality issue in Kern as elsewhere didn't go away. The problems in Fowler and McFarland appeared to parallel contamination problems discovered in several other communities in the county. The water industry still remained by far the most powerful and influential force in these areas, but the water quality issue had begun to effectively rally the water industry's critics. In 1986, six years after the original report was released and then withdrawn, a narrow majority of voters in Kern County supported Proposition 65, a water-quality toxics initiative that had direct implications regarding pesticide contamination. This occurred despite the fact that the water industry in the county, and for that matter agricultural interests and the chemical industry throughout the state, waged an extensive campaign in opposition. Water quality as an issue had begun to threaten the clout and reach of the agricultural wing of the water industry, even in an area like Kern County where water agencies and irrigation districts served as surrogate centers of power.

PRIVATIZING WATER QUALITY

By the late 1980s, water quality problems appeared to be increasing rather than decreasing in magnitude. The number of contaminants under review had grown, but the regulatory agencies such as EPA still moved slowly. The focus on pollution of surface waters expanded to include contaminated groundwater, yet policymakers and regulators found no effective way to reduce the sources of the contamination and provide a more thorough cleanup strategy. Thus, more than a decade after the passage of the original Safe Drinking

Water and Clean Water acts of the early 1970s, a water quality stalemate had developed.

It was inevitable that someone would emerge to take advantage of the stalemate and cash in on the problem. That someone has been the bottled-water industry, the fastest-growing segment of the beverage industry, and one of the most noticeable growth industries in the 1980s. Within just a decade, per capita consumption of bottled water has more than tripled, from over 317 million gallons consumed in 1976 to 1.23 billion gallons in 1985. Sales, meanwhile, have jumped from $275 million in the mid-1970s to about $1.5 billion in 1985. With growth rates averaging between 15 and 20 percent, the bottled-water market, which one securities analyst likened to "a play on the pollution industry," could ultimately rival the lucrative soft drink and beer markets.

As the industry grew in size in the early and mid-1980s, two countervailing tendencies emerged simultaneously. On the one hand, a number of small entrepreneurs entered the business, trying to capitalize on the growing concerns over water quality and changing consumer tastes. On the other hand, the industry also started to experience some consolidation, as mergers became commonplace and several multinational beverage companies, such as Coca-Cola and Anheuser-Busch, entered the business.

The expansion of the industry also reflected a change in the industry's marketing patterns and orientation. Prior to the 1970s, the bottled-water industry was composed of two quite distinct markets. The smaller part of the industry for much of its history was more directly related to the sale of beverage drinks including carbonated and sparkling mineral waters. This market, dominated by such companies as Perrier—which first came to this country in 1907 but took off in sales in the late 1970s—tended until recently to cater to a middle- and upper-class constituency.

The second and larger grouping, which now accounts for upward of 90 percent of the sales of the entire industry, has been characterized as the "tap water replacement" market. For much of this century, this market had developed as a replacement source for the local drinking water, primarily because of taste and odor problems in a number of communities throughout the country. As early as the 1880s, middle- and upper-class communities with heavily polluted sources, such as Newark, New Jersey, turned to tap water replacement substitutes. In the process, they spent exorbitant sums of money that could have paid the interest on any debts incurred in order to procure a new water supply.

The groundwater contamination crisis of the 1980s changed the nature of this industry. It catapulted tap water replacement sales into the billions of dollars, with this part of the industry expanding rapidly, particularly in California and the West. Both large and small companies, offering what they called an alternative "contamination-free" product, were quick to exploit and manipulate the fears that had emerged.

Sources for bottled water have included surface water—or "spring water" as the industry describes it—as well as groundwater. These are sometimes the same sources used by the water agencies. Some companies have even pumped from wells drawn from aquifers that have been contaminated in adjacent locations. Most bottled water, however, is treated more extensively than tap water, usually with GAC or ozone. The use of advanced treatment methods such as GAC is also crucial in achieving the elimination of taste and odor problems, as well as providing the basis for the industry's health-oriented marketing appeal and its claim of superiority regarding water quality.

Such claims have often been misstated. Like the regulations for tap water, regulations for bottled water have been established haphazardly. State and federal standards are varied, and there is no single regulatory body (such as the EPA) or legislation (such as the Safe Drinking Water Act) that provides a central regulatory function. Furthermore, there have been a number of abuses by bottled-water companies, some flagrant, both in terms of fraudulent claims and inadequate production safeguards. A number of these have led to consumer complaints as well as health department and district attorney investigations. These have been based on a range of problems, such as the presence of algae growth and foul odors, trace elements of various contaminants (including arsenic and nitrates), doctored laboratory results, and inaccurate or exaggerated claims.

Perhaps most significantly, bottled water has been subject to only a limited review. During the late 1970s, when states began instituting their own regulations in response to the limited federal role in reviewing bottled water, some bottled-water companies began to fear that the regulations "might erode the mystique they [the companies] trade on," as a *Business Week* article noted. By the mid-1980s, however, some of the larger companies welcomed regulation as a means to help consolidate the industry.

Still, the bottled-water companies remained defensive when new information regarding their product came to light. For example, a California Department of Health Services study in 1986 detected concentrations of methylene chloride in water stored in five-gallon plastic containers. The plastic containers, made of a polycarbonate resin, had substantially replaced five-gallon glass bottles since the mid-1970s when the Food and Drug Administration had approved the use of plastic containers. A bottled-water industry spokesman, in language reminiscent of the water industry, deprecated the findings, asserting that the methylene chloride levels were "well below the levels found in decaffeinated coffee."

The argument for a tap water replacement for health reasons has also been compounded by recent scientific studies, including those by a University of Pittsburgh biologist and an EPA chemist. These studies point to the possibility that potential carcinogens, such as THMs and TCE, could be absorbed through inhalation (such as while taking showers) as well as by ingestion (that is, by drinking). Thus, bottled water might at best reduce but not eliminate tap water contamination, given this possible alternate pathway for contamination.

Still, the aggressive marketing tactics of the tap water replacement companies, both big and small, have allowed them to keep the focus on the agencies. The rapid growth of bottled water companies has reflected the public's continuing fears and mistrust around the drinking water quality of agency water. The figures for bottled-water use in Phoenix—45 percent of the drinking-water public—referred to by George Britton in his speech before the NWRA, was not an isolated example. A *Los Angeles Times* poll suggested that use was not only as widespread in California, but also cut across class lines. The poll, undertaken in September 1986, indicated that four out of ten residents in the state drank bottled water or used a home filter system. In Los Angeles County, the figures were even more striking, with 48 percent purchasing bottled water or using a home filter system. Furthermore, income level was not the determining factor, even though the cost of bottled water could run as much as one thousand times more than tap water. Though taste factors were still important, particularly for upper-income residents, health considerations were critical, influencing both upper- and lower-income households.

With bottled-water sales skyrocketing, water agencies reacted strongly and waged their own counterattack. While suggesting that taste considerations were legitimate if people "can afford it," as one water utility official phrased it, water agencies denied the legitimacy of health factors. Some, such as the Metropolitan Water District of Southern California, developed expensive public relations campaigns to deny water quality problems. The water utilities also worked with health officials, state legislators, and the press to expose some of the more unsavory practices of bottled-water companies and develop legislation to come up with stronger standards.

Water quality advocates, on the other hand, have been relatively slow to respond to the emergence of the bottled-water "alternative." Though some key consumer and environmental figures such as Ralph Nader, Nader-ally Dr. Sidney Wolfe, and Jacqueline Warren have offered strong criticisms regarding the problems of regulation and misinformation about the product, others have either avoided or ignored the issue—or in some instances simply offered advice on how to evaluate different products.

By the late 1980s, the bottled-water industry had, to a limited extent, filled the vacuum created by the water quality stalemate. In the process, these companies, with their sensationalist advertising and aggressive marketing tactics, had exacerbated the situation. They

196

offered, on the one hand, a private solution—the solution of the marketplace, as one industry figure put it—while the public-policy questions regarding the source and treatment of the contamination remain unaddressed. This market solution, moreover, created significant inequities. It allowed those who could afford it—and even those who could not—to pay extraordinarily high costs for a health- and taste-related substitute for a public resource. These inequities have been compounded by the fact that one potential water agency "solution"—different treatment methods such as GAC that could address both health and taste considerations—has been attacked by the agencies as "too expensive." The unit costs per customer, however, are far less expensive than the private, bottled-water "alternative."

"By "privatizing" the issues and putting forth the solution of the marketplace, as the bottled-water companies have sought to do, the public discourse around water quality has been diminished. Many citizens concerned about water quality have focused on figuring out who provides the best bottled water rather than how to influence their water agencies and the policy-making process—a difficult enough task given the water industry's lack of accountability. Ultimately, the bottled-water "alternative" has deflected the terms of the debate and the definition of both the problem and the solution.

In this era of rapidly increasing bottled-water sales and water industry recalcitrance, the public-policy issues around water quality continue to remain difficult and unresolved. While some in the water industry have attempted to change direction concerning a range of water supply or allocation questions, the level of resistance to change in the area of water quality remains substantial. Part of this situation stems from long-standing political alliances and ideological biases between the water agencies and their allies in industry and agriculture. Even where the culpability around contamination is explicit, as in the spill from an Ashland Oil storage facility that sent one million gallons of diesel fuel into the Monongahela and Ohio river systems in January 1988, the water industry has been slow to respond.

At the same time, new players have come to focus on the issues of water, challenging the alliances and biases of the water industry. The confrontations over water quality have heightened those conflicts and made more visible the debates about water policy. These new battles have set in relief not only questions about the water industry's goals and objectives but the very purpose of its activities.

Chapter 6

The Outsiders:
Water Industry Critics,
Outcasts, and New Players

ROBERT REDFORD'S SEARCH FOR CONSENSUS

The setting, it turned out, was designed to influence the process. Deep in the Provo Canyon, with its sparkling brooks, majestic snow-capped mountain peaks, dense forests, and brisk, clear air, the fifty participants in the October 1985 "Water in the West: Understanding the New Era" conference sat back in their chairs sipping their chardonnay, picking at their strawberries, and watching intently as their host, Robert Redford, began his welcoming remarks.

"We need a balance between development and preservation," Redford told his guests. He pointed to the surroundings at his Sundance resort as just such an example. Of the four thousand acres Redford owns in the canyon, just a small portion of the land had been set aside for "development." This included his "time-share" cabins, discretely distanced to avoid a cluster effect; his conference center and restaurant, utilized by Redford's film and television institute; and his latest effort, the Institute for Resource Management, which was hosting this conference.

IRM was a particular kind of environmental mediation effort. It had emerged out of the protracted battles Redford and other environmentalists had waged with the energy and electrical utility industry led by Southern California Edison. Ten years earlier they had skirmished over plans to build a massive coal-fired power plant in the Kaiparowitz Plateau in the national parks area of southern Utah. Both Redford and his opponents at Edison had come out of the battle seeking to avoid future confrontations and to find the mechanisms for future agreement. Now Edison's chairman, Howard Allen, had become the chairman of IRM, with Redford its president and Redford aides staffing the organization.

"The idea behind this group," Redford told his audience, "is not to take on issues per se, but to bring opposite kinds of people together to create consensus." Three previous conferences had been held. One had involved the future of the electrical utility industry. In this instance, agreement had been reached around conservation as a "product"; that is, as a source of supply. The second gathering had focused on the question of whether to develop resources on Indian lands, or how to balance profits versus protecting the land. And the third group had met over the problem of offshore oil leasing, with the oil industry and the Sierra Club among others breaking bread and searching for that goal of consensus. "If people come together in the right circumstances," Redford concluded, "they'll respect each other. This country has declining respect."

The theme for this conference was the emphasis on the "new era" in water policy. "New winds are already blowing across the western landscape," the conference organizers argued in their initial mailing to participants. "The assumptions and policies of the past are being attacked by a wave of economic and political change that is taking place in the courts, states, cities, and tribes," the invitation went on. "Water, which has shaped the West more than any other factor, is flowing into a new era of competition and controversy."

The starting point for consensus in this new era, it was suggested, had to do with the emergence of water markets. The decline of the big water projects was another theme, highlighted by the fact that missing among the participants were representatives from the Bureau of Reclamation. Their absence, just ten or even five years earlier, would have made such a conference impossible.

The emergence of new issues and new players was another conference assumption. Environmentalists from such key groups as the Environmental Policy Institute, the Izaac Walton League, the National Wildlife Federation, and the Natural Resources Defense Council were in full force at the conference, as were a wide variety of water industry participants, elected officials such as Bruce Babbitt and George Miller, academics and mediators, tribal representatives, financial consultants, and government officials, including a representative from the Office of Management and Budget. The conference resembled a kind of partial who's who of the contemporary water scene, both old and new players, critics and defenders of the faith.

Yet despite the clean air, the exquisite surroundings, the willingness by most everyone to seek common ground, and even the presence of Redford (the conference concluded with a photo session, with Redford surrounded by the fifty participants; blownup copies were made available to each attendee), consensus was still elusive. Water markets seemed attractive but difficult to achieve, and there was some wariness about environmental impacts and equity considerations. Supply and pricing issues were equally as difficult to sort out. There were also missing themes, particularly water quality, and missing players, many of them locally based and new to water politics, which might have further hampered efforts at consensus.

When the conference was over, Redford was disappointed. "Is it the nature of the issue?" he asked his staff, who could only shake their heads and sigh and suggest that water was perhaps too complex, the transition too uncertain, the deals not yet sufficiently arranged. It was clear that the water industry no longer fully controlled the terms of debate, and that new players had become a part of the water elite. But the new forms of consensus had not yet jelled and a common agenda was still lacking. Following Redford's advice, a good time indeed had been had by all, but even that, alas, was not enough.

As the conference participants picked up their bags and returned to their water-related activities and jobs, there was a lingering feeling that all this had happened before and might happen again.

201

Although the conference organizers had conceived of the gathering as a kind of meeting of opposites, a unique opportunity for those on different sides of the barricades to forget their presumed ideological differences and find common ground, there was really a lot less separating the various participants than might have been anticipated. All of them, after all, spoke the obscure language of water politics. They had attended many of the same hearings, and even some of the same cocktail parties. There had even been earlier conferences with a similar intent, or meetings that drew on many of the same "experts."

The expertise ultimately was the common factor, the link among players. By talking the same language and sharing the same sense of exclusivity, the distance between players inevitably seemed to narrow. Some of the "outsiders" were already talking about a "third wave" of movement activity that could strengthen such bonds even further. While there were many in the water industry who remained implacable traditionalists, there were others who felt quite at ease in rubbing shoulders and even cutting deals with the "enemy," as environmentalists had long been viewed. Could consensus be far behind?

But not everyone had been invited to join, and that seemed to distinguish between those players who were welcomed, outcasts who had little input, and critics who were beyond the pale. As we left the canyon and headed onto I-15, I wondered whether consensus was really a matter of expanding the number of players or the more difficult problem of defining the objectives and purpose of water policy itself.

PRESERVATIONISTS, CONSERVATIONISTS, UTOPIANS, AND REFORMERS

Criticism of water policy and the role of the water industry has had a long and often contradictory history. With the rise of the public water agencies, and the related developments of irrigated agriculture, rapid industrialization, and urbanization, there emerged a series of social movements that contested the furious and unchecked pace of this expansion.

These movements often reflected differing sets of values and assumptions about urban, agricultural, and industrial change not only with respect to the water industry but among themselves as well. During the late nineteenth and early twentieth centuries, the conflicts over the pattern and pace of development culminated in a number of accommodations and adjustments as well as defeats for these various movements. At the same time, the water industry emerged as a stronger and more cohesive force, and water development became the central, unifying objective among both the public agencies and private interests.

By the 1950s and 1960s, the water industry was at the height of its powers, embarking on plans and projects that were enormous in comparison to earlier efforts. In this period, however, new opposition forces began to take hold. The politics of nature at first influenced these debates, though the emergence of an opposition that functioned outside the bounds of distributive, interest-group deal making threatened to unravel long-standing coalitions and local consensus-making capabilities.

During the 1970s, the critics gathered momentum, influencing policy discussions and ultimately gaining a foothold in administrative and legislative forums. The water industry was forced to adjust and reevaluate long-standing programs, as new players staked out a role for themselves in the circle of water experts and leaders. There were still those, however, who remained displaced from the centers of power in water policy, and whose own traditions were never successfully accommodated by the massive changes that had taken place in the post–World War II era.

Meanwhile, new issues and a different set of players, many of them community or neighborhood based, presented an altogether new challenge to the water policymakers. The critics, ultimately, had forced a debate around new agendas and the question of values and priorities, a debate that remains not easily resolved.

Similar to the water industry, the social movements that arose in the nineteenth and twentieth centuries—antecedents to today's various community and environmental movements—emerged in response to the forces of industrialization and urban and agricultural development. These movements—conservationist, preservationist, utopian, and reformist—sought to deal with the vast and rapid changes of the period. Resource issues were the key to some of those changes and they influenced the direction and priorities those movements were to take.

The earliest strategy for developing the land and shaping a resource policy in the Anglo settlement of the West was linked to the Mormon attempt to carve out a semiautonomous nation-state in the Great Basin Kingdom. To give cohesion to this new society in the Great Basin, the Mormon leadership emphasized a land policy based on irrigation and a cooperative organization of the land and water resources. "There shall be no private ownership of the streams that come out of the canyons, nor the timber that grows on the hills. These belong to the people: all the people," Brigham Young told Mormon farmers.

Pressed by U.S. government policy to open the territory to non-Mormons, and encroached on by mining and railroad interests, the Mormons reacted by strengthening their cooperative forms of social organization and intensifying their efforts to create a new society. These were primarily based on irrigation and a concept of harmony with the land and nature. The utopian character of the Mormon settlement was less an escape from industrialization than an attempt to create an alternative to the economic, social, political, and religious orders of the day.

The massive changes sparked by the first industrial revolution, including the early development of the West, were in part responsible for undercutting this Mormon experiment. The coming of the railroads, the mines, and ultimately large numbers of settlers precipitated the crises of the late 1880s when the U.S. government systematically expropriated the Mormon economic holdings and drove the leadership underground until an accommodation was arranged in the 1890s. Although the agreement focused on the disavowal of polygamy, an intended consequence of the government action involved the triumph of eastern financial and industrial interests who would not tolerate an autonomous utopian experiment in the West. The conversion of the Mormons away from the cooperative mode and toward capitalist forms of land and water development undermined the most significant attempt to establish a different form of water development from those that emerged by the turn of the century.

This utopian strand, largely ignored by the emerging preservationist and conservationist movements, quickly faded from view. Only a handful of individuals and advocates of communal organizations—including the dean of western exploration, John Wesley Powell, and Los Angeles socialist Job Harriman, who helped establish a utopian society in Southern California—continued to invoke the value of a cooperative form of development that would be nonantagonistic to the land and the existing resources of the region.

Many contemporary environmental groups have basically been uninterested in these utopian experiments and have instead traced their roots to the preservationist movement of the turn of the century. This hodgepodge of outdoor enthusiasts and defenders of nature against the advance of industrialization never did have a single organizational home or defined set of values or purpose. Even the Sierra Club, formed in 1892 as an organization of mountain climbers, was continually beset by contending factions and points of view.

The preservationist perspective, best embodied by its most persistent and effective advocate, John Muir, did, however, strike a chord throughout the country just before World War I. It developed a strong national following in its celebration of nature as a discrete resource that needed to be protected from the forces of urbanization and industrialization. By advocating a park system and a wilderness policy, the preservationists sought to remove from the plans of the engineers and other development advocates a range of undeveloped natural areas such as forests, watersheds, rivers, and pristine valleys.

All of these areas fell into the general category of wilderness. The wilds had an absolute value precisely because of the mistrust of industrialization and development that cut across class and regional lines. As Muir portrayed it, communion with this form of nature was the highest form of human activity.

But the push for development, particularly in the West where resources were still relatively untouched, had strong and powerful backers. It involved the railroads, land developers, cattle interests, timber merchants, financial investors, and a wide assortment of other speculators and resource development advocates who were rapidly shaping the region. Much of this development was chaotic and contradictory, pitting different interest groups, such as cattle ranchers and farmers, against each other, and often forcing the federal government and the Congress to intervene. While the preservationists promoted federal government intervention against the speculator through the establishment of national parks and forests, other points of view, equally critical of the unbridled speculation, also emerged around the question of development.

These conservationists, or utilitarians, also had a relatively diverse organizational presence and set of themes. Conservationist ideas came to be associated with the approach of certain individuals such as Gifford Pinchot, or certain governmental organizations such as the Bureau of Reclamation and the U.S. Forest Service.

In the water area, conservationists advocated the concept of "multiple use." They urged that each water development project be allowed to incorporate differing features such as power generation, irrigation, or flood control. Such an approach was strongly opposed by the Army Corps of Engineers, the primary water development agency at the time the Conservationist movement first flourished (1900–20). The Bureau of Reclamation, on the other hand, whose first commissioner Frederick Newell was a leading conservationist and multiple-use advocate, embraced the concept from the outset. It saw the possibility that revenues from power generation could subsidize western irrigation, the primary focus of the bureau's activity.

The more expansive notion of the federal government's role did not suggest, however, that the conservationists were interested in attacking private interests. The Conservationist Movement was not a reaction against industrialization and the emergence of the

206

corporation, but rather a desire to rationalize and improve the system, to maximize productivity. Thus, the slogan "the greatest good for the greatest number," widely used among conservationists, was less a populist appeal than a notion of capitalist efficiency.

Support for public intervention was also a central feature of the range of reform movements that sprang up around the same time as the preservationist and conservationist points of view made their bid for public support. More critical of the structure and consequences of the new industrial order, groups like the Eugene Debs–led Socialist party and the Industrial Workers of the World (IWW) often conflicted with the conservationists, who saw such groups as interfering with the possibilities of greater productivity. Unlike the preservationists, who wished to protect nature from the encroaching forces of industrialization, the socialists wanted to restructure the industrial order. They were supported by a variety of social reformers, public health advocates, and muckraking journalists and writers who exposed the excesses of industrialization and the enormous problems of urbanization that plagued the cities of the late nineteenth and early twentieth centuries.

These contending movements attempted to articulate a more coherent approach toward resource policy, urbanization, and land and water development. Sometimes, the lines between groups blurred, while at other times their differences were substantial and became the basis for conflict. When Pinchot, for example, organized the National Conservation Association to develop public support for conservationist principles such as multiple use, he discovered to his surprise and consternation that a number of the affiliated constituent groups, including such middle-class women's organizations as the Daughters of the American Revolution, were far more inclined to identify with the preservationist ethic: "to save resources from use rather than to use them wisely," as historian Samuel Hays put it. While conservationists and preservationists had both supported efforts to establish national parks and forests, they divided over its implications as in the famous conflict over whether to preserve a park or build a water development facility in California's Hetch-Hetchy Valley. Though all the movements were concerned

207

with the problems associated with speculation and land grabbing, they ultimately sought out different ways to accomplish what sometimes turned out to be different objectives.

During the New Deal there was a partial merging of these different groups and perspectives. Under Franklin Roosevelt and Secretary of Interior Harold Ickes, a federal program of water development emerged as a policy designed to stimulate regional economic development as well as create jobs. Though Ickes had been critical of Pinchot regarding some earlier disputes that had embroiled the Progressive movement, the new secretary became, as head of the Interior Department, the ultimate conservationist. BuRec projects were now structured to include everything from power generation to water reclamation and irrigation. Both cities and farms benefited from these projects. They were designed, in part, to stimulate various local economies, from the Pacific Northwest to California and the intermountain West. At the same time, Ickes also expanded the parks system and was able to deflect potential preservationist misgivings by modifying or eliminating development plans in such remote areas as Kings Canyon in Southern California.

The New Deal coalition incorporated the labor movement and various social reformers, as well as the preservationist and conservationist advocates who had increasingly aligned themselves with particular parts of the bureaucracy. The terms *conservationist* and *preservationist* were, in fact, used interchangeably. The two largest groups, the Sierra Club and the Wilderness Society, focused less on water development and more on the expansion of the park system that Ickes encouraged.

In the postwar period, elements of the coalition began to unravel. The New Dealers were placed on the defensive, with attacks from both Congress and the water industry. These were designed to reshape water development by eliminating or restructuring such social policies as the 160-acre law or public power development. The new battles that emerged during this period pitted the bureaucracy against its one-time advocates, primarily preservationist-minded groups such as the Sierra Club. Ironically, the multiple-use concept, which had become largely integrated into resource policy, also came to be adopted by a wide variety of development interests. These included industrial groups who justified their dumping and discharge activities on the basis of the old conservationist principle that rivers and streams could be defined by their economic utility.

The big battles of the 1950s and 1960s over Dinosaur National Monument and the Grand Canyon were in part a transition by the preservationists-cum-conservationists away from reliance on the bureaucracies and the government. Both those battles were highly visible and involved substantial public protest. The greater the public mobilization, the more it restricted the ability of the leadership of such groups as the Sierra Club and Wilderness Society to work out compromises. When agreements were made, further concerns and frustrations arose among the membership of these groups.

The merging of interests between conservationists and the bureaucracies had fallen apart. Water development itself had become the target, as the old-style conservationists and preservationists found their long-standing ties with government agencies under attack. New social movements had emerged, ready to challenge the assumptions of development and suspicious of what came to be known as the "system."

THE ENVIRONMENTAL DECADE

Though contemporary environmentalism has often been traced to such events as the massive Earth Day demonstrations of 1970 and the 1969 passage of the National Environmental Policy Act, this movement also had roots in the activities and events of the 1960s. The most visible of the old preservationist groups, the Sierra Club, split at the end of the decade, in part because of its own evolving activist impulse. Such groups were influenced by that decade's movements, which strongly mistrusted the role of the bureaucracy. That activist spirit also influenced the founding of several new organizations, such as the Environmental Defense Fund, Friends of the Earth, and the Natural Resources Defense Council. These groups were primarily staffed and led by scientists, lawyers, and technical experts. And, in those early, heady days of the "Environmental Decade" of the 1970s, these professional environmentalists shared a kind of activist spirit and a critical assessment of the industrialized and "petrochemicalized" postwar society with their more radical counterparts in the New Left and "Youth culture." Together, these groups seemed to welcome the vision of a new, environmentally benign alternative order—an "ecotopia," as one bestselling novel called it.

There was a strong utopian strand to these social movements, similar in some respects to the Mormon vision of a new order nearly a century before. Both the 1960s "counterculture" and the more politically inclined organizations and movements of the New Left looked to cooperative forms of social organization and a reaffirmed notion of the value of the land. They sought to overcome the distinction between urban and rural, and already raised concerns around "growth" and "quality of life" that came into more prominence during the 1980s.

"Green" became the symbol of this new politics. This was not so much the preservationist ideal of an untampered Nature, but a desire to redefine urban and rural spaces. The influence of the new movements, though indirect and fleeting, provided the new environmentalism with ideas about challenging the existing industrial order and its increasing levels of environmental degradation. The images of Cleveland's burning river, Santa Barbara's oil-slicked beaches, the moving slime of Arthur Kill, or the deadly spray of DDT were powerful reminders of the need for a new environmental agenda. Even the water industry's proudest accomplishments, its engineering feats such as Hoover or Glen Canyon dams, became fair game for a new generation of "eco-activists" for whom technology and engineering solutions had become instruments for negative impact on the environment.

During the Nixon and Ford years, the organizations of the New Left and counterculture began to fade. Not so the new environmental groups. They joined with a range of rejuvenated "preservationist" and "conservationist" organizations, such as the Sierra Club, Audubon Society, the Wilderness Society, and the Izaac

Walton League, to emerge as powerful new players influencing a range of issues. To judge by the degree of legislative activity and technical material generated, resource issues were among the most prominent for the new environmentalists. Each of the groups became adept at lobbying to influence legislation, using litigation to block or redirect water projects or regulatory actions, and developing expertise to counter water industry claims and influence the design of water policy. Preservationist arguments about protecting scenic resources such as rivers and streams remained significant, as the groups pushed hard to make "instream use" part of the planning and regulatory process. Conservationist themes, especially those concerning "efficiency," were also employed. Cost-benefit analysis, for one, became widely used to attack project subsidies and isolate the more marginal water projects.

By the mid-1970s, the environmental groups had succeeded in interrupting the water industry's long-term objectives and even some short-term goals. Projects such as Garrison, the Central Arizona Project, the Central Utah Project, and others from the postwar era of large-scale water development, became subject to lengthy delays and hefty cost increases, particularly in this period of high inflation. In a few cases, projects were terminated because of a court or administrative action. Most of the environmental groups were centralized, with a strong presence in Washington. One important new organization, the Environmental Policy Center, actually split off from its parent group, the Friends of the Earth, in order to focus exclusively on Congress and the federal government.

The more influential these groups became, particularly in the legislative arena and the courts, the further they drifted from the large and relatively inchoate constituencies backing environmental reform. A number of local "single-issue" groups primarily engaged in opposition to specific projects also emerged during the 1970s, but they were largely removed from the debates in Washington and the development of new legislation.

When Jimmy Carter came to Washington in 1977, his assessment of the strength of environmental sentiment, especially in the West, failed to differentiate between the organized environ-

211

mental groups and lobbies and the diverse and relatively unorganized environmental constituencies. The development of the water project hit list, designed in part to show Carter as an "outsider" taking on the Washington establishment, was in effect produced by several of Washington's newest insiders, career-oriented environmentalists who had learned to walk through the corridors of power. Without any effective public mobilization and strengthening of links with local critics of the water industry, the environmental groups were as surprised as Carter with the backlash that resulted.

Though maintaining some success during the Carter years in slowing down water development, the environmental groups were increasingly on the defensive as major industrial interests, led by the Business Roundtable and the Western Regional Council, went on the offensive against regulations and the limitations placed on resource policy. By the end of the Carter years, the administration was considering "fast-tracking" essential resource projects, spending billions on new resource developments, and launching a major effort toward deregulation. This shift toward industry was largely overwhelmed during the 1980 campaign by Ronald Reagan's more encompassing prodevelopment rhetoric.

By the time Ronald Reagan took office, many of the environmental organizations were ready to proclaim the end of the Environmental Decade. Groups spoke of the need now to simply maintain the status quo in legislation and regulatory controls. The environmental groups had become even further removed from the locally based citizen groups to focus more fully and obtain their cues from policymakers in Congress, the courts, the federal bureaucracies, and the media. These policymakers were quick to accept the Reagan interpretation of the need for regulatory reform and a new round of resource development. When James Watt and Anne Gorsuch assumed their respective roles at the Interior Department and EPA, both the water industry and environmentalists were ready to resume their debates along the lines of an industry-inspired retrenchment.

THE THIRD WAVE

To start with, it was assumed that the market was king once again. The early talk from the Reagan administration seemed to bolster the contention of environmentalists who argued that market economics rather than environmental advocacy as such would play better politically with Congress and the media in this more conservative period. The champions of this new approach among environmental organizations argued that they were drawing on a long-standing "conservationist" tradition in using economic positions to accomplish environmental goals.

This tradition was strongly reinforced by the publications of a number of academics and think tanks, most especially Resources for the Future, whose studies were seen as reinforcing the criticisms of the conservationist groups. RFF published a series of books and monographs designed in part to explore what it defined as the "externalities" of production, that is, the by-products of industrialization, including pollution. RFF identified these as stemming from a failure of the market, which in turn would require some form of government correction. RFF also used cost-benefit analysis and other related theories to describe the economic value of resource development. The RFF approach was used by a number of the researchers whose material formed a large component of the National Water Commission Report, and it was widely incorporated by many of the environmental groups of the 1970s.

During the Reagan years, economic arguments were given even more prominence within the environmental movement, particularly among the professionally staffed organizations such as the Environmental Defense Fund. The EDF position, as it evolved during the early and mid-1980s, gradually expanded from a political calculation that the Reagan era required a lessening emphasis on regulation to a full-blown perspective on markets, efficiency, and environmental protection. According to Tom Graff, a senior attorney in the Berkeley office of EDF and its leading "market" advocate, government's role could be reduced by shifting the definition of water from a public and subsidized resource to an economic commodity. By allowing water rights to be bought and sold, Graff argued, the economic advantages to the more marginal users, particularly irrigated agriculture, would become apparent. Meanwhile, the leading proponents of new development—the urban interests in places like Phoenix, Denver, and Southern California—would recognize the attraction of substituting market transactions, where the water costs would be lower, for the big development projects whose costs continued to spiral. Such transitions would have unintended but welcome environmental benefits, while at the same time underlining the bankruptcy of traditional water development strategies.

EDF's first opportunity to develop this approach in the water area was the conservation issue in the Imperial Irrigation District. EDF's advocacy of a water SWAP between IID and MET was at first criticized by the water industry though applauded by market advocates.

EDF's position soon came to the attention of a Montana-based institute, the Political Economy Research Center, or PERC. The PERC group had become the leading exponents of the market-oriented, "new resource economics." A senior associate of this conservative, pro-Reagan think tank, Terry Anderson, wrote approvingly in the *Wall Street Journal* of EDF's market approach, while criticizing the water industry's reliance on the old system of subsidies and public intervention.

Within a short period of time, EDF and the new resource economists had begun to fashion an alliance, which Graff characterized in one article for the *Los Angeles Times* as the "conservationist-conservative alliance." Graff became the featured speaker at a PERC conference and EDF staffers spoke positively of the contributions of the new resource economists. By the mid-1980s, the conservative-environmental alliance extended to several other groups who had become attracted to a politics based on the central role of the market. Even Resources for the Future, long an advocate of government regulation, began to talk of externalities as stemming from the "absence of private property rights" rather than market failures, as RFF economist Roger Sedjo told a PERC gathering.

EDF itself had initially advocated markets in order to criticize the water industry's reliance on its development scenarios, as the environmental group had done during the Peripheral Canal campaign. But by the mid-1980s, EDF had modified that criticism to be more "constructive," becoming in effect a surrogate advocate of a more efficient and "contemporary" water industry. At the height of the Kesterson controversy, for example, EDF signed an agreement with the Westlands Water District to jointly explore possible technical solutions to Westlands drainage problems. The next year, with the Metropolitan Water District under attack for its hostility to water quality regulations and pro-industry biases, EDF worked out an arrangement whereby MET would help finance a "source reduction" study that could pinpoint economic incentives for industry to reduce its volume of hazardous wastes into the groundwater supply. And then, soon after that, the group negotiated an arrangement with the Kern County-based Berrenda Mesa Water District, controlled predominantly by a handful of large agribusiness entities, to promote that agricultural district's attempt to market some of its water entitlements at a substantial profit.

These arrangements became the cutting edge of what EDF's executive director Frederic Krupp described in the *Wall Street Journal* as a "third stage of environmental advocacy." According to Krupp, the first two stages of environmentalism corresponded to concerns over conservation (the Theodore Roosevelt era) and pollution (the post–*Silent Spring* period). This third and current stage "is not satisfied with the precast role of opponent to environmental abuses," Krupp wrote. "Its practitioners recognize that behind the waste dumps and dams and power plants that threaten major environmental harm, there are nearly always legitimate social needs— and that long-term solutions lie in finding alternative ways to meet those underlying needs."

This concept of the "third wave," as it came to be called, quickly became a magnet for the environmental organizations, either attracting or repelling different groups and participants, each trying to adjust to the Reagan era. The fear of being tagged an obstructionist, or an "aginner" as Wilderness Society leader Howard

Zahniser phrased it in the 1950s, had been a long-standing concern of environmentalists. It had been a primary motivation—along with the recognition of "political realities"—for making compromises and trade-offs, such as the Echo Park/Glen Canyon experience in the 1950s. EDF basically turned this fear on its head and suggested that environmental groups could become direct participants in formulating policy "to do the job that the water agencies should be doing themselves," as Graff commented.

A number of environmental groups quickly embraced the third wave concept. "Third wave" conferences were hosted, joint water industry/environmental meetings arranged, and political talks over water policy matters, characterized as "peace negotiations," held behind closed doors. A revolving door for those who circulated between environmental groups, government agencies, and corporate interests facilitated such exchanges, as did the rapid rise of environmental mediation groups, of which Redford's IRM was just a small example. Figures like Harris Sherman and Joseph Browder exemplified this new environmental career ladder. Sherman made the transition in less than a decade from the Denver office of EDF to the head of the Colorado Department of Natural Resources under Richard Lamm to the law offices of Fried, Frank, Harris, Shriver, and Jacobson, which counted numerous resource developers among its clients. In a similar manner, Browder, a founder of the Environmental Policy Center and a major figure within the environmental movement, had been a key Carter appointee in the Interior Department. He shifted from there to a consulting business, whose clients included several big resource developers. Browder also tried his hand at mediation, particularly between his corporate clients and Indian tribes.

Most of the largest environmental organizations, EDF included, had gone through important transitions in the mid-1980s. These were symbolized by the methods used to select new leaders for these groups, or "chief executive officers" as one environmental document called them. That search, which included the use of professional search firms, emphasized the need for managerial rather than activist skills, the ability to fundraise rather than mobilize.

"We're looking for a person who's very strong in finance and budgets, who has a track record in management, who can offer entrepreneurial leadership, who is alert to changes in the marketplace," stated Sierra Club leader Michael McClosky of his group's search for a new c.e.o.

Some groups became heavily dependent on outside sources of funding, such as foundations, and made staffing and priority decisions based on what those sources were willing to fund. For example, Peter Carlson, one of the leading environmental lobbyists in Washington around water project issues, who also had the most extensive ties to local groups, was dismissed by the Environmental Policy Institute (formerly the Environmental Policy Center) in 1987 because of the lack of foundation funding for his kind of activity. Over the years, EPI, like many other nationally oriented environmental groups, became heavily dependent on these sources, in lieu of a strong membership funding base. The foundations, moreover, were interested in the development of technical expertise rather than grass-roots-type activities. They were also more likely to fund specific projects than provide general support for an organization. Those needs for organizational survivability and expansion, given the definition of organizational purpose and fundraising realities, played an important part in the EDF–water industry agreements, which also helped EDF in its funding appeals to major donors and foundations.

The strongest critics of the third wave, symbolized by EDF's arrangements, were locally based groups and movements who were fast becoming the water industry's most implacable opponents. In the Kesterson situation, organizations such as the California Institute for Rural Studies and Fresno-based activists led by veteran union organizer and 160-acre advocate George Ballis, identified the concentration of land ownership and the nature of farming practices in Westlands as the culprit. They urged that some of Westland's farmland—marginal without the CVP water—be taken out of production, rather than focus on a technical solution to the drainage contamination, such as desalting, as EDF proposed. In the Berrenda Mesa situation, these and other rural-based water industry critics emphasized pricing reforms and the elimination of subsidies rather than profit-inducing market sales as a way to generate greater "efficiencies." And, with the MWD source-reduction study, urban water quality advocates, such as the Los Angeles–based Citizens for a Safe Drinking Water, pushed for more effective regulatory procedures and direct public intervention to address the environmental hazards of industrial production. This "social governance of the means of production," as environmental analyst Barry Commoner called it, contrasted with the EDF/MET incentive-based, industry-oriented operation that relied on the market to somehow reduce such hazards.

For the water industry, the third wave was seen as an interesting and appealing though limited shift on the part of the environmentalists. In each of the three EDF arrangements, the water agencies based their involvement on *public relations* purposes for which they quickly took advantage. Westlands, for example, had been in serious trouble with Congress, but was able to use its EDF connection "to do for us what we couldn't do without them," as Westlands manager Gerald Butchert characterized it. Even their tentative forays into the world of water markets did not eliminate for the agencies their long-standing bias in favor of construction of new water development facilities or hostility toward water quality legislation, positions all three of EDF's water industry partners continued to advocate.

Most importantly, the water industry's limited alliances with third wave environmentalists did not seriously alter the closed nature of water policy decision making. Long-standing problems of equity, water quality, and accountability continued to be basically ignored by the water agencies until confronted with substantial public opposition. Some environmental organizations had become "new players" in the area of water policy, but this only highlighted the "outsider" role of all those groups and constituencies who continued to be excluded from the process.

THE OUTCASTS

While the water industry has been concerned with development and environmentalists with rationalizing the system to avoid the excesses of development, others, such as Indians and rural Hispanics in the West, have seen water as central to a way of life related to tribal or community values. "Water is part of living and part of the way we make a living," one resident of the Upper Rio Grande Valley of New Mexico told a University of Arizona research team. "Water rights are sacred."

Yet, over the years, the systematic development of water resources took place without the participation and with little regard for the values of those who had used the water and tilled the land. Indian tribes and Hispanic and Mexican villages on both sides of the border were adept irrigators. They developed both communal and cooperative forms of organization. They effectively adjusted to dry- and wet-year cycles and other variations that influenced the nature of their water supply. The coming of the Anglo settlers in the mid- and late nineteenth century was largely though not entirely responsible for undercutting these practices (the earlier rise of the ranchos, for example, had had a negative influence on the Mexican cooperative ditch systems), and creating an alternate method of water development based on a different set of values.

Indian tribes, of course, were immediately affected by the nineteenth-century establishment of land reservations. These were often in areas considered most inhospitable for development, with the tribal lands either reduced in size or formed outside their traditional boundaries. Water became central to the tribes' cultural and economic survival. The Indians were provided some modest support in the form of a 1908 decision by the Supreme Court known as the Winters Doctrine. This decision grants Indians the rights to all the water "which arise upon, border, traverse, or underlie a reservation." This water has to be made available in sufficient quantities to meet the needs, including future needs, of the reservation lands.

The water industry, though, ignored the Winters ruling and undertook its projects without attempting to satisfy the ruling's re-

219

quirements. The Bureau of Reclamation's projects on the Colorado River or the Army Corps of Engineer programs proceeded without Indian participation or recognition of Indian rights. Local water industry groups were often hostile to Indian claims and attempted to influence state policymakers to ignore or exclude their rights to the water. It was not until the 1960s and 1970s when a series of court cases, beginning with the famous California vs. Arizona ruling of 1963, which granted and quantified rights for the Colorado River tribes on the basis of "practically irrigable acreage," that the water industry was forced to acknowledge and contend with Indian claims.

By the mid- and late 1970s a degree of panic about potential Indian water rights had set in among the water interests and the larger development forces such as agriculture, the mines, and the urban interests. In Arizona, for example, the "practically irrigable acreage" standard, when applied to the reservation areas for the Navajos, Papagos (who later renamed themselves Tohono O'odham to correspond with their own cultural usage), and other tribal groups, would, according to one estimate, entail "more than ten times the amount of the annual dependable supply of water in the state even if only one-third of the reservation lands were 'practically irrigable.'"

Indian water rights quickly jumped to the top of the agenda of many water industry groups and corporate interests, such as the Western Regional Council. Efforts at environmental mediation broadened to include the "Indian issue." The emphasis here was on convincing Indians to consider selling their water rights, perceived by many of the mediators to be the only way out of the impasse. The Bureau of Reclamation, local congressional representatives, and water industry beneficiaries of such projects as the Central Arizona Project, Central Utah Project, and Colorado's Animas–La Plata attempted to restructure those projects so that the quantification of Indian water rights would be dependent on completion of the projects. This strategy was effective in increasing project funding levels by gaining support from skeptical members of Congress who were sympathetic to potential Indian water development.

Ultimately the moves to negotiate and mediate in order to quantify Indian rights and thus end uncertainty dominated the efforts of the water industry in the late 1970s and 1980s. In certain instances, the water industry groups went to the courts to try to limit the amount of water that tribes could claim. They argued that the tribes had neither the economic means nor land base to support widespread irrigation possibilities, and that the "practically irrigable" standard needed to be narrowly conceived.

The quandary for the Indian tribes was that the quantification choices presented only limited and frequently unfavorable options. To reject negotiations would likely mean expensive and lengthy litigation with no access to the contested water rights in the interim. In addition, these cases would be heard in increasingly unpredictable courts, particularly with the large numbers of Reagan appointees at the District and Appeals court levels.

Quantifying also presented a number of problems. For one, the successful maneuvers of the Tohono O'odham and Ute tribes to link their water rights with BuRec projects (phase three of the CAP, and the Bonneville and Ute Indian components of the CUP, respectively), had created strong misgivings among members of both tribes about distant, unpredictable water sources designed chiefly to serve other beneficiaries. In the case of the Tohono O'odham, furthermore, there was far more interest in drawing on the local groundwater, something tribal members were limited in doing according to the terms of the settlement. Ultimately, the strongest fears and objections to quantification and other forms of agreement had to do with the lack of full participation by tribal members and concerns over the role of outside Anglo experts, albeit sympathetic ones, such as lawyers and engineers, as well as the tribes' long-standing outside arbiter, the Bureau of Indian Affairs.

This sense of powerlessness and disenfranchisement, which had long characterized reservation life, was particularly poignant when it came to issues of water. Both water and land were sacred to nearly all Indian cultures. This was a belief that had survived and even grown stronger since the development of the reservation system. Quantifying Indian water rights placed pressure on tribal govern-

221

ments to develop farming practices for purposes of economic development and as a demonstration of the need for water. These pressures at times led to attempts at irrigation, such as the Navajo Indian Irrigation Project (more capital intensive, larger-scale operations), at variance with tribal experience and inclination. On the other hand, the farming methods more conducive to Indian traditions suffered from such problems as a lack of access to capital, technology, and markets, even on a limited scale.

The other alternatives to farming, especially leasing or marketing the land or water, seemed even bleaker to many tribal members. This was particularly true in those western states where the doctrine of prior appropriation prevailed, and the tribes felt under enormous pressure to demonstrate some use of the water or lose their rights to it. Those pressures were exacerbated in those cases where links between Indian water rights and the big federal projects had been established. Both the Bureau of Reclamation and the Bureau of Indian Affairs, in such instances, joined in the push to demonstrate beneficial use.

Marketing or leasing arrangements were frequently proposed as a way to establish such use. This approach was often favored by the non-Indian parties. And although some members of such tribes as the Northern Utes and Ute Mountain Utes were willing to explore the market option, nearly all tribal members worried that these arrangements would violate their culture. "By selling the water," some Northern Utes would say, "[we] would be killing it."

The powerlessness was as much a reflection of an alien decision-making process as the problem of the limited options. The system of representative government imposed on the tribes by their federal protector had already created distance between tribal members and their designated decision makers. Moreover, the tribal leaders themselves had limited access to water policy decision making, at times even playing secondary roles in the negotiations to quantify their own tribe's water rights. The terms of negotiations and decision making—assigning a money value to the water, quantifying rights, use of effluent water in place of fresh water, and so on—often remained outside the historical framework of Indian experience. Ironically, while the water industry fretted about Indians inserting themselves into the process and claiming a piece of the pie, tribal members were becoming increasingly alienated by a water system that bore little resemblance to their own experience and sense of worth.

While the question of Indian water rights has often been viewed as a unique situation because of the status of reservations, farmers and landless agricultural workers south of the U.S. border felt similarly powerless with respect to the decisions and activities of the water industry from the north. Mexican interests in areas like the Mexicali Valley, where the Colorado River flows on its way to the Gulf of California, have become heavily dependent on water development activities in places like Yuma, Arizona, the Imperial Valley in California, and, in many ways, on the practices of landowners and water users throughout the seven Colorado River Basin states.

As far back as the turn of the century, American land development interests, primarily the syndicate headed by *Los Angeles Times* owner Harry Chandler, began to play a significant role in the Mexicali Valley. The Chandler syndicate controlled 860,000 acres south of the border plus far more modest holdings in the Imperial Valley. It hired an ex–South African general to manage its properties and imported non-Mexican labor, including Chinese, Japanese, and Philippine immigrants, to farm the land, often as tenants.

The issue of the use of the river for irrigation on both sides of the border was compounded by the presence of the American landowners. The Colorado River Compact of 1922, which divided up the river north of the border, had failed to address the question of allocations to Mexico. Chandler's *Los Angeles Times*, meanwhile, became a major opponent to the All-American Canal facility for the Imperial Valley. This project, part of the 1928 Boulder Canyon Act that also authorized Boulder (subsequently Hoover) Dam, would, when completed, have the effect of limiting the flow of the river into the Mexicali Valley and the Chandler land syndicate.

The development of strong nationalist sentiment in Mexico during the 1930s, particularly around the nationalization of the oil industry, contributed to the emergence of a widespread movement of landless Mexican laborers in the Mexicali Valley who focused on the Chandler properties. A series of sit-ins and land takeovers from 1936 to 1938 precipitated a crisis over the disposition of those lands. The Mexican government finally intervened to buy out the properties through a nationalization decree and redistribute the land to those who had seized it.

The "assault on the land," as the Mexicali Valley actions were called, also put pressure on the Mexican government to intervene more broadly over rights to the Colorado River. During the early 1940s, a series of bilateral negotiations were held to review the range of problems between the two countries. These included Mexican entitlements to the Colorado River as well as issues related to the Rio Grande, and a labor importation policy—the "bracero" program—that was designed to serve agricultural interests in the Southwest. Water industry interests, represented through the organizations of the seven Basin States, reluctantly agreed to allow a guaranteed amount of 1.5 million acre feet to remain in the river for Mexico. California interests at first refused to sign the agreement.

This water industry reluctance ultimately translated into a narrow interpretation of the agreement, particularly in terms of the quality of the water flowing south. The water industry, led by BuRec, claimed it was under no obligation to provide decent quality water to the Mexicans. That attitude culminated in the development of a drainage project in the Wellton-Mohawk Valley in southern Arizona. This project dramatically increased the salt content of the river, which was already heavily saline. The water that flowed into the Mexicali Valley was becoming nearly unusable.

The completion of the Wellton-Mohawk project in 1961 had immediate repercussions south of the border. Within five years, 50 percent of the Mexicali Valley had such a salt buildup that crop yields had been lowered significantly. Agitation among local farmers and landless laborers increased. As it did thirty years earlier, the Mexican government reluctantly intervened after the national press

224

had picked up on the issue and linked it to the range of U.S.-Mexico problems requiring negotiation. By the early 1970s, the Nixon administration was ready to work out an arrangement as part of a larger set of issues facing the two countries. Once again the water industry interests in the Basin States gave their approval only after it became clear that the solution—federally funded desalinization facilities rather than restrictions on irrigation practices and other uses responsible for the salt buildup—would not affect water industry activities.

The problems for the Mexicali Valley, however, were not over. Through the 1970s and early 1980s, the Bureau of Reclamation, in conjunction with the water industry interests in the Basin States, maintained a policy of keeping Colorado River water storage levels high both for protection against future drought and to accommodate recreational interests at Lake Mead (Hoover Dam) and Lake Powell (Glen Canyon Dam). Moreover, high storage levels also provided for substantial power generation. This was a source of income for the water project beneficiaries as well as electrical utilities who received a share of the power. During the 1960s and 1970s when Lake Powell was being filled, the flood control implications of this policy were not readily apparent. But once the reservoirs were filled, as they were by 1980, the problems emerged with a vengeance.

During the winter of 1982–83, heavy snowfalls produced high flows in the river that turned into a series of floods in the late spring and summer of the following year. These floods were of catastrophic proportions, especially for the people of the Mexicali Valley. The floods were stimulated in part by forced releases at Hoover Dam, where BuRec had continued to maintain its high-storage policy. In one particularly disastrous release, the bureau had even failed to notify Mexican authorities. This created scenes of panic and disaster in the Mexicali Valley that received scant attention in this country. Most of that attention had been centered on the flooding problems in areas like Lake Havasu, where developers had sold lots on the flood plain at the river's edge, despite formal warnings from the bureau.

The Colorado River floods of 1983 had a number of victims.

Five people in the Mexicali Valley were killed; hundreds of people lost their homes, their lands, and their animals. The massive flood-created erosion washed away entire fields. More than fifty-five thousand acres were under water. This also had the effect of reintroducing the problem of salinity in areas where it had been brought under some control. Hardest hit were the landless agricultural workers, many of whom had squatted on the land and been forced to live and farm on the river's edge because of the huge salt buildup that had occurred after Wellton-Mohawk. Once again, pressures were brought to bear on BuRec and the water industry to modify policies. Although future storage levels for wet years were to be reset, the activities in the Basin states that have contributed to the problem have yet to be more thoroughly reviewed.

In areas like the Upper Rio Grande Valley, where those of Mexican descent came to settle and farm the land for several hundred years, another kind of victimization has emerged in recent years. Both the Pueblo Indians and the Latinos or "Mexicanos" of the Upper Rio Grande had engaged in irrigation for years before the Anglos had arrived. Many of them had organized themselves into community ditch organizations called *acequías*. Their concept of cooperative organization was, as one local community organization noted, "far more than just a means of water distribution . . . [it is] the basic socioeconomic unit out of which community life in rural northern New Mexico has evolved."

At the same time, the Upper Rio Grande Valley has been an area of interest and contention for the Anglo-dominated water industry for more than forty years. When the Upper Basin States of the Colorado River divided up their share of the river in 1948, New Mexico was allocated 11.25 percent of the water. Along with the other Upper Basin States, New Mexico immediately began to devise ways to develop and use its allotted water, partially in reaction to the possibility of increased use in the Lower Basin, especially California.

The key to the New Mexico water industry was its plan for an

226

interbasin transfer across the Continental Divide into the Rio Grande system. This would provide a large supplemental water supply for different interest groups, from the urban growth areas of Albuquerque and Santa Fe to the agricultural interests in the Upper Valley. The proposal devised to accomplish this, the San Juan–Chama Diversion Project, immediately faced resistance in Congress as a costly, oversized project with a potentially negative cost-benefit ratio. San Juan–Chama was authorized in 1962 only after it was justified as beneficial to poor and needy communities, including the Hispanic farming communities and the Pueblo and Navajo tribes in Taos County. San Juan–Chama was in fact specifically tied to the legislation establishing the Navajo Indian Irrigation Project.

At first there was some initial interest and support among Hispanics for the project on the assumption that an additional water supply might help sustain and possibly expand the varied kinds of farming in the region, most of which was small-scale and even part-time. But resistance developed when it became clear that much of the decision-making process in the key project-related organizations, such as the local conservancy district, would likely be in the hands of Anglo landowners and developers. Further, the leading official within the water industry, state engineer Steve Reynolds, had initiated an adjudication process through the courts that could negatively affect Hispanic water rights and potentially pit the Pueblos against the local Hispanic community.

These emerging conflicts, spelled out in John Nichols's novel *The Milagro Beanfield War*, had an enormously detrimental effect on the culture and regional life in the Upper Rio Grande. It created strong antagonisms between Indians and Hispanics where few had previously existed. The expensive and draining litigation process also disrupted long-standing cultural traditions. Water was being transformed from a sacred resource that was shared as community property into "a political and economic commodity," as one local Hispanic activist put it. The conflicts that emerged over how to divide up the San Juan–Chama water caused "untold upheaval in the social relations of two peoples," the activist declared, "two peoples that have coexisted, side by side, before the arrival of Anglo government, who now presumes to decide the future of a people it knows little about."

There is a terrible irony related to the San Juan–Chama chain of events. Here was a project designed by the water industry from motivations ("use it or lose it") long associated with its approach toward development. Yet it was being authorized, ostensibly, to provide support for several outcast communities. These communities, whose traditions of cooperation and spiritual values associated with water have been alien to water industry perspectives, have now been thrust into a situation where the culture is being undermined and the only "solution" is to adopt the water industry's approach on development.

The Hispanic communities in the Upper Rio Grande have partially resisted that process, however. They have mobilized their forces to challenge water industry actions. On a couple of occasions they have been able to block additional water development projects. Drawing on a tradition of resistance in the Upper Rio Grande, where land and water rights have been central, and utilizing the limited political means at their disposal, the communities have survived and maintained their strength. Like the tribes of the Southwest and the farmers and landless squatters of the Mexicali Valley, the Hispanics of the Upper Rio Grande are outsiders removed from the locus of power who present a different and alternative way of thinking about and using water.

THE RURAL OPPOSITION

The historical promise of social reform associated with the origins of federal reclamation law was linked, in part, to a social vision of a democratic, cooperatively based agriculture strengthening and stabilizing rural communities. But as reform gave way to the prerogatives of large-scale irrigation and water development, those who shared that vision ultimately became some of the water industry's fiercest critics. This rural opposition, which emerged as an important social force in North Dakota, Minnesota, Wisconsin, California, and elsewhere during the New Deal era, has continued to make its influence felt as the issues concerning development have shifted and new movements have emerged.

Two of the most important figures in this opposition have been Carey McWilliams and Paul Taylor. Both McWilliams and Taylor took the promise of social reform to mean increased possibilities for small farm development as well as improved working and living conditions for farm workers. Their advocacy was in part a reflection of the times. The late 1920s and 1930s were a period of contention in the agricultural lands of California and Arizona. A series of bitter strikes in places like the Imperial and Salinas valleys were met with a fierce and at times violent response from agricultural interests. Agricultural grower groups such as the Associated Farmers in California developed strategies designed to keep out unions and maintain a flow of cheap, imported farm labor, particularly from Mexico. At the same time, these groups attempted to restructure the plans for the Central Valley Project and other water development projects in order to eliminate or modify any acreage limitations or other reform-oriented conditions.

McWilliams, who became head of the California Department of Housing and Immigration during the administration of Democratic governor Culbert Olson (1938–42), directly challenged the agricultural industry's labor and social policies. He became one of the most insightful analysts and critics of California agriculture and its politics of water. His books, such as *Factories in the Field* and *California: The Great Exception*, detailed the rise of the concentrated land holdings and industrial forms of organization that came to characterize irrigated agriculture in California. He quickly became a target of the agricultural groups who defined him as the "number one pest" in the state. They immediately sought to dissolve his modest reforms of rural housing and conditions in the agricultural labor camps after a new governor, Earl Warren, took power and removed McWilliams from his position.

Paul Taylor was an equally disliked and targeted opponent of the agricultural groups. A University of California economist, Taylor early on locked horns with California agriculture when he detailed the huge size of the unharvested surpluses rotting in the fields

229

in the midst of the Depression. By the 1940s, Taylor had become the foremost advocate of the 160-acre provision and the importance of small-scale farming and rural cooperatives in maintaining a more democratic and participatory rural culture. This perspective formed the backdrop of a key and influential study of small rural communities by Walter Goldschmidt entitled *As You Sow*. Originally commissioned in the waning years of the New Deal by a federal agency, the Goldschmidt study contrasted the towns of Dinuba and Arvin. What Goldschmidt found was that the small farm community town of Dinuba was associated with a far richer community life. Arvin, on the other hand, due to its industrialized farming patterns and the availability of newly developed CVP water, had a much poorer community life, a higher level of poverty, and greater land concentration.

Taylor, Goldschmidt, and other critics of land concentration such as Marion Clawson, who studied landownership patterns in the Central Valley of California, saw the 160-acre law, imperfect and as poorly enforced as it was, as the best social tool to achieve a flourishing, democratic community culture in rural areas. The transient life and economically depressed conditions of agricultural labor, these critics argued, was a function of land concentration and industrialization. These patterns served to rob rural communities of any ability to maintain thriving or stable local institutions. They became fully dependent on the single large-scale, corporate-style landowner, a rural version of a company town. One of Taylor's students, George Ballis, became a leading advocate of unionization of farm workers and helped link the issues of the 160-acre law with farm worker organization.

Though the farm worker union drive of the late 1940s ended in defeat, and the 160-acre provision, though maintained, never became properly enforced once the Central Valley Project came on line, critics such as Ballis and Taylor continued their efforts to link those issues and challenge the practices of the water industry. The fears of concentration proved founded when the arrival of the CVP reinforced patterns of industrialization. One study undertaken in the mid-1980s retraced the ownership patterns analyzed in Marion

Clawson's acclaimed investigation in the 1940s of land concentration in several Central California counties. The new study discovered even greater tendencies toward concentration that resulted directly from the availability of the CVP.

The group that undertook the updated study on landownership, the California Action Network, formerly the California Agrarian Action Project, had first become interested in water issues during the mid-1970s. At the time, the 160-acre issue was in the news because of a lawsuit brought by George Ballis over failure to implement the acreage provision with respect to the Westlands Water District. The CAN group had been involved with farm labor employment issues, and the more they explored the structure of the agricultural industry, the more they ran into the issue of water. They were aware of Ballis's lawsuit and the 160-acre issue and decided to see Paul Taylor to understand how the issues joined together.

"It was like a revelation," CAN-organizer Don Villarejo recalled the moment. "We spent the whole day with Taylor and would have stayed longer. He laid out to us and got us to understand the significance of water." After the Taylor session, the group proceeded to organize a series of community events around the 160-acre law. They ultimately began to incorporate, as part of their agenda, issues of farm labor, land concentration, water development, and eventually pesticides and the quality of water in rural communities.

By the 1980s the group had extended its network to rural communities in several counties. It had also developed a base in the cities of Fresno and Bakersfield. The group quickly established ties with organic farmers, antipesticide groups, farm labor organizations, and water industry critics both in urban areas and in rural communities outside the Central Valley where CAN concentrated its efforts.

This multi-issue approach brought the organization into many conflicts with the water industry. CAN particularly focused on the disparities of wealth and poverty in rural communities, exacerbated by the consolidation of an industrial farming system based on irrigation. It played a significant role during the Peripheral Canal

231

campaign when its research regarding inequities in the State Water Project and the favored role of a handful of giant multinational corporations in the Kern County area was popularized by canal opponents. The group first began developing a community organization in the Fresno area when it focused on DBCP contamination in numerous groundwater wells in the area. The group had also been instrumental in making public the multiple ties and questionable relationships between the University of California and California agribusiness, which resulted in an important lawsuit and some needed reforms. By the time CAN celebrated its tenth anniversary in 1987 with a keynote speech by Texas Agriculture Commissioner and farm populist Jim Hightower, the group had successfully inherited Paul Taylor and Carey McWilliams's mantle. Its activists had become the new "pests" of the agro-industrial wing of the California water industry.

As CAN extended its roots in the Central Valley, it also developed ties on the national level with similar groups seeking to create a rural opposition to an increasingly concentrated and industrialized agriculture. During the Carter and Reagan years, these oppositional groups had coalesced into a network of organizations called the Rural Coalition. These included farm labor organizations in places like Texas and Arizona, the Federation of Southern Co-ops, and an important oppositional group in the Midwest, the Nebraska-based Center for Rural Affairs.

Similar to CAN in California, the Center for Rural Affairs was part research effort, part advocacy, part organizing. It had been organized in 1973 during the boom period for midwestern agriculture in the wake of the Russian grain deal of the early 1970s and the inflation in the prices of commodities and agricultural land. Center staff recognized early on that the boom conditions had also set in motion changes in ownership and agricultural practices in Nebraska and elsewhere in the Midwest. They particularly focused on the rise of the center-pivot systems in the western part of the state. Their 1976 study, *Wheels of Fortune*, first identified the speculative nature of center-pivot activity and the growing role of outside investors and more concentrated holdings in those areas where center pivots had been widely adopted.

Like Paul Taylor, the center traced the connection between water development and the squeeze on the family farmer. Similar to CAN, they also became critics of proposed big water projects, including the variety of interbasin transfer schemes concerning the Ogallala aquifer. The center saw these plans of the army corps and the Great Plains water industry as intending to increase the patterns of a speculative and more concentrated irrigated agriculture. The divisions that emerged over water development represented essentially a conflict between the family farm and the industrialized irrigated system.

While recognizing the right to private property, the center and its allies also argued that "there is also a social mortgage on all private property requiring that in return for protection from encroachers, the public holds the owner responsible for the wise use of the land. Beyond this individual responsibility, however," the argument continued, "is a larger responsibility on all of us for constructing social systems which distribute the fruits of the land equitably. It is not enough to produce more from the Ogallala aquifer, if what we produce is used to foster food dependencies and social injustices around the world, and if by doing so we diminish the lives of future generations."

This concern for equity and wise use, an agriculture that could be "both environmentally sound and socially just," was the central feature of this new-style prairie populism. The center itself, a product of discontented family farmers and activists from the 1960s and early 1970s with roots in these rural communities, attempted to develop links with a variety of movements among farmers and in the cities. They helped to successfully launch a movement in the early 1980s that challenged the role of the out-of-state investors such as Prudential Life Insurance. In 1982, Nebraska voters passed a center-supported constitutional amendment, Initiative 300, which forbids the purchase of agricultural land by corporations, a victory that took the large agricultural interests and out-of-state investors by surprise. Subsequently, these interests have attempted to undercut Initiative 300 through court challenges and a possible new initiative election. In the process, a major debate has unfolded about the structure of agriculture and, indirectly, the role of water development.

By the late 1980s, the center-pivot system was in serious trouble. The concepts of a regenerative or sustainable agriculture based on the family farm no longer seemed just an illusory yearning for some preindustrial past. Similar to the debates over pesticides and water development in California, the rise of rural opposition movements had helped focus the debates by linking environmental and equity issues, problems of land ownership, water supply, and water quality. The combination of activism and research, and the cross-fertilization between family farm values and the democratic, participatory, and visionary appeals that traced back to the 1960s, provided a compelling base for a new movement. The water issue, still obscure and controlled by a narrow set of interests, was beginning to receive more visibility and a wider base of participants.

COMMUNITY POLITICS

Perhaps the most surprising and unanticipated critics of the water industry have been locally based grass-roots groups addressing issues that affect their local neighborhoods and communities. Historically, the water industry has been most successful at the local level in promoting particular development projects and the water industry's agenda in general. Local chambers, rotary clubs, trade associations, and special interest groups have been enlisted as part of an organized campaign to convince federal agencies, like the corps and BuRec, or Congress and state legislatures, that a powerful political consensus existed in support of a particular project. These efforts were led by the public agencies and private-interest groups that stood most to gain from the project's completion.

This effort at local consensus politics was rarely challenged during the heyday of the water industry from the 1940s to the 1960s. A handful of organizations, most notably the League of Women

Voters, would, from time to time, adopt a stance different from that of the water industry. Their efforts were often based on a search for project efficiency and a desire to rationalize the organizational setting for development—by establishing, for example, a centralized administrative authority.

The most troublesome issues for the water industry in its search for consensus were those related to problems of contamination. In these cases, conflicting parties such as industry and residential groups were far less willing to accede. The water agencies themselves, frequently caught between conflicting pressures, often attempted to remove themselves as an active participant and possible source of criticism.

That situation began to change during the 1970s and 1980s with the concurrent rise of both the contemporary environmental movement and a local grass-roots community politics focused on such issues as toxics and water quality. Local environmental groups that became active during this period had less to do with the agendas and organizational biases of the national groups and involved themselves more with responding to a particular development project or problem of contamination. Those groups, moreover, that formed specifically around a "toxics" issue tended to be novices about both water and environmental politics.

During the 1970s, the toxics issue quickly spread throughout the country. Episodes in Love Canal in New York State, Hardman County in Tennessee, and Stringfellow in California were at first considered isolated events. But soon groups began to spring up in every region in the country to respond to new problems of contamination. In 1981, Lois Gibbs, the housewife who led the fight at Love Canal, established the Citizen's Clearinghouse on Hazardous Wastes in response to the hundreds of letters and phone calls she had received from individuals concerned about a particular toxics issue in their area. Within a few years, the clearinghouse was providing information and support for dozens of organizations in places like Jacksonville, Arkansas; Evansville, Wyoming; Columbia, Mississippi; and Grand Island, Nebraska. The leadership of many of these groups came from self-described housewives, active previously in groups like the PTA rather than in political or environmental causes. These activists had become outraged at the impact the contamination of the local water supply would have on their lives and those of their neighbors.

This process was particularly striking in the case of Stringfellow, where a Glen Avon, California, housewife, Penny Newman, became one of the most persistent and capable critics of water industry and governmental response to a toxics crisis. The "acid pits" of Stringfellow, as they came to be known, were first developed when an industrial waste-disposal site was opened in 1956 in Riverside County by the Stringfellow Quarry Company. The first major dumper at the site was the U.S. Air Force, which deposited chemicals used for refurbishing missiles at the nearby Norton Air Force Base. For over sixteen years, Stringfellow received huge quantities of hazardous materials—between thirty-two and thirty-four million gallons of liquid wastes: heavy metals, organic solvents, pesticides (including DDT), and large amounts of sulfuric, nitric, and hydrochloric acid (whence its name the "acid pits"). These wastes were deposited by chemical companies, aerospace industries, agricultural concerns, steel and aluminum companies, plating operations, and the U.S. Air Force, among others.

In 1969 heavy rains caused a local earthen dam to overflow. The spill carried wastes into the nearby community of Glen Avon, a small suburban community a few miles northwest of Riverside, in the heart of the Inland Empire to the east of Los Angeles, the fastest-growing urbanizing area in the state. Soon after the flood, local residents created an organization called the Mothers of Glen Avon (which later incorporated as the Parents of Jurupa) to protest the inaction of the local agencies.

In 1972 the site was voluntarily closed after signs of contamination were detected in several wells, including one serving the Glen Avon school. Over the next several years various government agencies got into the act, hiring consultants, issuing reports, and moving slowly, if at all, toward a cleanup strategy. In this period, some of the local residents, Penny Newman among them, began to compare notes regarding the possible health consequences of the spill and the contaminated wells, and speculated about whether the problems were far more extensive than the water and government agencies, the dump site operator, and industrial groups had been suggesting.

During the late 1970s, another round of heavy rains forced government agencies to undertake emergency removal of the liquid wastes spilling over from the site—more than five and a half million gallons during the rains of 1979 and early 1980. The new rains also had a dramatic effect on Newman's own life, as one of her sons, during and after the discharges from the site, suffered asthma, dizziness, headaches, and blurred vision. Newman, who had been president of the local PTA and active in the Jurupa Junior Women's Club, began to suspect, as did a number of other residents, that the health problems affecting their children and themselves related to the acid pits of the nearby quarry.

In 1979 Newman and several other concerned residents involved in a variety of community organizations decided to form an umbrella organization, Concerned Neighbors in Action. They held a series of meetings, including one with the executive director of the local Regional Water Quality Control Board. This water official told residents that they were "overreacting" and that "everything [was] under control."

That kind of response by a water official had been heard before. When the site was first established, residents were told that the waters could never percolate down into the groundwater since an "impermeable layer of clay" blocked its passage. After contamination began to be detected, the various agencies, including the local utility, responded slowly, denying that the contamination could spread. Early cleanup proposals were put on hold, and even after the second wave of floods and spills into the community in 1979–80, the regional board among others continued to advocate a containment rather than full cleanup solution.

After the passage of Superfund, Stringfellow began to receive more attention. The site became a political football. In the early 1980s, Anne Gorsuch of EPA considered withholding cleanup funds for Stringfellow in order, it was alleged, to embarrass California governor Jerry Brown who was then running for a U.S. Senate seat. The regional water agencies also took an interest in Stringfellow as a potential source of funds for an industrial brine line, or sewer line, that would extend from San Bernardino through the Santa Ana river corridor to the ocean. By getting Stringfellow included in the system, one designed to accommodate new growth in the region, the agencies hoped to obtain Superfund dollars. The problem, according to residents, was that such an approach did not contain and effectively deal with the site, which was the source of the problem. There were also objections to the idea of pumping the wastes in the ocean.

While different parties jockeyed over disposition of the site, the residents became increasingly concerned that the problem was not just the question of spills but the ultimate contamination of their drinking water supply. Many residents in the area were served by private wells and they now began to insist that the wells be tested for contaminants. After some reluctance by state and regional authorities, the results came back confirming everybody's worst fears. The wells were indeed contaminated with both high levels of TCE (upward of three hundred parts per billion) and chloroform. Later results also pointed to levels of radiation in some wells.

It was the discovery of radiation that probably had the biggest impact on the local communities. Residents discovered, soon after the radiation problem became public, that their community had become redlined by FHA. Property values plummeted and a number of businesses went under. The California Department of Health Services finally acknowledged the seriousness of the situation and agreed to provide bottled water for residents. The local water utility had become an obstacle in getting recognition of the problem. At community meetings the local utility manager declared that people had to expect some level of pollutants in an industrialized society. There is no correlation, he said on one occasion, between improved health and clean water.

The conflict between residents and the water utilities came to a head with the publication of a report for the Congressional Office of Technology Assessment by a University of California professor from the Department of Mechanical Engineering, G. J. Trezek. Trezek reviewed the history of the Stringfellow site, detailing how the risks to health and the environment "resulting from the migration of toxic wastes from the Stringfellow Acid Pits remain poorly understood," and declaring that cleanup actions had been ineffective in protecting the water supply of Glen Avon. The actions that had been undertaken in the twelve years since the site closed, Trezek stated, "focused on the removal of contaminated surface and groundwater, rather than on preventing groundwater from becoming contaminated." Finally, Trezek pointed out that the Stringfellow site had been known to lie on the Chino Basin, a large underground water basin whose wells were used extensively in the area east of Los Angeles. The Chino Basin had begun to figure in plans for the Metropolitan Water District, which was considering storing up to a million acre feet in the underground basin. Since the plume was moving in unpredictable ways, particularly toward Glen Avon and possibly further along the path toward the Chino Basin, Trezek recommended a major monitoring program in the vicinity of Stringfellow to determine the movement of the plume.

The water industry, which had failed to respond earlier concerning the Stringfellow cleanup issues, immediately mobilized to attack Trezek and his report. They dismissed the concerns about plume movement as sensationalist and irresponsible and ignored the issue about monitoring. The water agencies, furthermore, addressed only the issues of the Chino Basin, where much of the news media attention had focused, and not the possible problems elsewhere, especially Glen Avon and the other towns directly affected.

Newman and her organization were outraged by the posture of the water agencies. "The mere fact that my small community of 5,000 to 8,000 was slowly, but surely, being poisoned by extremely deadly chemicals wasn't enough to warrant hearings . . . or to have representatives from water agencies even comment," Newman declared. What outraged Newman and her group most were the continuing assurances from the regulatory agencies and water industry managers that the movement of the water would not present *more* of a problem, and that natural geologic barriers and other technical explanations suggested the problem had been contained. "We have heard that over and over and over again in the last decade," Newman said in anger to one reporter's question. Her experience convinced her that the water industry, as well as some of the recalcitrant government agencies, had become as much an issue as the String-fellow dumpers who had brought on the problem in the first place.

Once the fuss over the Trezel report died down and was largely forgotten, the water industry basically disappeared from the scene. When Trezek did a followup report in 1987, he pointed out that the problem had indeed become more serious for Glen Avon. He didn't raise the question of the overall Chino Basin, however, but instead focused on the local cleanup issues. With that omission, Newman commented, "you could hear a huge sigh of relief" from the water industry and their satisfaction that Stringfellow no longer appeared to be a cause of concern for them.

Newman herself not only became a leader in her community but became increasingly visible on the state and national levels as an outspoken critic around water quality and toxics issues. It was the involvement of people like Newman that provided the back-ground to the emergence of new networks of community groups and activists who were increasingly becoming an important political force in their communities and states. Their perspective—action through mobilization rather than a more exclusive reliance on ex-pertise and lobbying—was an essential component of these move-ments. They became the newest and most forceful members of the water industry opposition. And the intensity of their concerns and their rapid growth has contributed to the mood of uncertainty and transition that characterizes today's era of water politics and water policymaking.

PART FOUR

Water Policy Confronts Itself: A Conclusion

Chapter 7

A New Era?
Prospects for Change

THE WATER INDUSTRY IN TROUBLE

At a certain point in the discussion, the chairman decided to intervene. Metropolitan Water District leader E. Thornton Ibbetson, then in the last months of his second and final term as board chair, told the assembled directors that this was a matter about which he, the chairman, felt quite strongly.

The MET board members were discussing Proposition 65, a statewide initiative that would be voted on a few months hence in the November 1986 elections. Officially titled the Safe Drinking Water and Toxic Enforcement Act of 1986, Prop 65 was the product of an uneasy alliance between community groups, including Penny Newman's organization, environmental organizations, and some Democratic party politicians, most notably the deputy and key advisor to Los Angeles mayor Tom Bradley, who was running for governor. The initiative called for a prohibition on the knowing discharge or release into the drinking water supply of chemicals known to cause cancer or reproductive toxicity, with a series of warning and enforcement provisions as well.

When the measure first came to the attention of MET, district officials had been able to obtain a "public exemption" clause that exempted the water agencies and other public utilities from the initiative. (MET, especially, would have been vulnerable because of its THM problem resulting from the chlorination process.) The measure, however, did still directly affect other parts of the water industry, particularly agriculture, which was concerned about the potential impact on pesticide use. The business community had also begun to mobilize against the initiative, led by oil and chemical companies such as Standard Oil of California.

It was this effort to establish a unified opposition front among business and industrial interests that had caught Ibbetson's attention. "I recently received a letter from the J.G. Boswell people," the chairman told board members, referring to a "Dear Ibbey" letter sent by the agricultural company's corporate counsel Ed Giermann. The Boswell lawyer was a leader in the campaign against Prop 65.

Giermann had complained in the letter that the provisions of the initiative would "at least make doing business in California substantially more difficult; at most, it could shut down elements of manufacturing and farming." Giermann then urged Ibbetson and the MET board to join the opposition campaign. In a postscript, he attempted to personalize the issue by writing, "Ibbey, inasmuch as you have farming interests in the Imperial Valley, you will appreciate the enclosed list of agricultural chemicals affected by the initiative."

There was some irony in this solicitation by Boswell. Just four years earlier Boswell had been a major nemesis of MET's during the Peripheral Canal campaign. There had been a number of sharp exchanges between Ibbetson's predecessor as MET chairman, Earl Blais, and then-president of the Boswell Company, Jim Fisher. In the intervening years, however, water industry groups, including MET and Boswell, had attempted to reestablish consensus efforts, particularly over water supply matters. Now, with Prop 65, Boswell was trying to extend that effort into the water quality arena.

Ibbetson, for one, was a strong advocate of this united water industry/business oppositional front. "We have to oppose this initiative," Ibbetson argued forcefully. "Our business friends at the Chamber and the Business Roundtable have lined up against it. If this initiative passes, the water industry will be in trouble. Big trouble."

Though Ibbetson had the willing ear of most of the MET directors, it turned out to be a more difficult task than anticipated to mobilize this opposition front. Business interests had already contributed substantial funds to the opposition campaign, and the no side would ultimately raise more than four times the amount than the initiative proponents. But the opponents, who had hired the Russo-Watts (campaign firm) of Peripheral Canal fame, had wanted a far larger financial war chest. Several companies, it turned out, were fearful that by contributing heavily to the No on the Prop 65 campaign or by taking a high profile around the issue, they might get tagged with the polluter label.

Many of the water agencies and utilities also feared being too identified with the opposition campaign. "If we oppose Prop 65," MET's legislative lobbyist argued at another board gathering, "that will hurt us in Sacramento before the legislature." MET's vulnerability on the issue was also a problem. Its incoming board chairman, E. L. (Les) Balmer, for example, had been a longtime managment executive for Standard Oil of California and held substantial stock in the company. This fact was noted by one environmental group, Citizens for a Better Environment, which sent an open letter to Balmer raising potential conflict of interest concerns.

Ultimately, MET and several other urban water agencies decided to remain neutral on the issue, though the sympathies of many of the board members, like Ibbetson, clearly lay with the industrial interests. The agricultural water agencies, on the other hand, were united in their opposition. In areas like the Central Valley and Kern County, the agricultural forces launched a major effort, lining up politicians and the press, and declaring that passage of 65, with its antipesticide implications, could be a disaster for the area. But to agriculture's surprise, opposition to 65 not only failed to generate the number of no votes expected but in agricultural areas like Kern, San Joaquin, and Yolo counties the water quality measure actually received a plurality of votes.

When the votes were counted, Prop 65 had passed by landslide proportions, winning by a nearly two-to-one margin. Support had also been regionally broad based, with strong backing in both the northern and southern parts of the state, unlike other water-related measures. The old consensus mechanisms of the water industry and their business allies had not worked as effectively as had originally been hoped.

For the water industry, and especially the utilities and agencies who had become more visible to the public, an awkward and difficult transition, symbolized in part by the Prop 65 campaign, had begun to occur. Most everyone in the water industry recognized that conditions were changing. The concept of the "water industry in trouble" had almost become a truism of contemporary water politics. But the question remained, would the water industry really be willing to change?

OPENING UP THE PROCESS

By the late 1980s, the water industry struggled to remain a closed and largely invisible policymaker. Its success in removing itself from public scrutiny had stemmed from the perception that its decisions were outside the political arena and required technical expertise in order to best accomplish these nonpolitical goals.

In truth, the decisions of the water industry are highly political. They are biased in favor of certain interests such as urban developers and large landowners. They have influenced the parameters and direction of both urban growth and agricultural development and in the process have affected the quality of life on the farm and in the cities. Instead of seeking to clarify alternatives, water agencies have sought to circumscribe them.

Now the water industry, this overlap of public agencies and private interests, has reached an impasse. The decline of the economy in areas such as agricultural exports and public expenditures is one reason; so too has been the rise of opposition movements that have attempted to place on the agenda the issue of values and the impact from water development on the environment and the community.

246

As a consequence, the water industry has sought to make adjustments. Public "outreach" skills have been emphasized. Water "reallocations" rather than "new allocations" have been pursued in the form of water markets. Privatization measures have been explored. Some of these programs have represented a shift in power within the water industry, as urban development interests continue to pursue the possibility of expansion. Other programs have simply sought to maintain the level of power, whether in terms of public expenditures for pet projects, sustaining the system of priorities that have favored water supply over water quality options, or keeping intact local consensus and influence on the regional or national level.

As the politics of water evolves from its closed, technical and locally oriented consensus, there has still not emerged a full-blown alternative perspective or scenario. The politics of the moment predominates. The issues of water—water development, water quality, the pattern of urban, industrial, and agricultural development—are preeminently social issues. They address value systems. They influence the quality of life. The debates over the future direction of water policy are really debates about the direction of social change.

The key political unit within the water industry is the public water agency. Water agencies come in a variety of forms: from municipal water departments, to irrigation districts, to water and sanitation bureaus, to county water authorities, to groundwater management districts. In Southern California, there are more than three hundred separate agencies. In New Jersey more than six hundred water suppliers serve cities and towns; in Connecticut, as many as four hundred.

These agencies are the mainstay of the water industry. Their local leaders, members of their boards, are often drawn from the business and political elite in their communities. Some but not all of these figures have a direct interest in the activities of their industry while most have ended up making a career out of participation in water matters.

These leaders, who represent the public side of the water industry, are likely to be appointed or elected to office, depending on the agency. Though many are elected, there are very few contested elections, including first-time elections. When a slot does become open through the retirement or death of the previous incumbent, the existing board frequently appoints the new board member prior to the next election. This allows each first-time candidate to run as an incumbent. Even with elections, then, the agency's leadership group has become self-contained and self-perpetuating over the years.

The leaders of these public agencies have often tended to be middle-aged or elderly white men. Many of them have held their positions ten years or more, some as long as thirty or forty years. Agency managers, also nearly exclusively white and male, have largely been engineers, though both lawyers and those with a financial background have played more of a role in recent years. These agency managers and directors have worked closely with and come to resemble in both background and perspective the assortment of private-sector figures who attend many of the same water industry gatherings and together constitute the membership of the various water industry groupings, such as its lobbying organizations and trade associations.

The public agencies tend to be mirror images of private water utilities. These investor-owned utilities, unlike their counterparts in the electrical utility industry, are far fewer in number than the public agencies. They are still significant, however, in certain areas of the country and play an important political role through their lobbying organization, the Association of National Water Utilities.

All the agencies see themselves as serving specific and distinct interest groups, whether agriculture, urban interests, industry, or development interests as a whole. Historically, the engineering and development-oriented biases of the water industry provided a strong unity of purpose and common identity among the agencies and related private sector interests. This has helped establish the water industry as a kind of narrow fraternity, an exclusive club that solicits the public on those occasions when additional support is required.

Through much of the twentieth century these agencies and the water industry as a whole maintained a limited though cordial relationship with the press, who treated the water story as one that involved dull, though perhaps important, civic organizations and their activities. Press stories, in fact, were often rewrites of handouts provided by the agencies, while utility managers or board members were relied on as "experts" to define the issues and set the context.

At times, the press was mobilized, along with other local institutions and interest groups, to establish consensus around a matter of particular importance. In Onandaga County in New York State during the early 1960s, for example, the water industry was quite effective in enlisting the aid of the region's two largest newspapers, as well as a number of smaller local papers and TV and radio stations, to support the construction of an expensive set of facilities to bring water from Lake Ontario to the city of Syracuse and other suburbs and small towns in the county. This project was designed explicitly to accommodate new and anticipated growth in the area. It was perceived by local development interests as crucial to their short- and long-term objectives.

From the outset, the newspapers and the radio and TV stations were continually filled with stories, interviews, and promotional blurbs designed to answer questions and solicit support for the project. In fact, the chairman of the key water industry group, the Onandaga County Water Agency, was also the editor of one of Syracuse's two daily newspapers. His role in promoting the project ultimately contributed to having a county water facility named after him.

Up through the 1970s, the press continued to be seen as an extension of local water industry coalitions. This was particularly true in the South and the West, where local coalitions were established to work with and promote projects designed by the two large federal water agencies, the corps and the Bureau of Reclamation. In these areas, the press helped define water issues in a more symbolic and emotionally charged way, particularly when the individual projects at stake were under scrutiny. The dangers of floods or drought were heavily emphasized to reinforce the argument that the structural solutions offered by the water industry were required to offset these natural and calamitous occurrences.

During the period of the Carter hit list, when the water industry organized a counteroffensive to offset the attacks on some of the key corps and BuRec water projects, the press helped the water industry rebound. The *Los Angeles Times, Denver Post, Arizona Republic, Albuquerque Journal, Salt Lake Tribune,* and other newspapers portrayed the hastily assembled list and programmatic thrust of the Carter initiative as an assault against regional and local interests. The press continued to describe these water projects as benefiting the community as a whole rather then a specific set of economic interests—something that ipso facto required defense against a politically conceived attack based in Washington.

The countermobilization orchestrated around the hit list was in some respects the last successful attempt to portray water issues in consensus terms. The terms of water development had already been challenged during the 1970s on both environmental and economic grounds. The closed and self-contained decision-making processes associated with the water industry were also criticized. The water agencies throughout this decade were being told to "open up the process" in order to break some of this insularity—advice most water industry leaders ignored. "The water industry is managed mostly by engineers who are production and distribution oriented," one water manager commented critically about his counterparts. "They don't get involved in the society of the people they serve. They forget we sell service, we supply people's needs; we don't sell water—we clean it up and distribute it."

By the 1980s, water industry gatherings were filled with discussions about "public participation" and "relating to the public." Consultants and media experts were brought in to advise industry gatherings about how to change the perception that the water industry was closed off to the public. "Public involvement" firms like the Los Angeles–based James Ragan Associates were hired by various agencies to handle potentially contentious public meetings, and assure the public that it was being heard.

Some agencies, like the corps, had already been persuaded that a controlled public participation program could create greater support for their programs and goals and provide greater legitimacy for the agency. One official from the Denver Water Department, a water agency with a long track record in behind-the-scenes maneuvering and decision making, proclaimed this new message in a 1976 article for a trade publication. "Citizens of the 1970s," he wrote, "demand full disclosure, open public meetings, and opportunities to become involved in the decision-making process with full information so they may arrive at intelligent decisions."

By the 1980s, in the wake of challenges from environmentalists, conservatives from the Office of Management and Budget, and other water industry critics, public participation and a higher water industry profile had become largely accepted. "It's like a safety program," one consultant told a gathering of utility managers of public participation programs. "It's good risk management."

Despite the interest in improving its public image, the water industry, however, has been slow to substantively alter either its methods or goals. During much of the 1970s and 1980s, it continued to rely heavily on the engineering impulse. Its concept of development—building more facilities, relying on structural rather than nonstructural approaches—was linked to the notion that providing additional water was essential for continued expansion and growth, whether agricultural, industrial, or residential. The purpose of the water industry—its short- and long-term goals—continued to revolve around insuring that such expansion could take place. To challenge the notion of development seemed, to many in the water industry, to challenge their very reason to exist.

Yet it had also become clear during the 1970s and 1980s that this water development scenario had become problematic. The effectiveness of the mobilization against the Carter hit list had only postponed what to some in the water industry appeared to be the need for certain changes to salvage at least some of the goals of development. The discussion over politics and process and public participation was in part a discussion over how to most effectively make that transition.

The emphasis on public relations served in part to modify the engineering impulse that had so long dominated the water utilities. Several agencies began to place nonengineers—lawyers, public relations or politically inclined administrators, even financial people—in top management positions, a shift that also began to occur within the federal agencies as well. Simultaneously, a number of agencies decided to adopt a high public profile rather than the low-key, relatively invisible role that had characterized both the utilities and the water industry as a whole.

This higher profile policy had emerged partly out of necessity. The low profile, behind-the-scenes approach to water issues had already begun to fade during the 1970s, primarily from the challenge of the environmental organizations who had become adept at influencing their primary constituency, the press and policymakers, particularly on a national level. The bureau and the corps were the first to feel the effects of the influence of the environmental groups, though, by the 1980s, that influence had also extended onto regional and local levels. The quiescent and loyal press of an earlier era now began to respond to the issues raised by environmentalists, hastening the transition. State legislatures and local government officials could no longer be automatically considered part of the consensus coalitions that had characterized the support for water development in the past. Water was becoming a contentious rather than consensual issue, even on the local level.

The higher profile did not necessarily translate into a new set of policy initiatives. The engineers were still prominent and the organizational bias of the utilities was still development oriented. Many utilities, particularly utilities in the East and Midwest, also faced continuing infrastructural problems requiring the upgrading and construction of new facilities—tasks presumed for engineers. The emergence of water quality as an issue, which had taken the water industry by surprise, also had not resulted in any shift of priorities. Utility managers, despite their interest in public relations, continued to remain suspicious of the public's interest around quality issues, and tended to blame activists, the press, and their corporate competitors—the bottled-water industry—for creating scare tactics that manipulated the public. Public participation, it turned out, meant establishing water utility legitimacy, not new policies.

A few utilities recognized the merit of appearing to seek out compromise and possible accommodation on certain issues with key antagonists, particularly those environmental groups who were equally interested in establishing a meeting ground with the water industry. Environmental mediators, including organizations like the Metropolitan Water Roundtable in Denver or Redford's Institute for Resource Management, and individual consultants, such as Washington, D.C.–based Joan Kovalic, became available to facilitate such exchanges. These contacts appeared most fruitful when linked to the question of "markets" and certain other economic initiatives. If the establishment of "markets" or the efforts toward "privatization" meant economic benefits or the continuing flow of new water supplies, the water industry expressed interest. For the environmentalists, economics had become the key to altering the orientation of water policies.

This limited effort at public participation, then, did not change the terms of decision making, only the profile of the water industry. The emergence of markets, privatization, and related economic matters as issues, furthermore, took the transition out of the realm of politics and brought it into the economic sphere.

THE PROBLEM OF EQUITY

By the Reagan years, economic factors had come to dominate the discourse around water. During the late 1970s, the political debates around water centered on the increasing expense of constructing major facilities as well as the question of price. The intricate pattern of subsidies, particularly those for agriculture with respect to the federal programs, and for industry and new urban developments on the regional and local levels, was increasingly challenged on the grounds of both efficiency and equity. The Westlands Water District, for example, went through lengthy conflict over pricing issues that was debated in Congress, the administration, and the courts.

When the Reagan administration took office, pricing issues flared both inside and outside the administration. Westlands, for one, continued to figure prominently in these disagreements. The sustained effort by Westlands critics to push the government to charge a higher price for the heavily subsidized water—in an area that was generating severe drainage problems—was ultimately over-ridden by rulings within the Interior Department. The rulings were shaped primarily by the Interior Department Solicitor Ralph Tarr, who had also been a crucial player on the matter of exemptions around the "hammer clause."

These pricing matters had become, particularly for agriculture, the primary focus for lobbying and influence peddling by the water industry. In most specific policy matters, administration officials were prevailed upon to oppose congressional efforts to intervene on pricing matters. The one small victory for the pricing subsidy critics was the 1987 decision of the Department of Agriculture to revise the way it determined benefits from federal water projects. "In the past, these prices have included the effects of the government's own price-support programs for surplus crops," commented Wayne Marchant, the principal deputy assistant secretary for water and science in the Interior Department. "As a result," Marchant continued, "project benefits from production of surplus crops have been over-estimated, in some cases making uneconomic projects appear viable."

This ambivalence of the Reagan administration extended into the legislative arena. There, the pro–water development forces within the administration were often able to prevent the elimination of subsidies for surplus crops or block attempts to revise the low cost of hydroelectric power generated at BuRec-operated dams such as Hoover. A stalemate of sorts in fact had developed. While some changes, most significantly cost sharing, were partially imple-mented, most pricing initiatives to restructure government subsidies were defeated or deferred.

The problem of pricing inequities exists at the state, regional, and local levels as well. Long-standing policies used to determine local rate structures in urban areas, for example, have contained a number of inequities. These have disguised the real cost of water and created a series of advantages for certain users, such as industry and new residential developments in the suburbs or outlying areas.

During the nineteenth and early twentieth centuries, many cities were reluctant to impose fees and rate charges that would reflect the actual costs of obtaining the new water supplies and constructing the distribution facilities to accommodate residential and industrial growth. Rates were often designed with their built-in subsidies to further stimulate that growth. A more equitable pricing system, on the other hand, was thought by many civic leaders and industries to have a negative effect on growth.

Many of the initial rate structures in most metropolitan areas relied either on a flat or a declining block rate. In these cases, the largest users would be charged either the same amount or a lesser rate than the smallest users. Furthermore, several of the flat-rate structures were instituted without any form of metering for private dwellings. This occurred in places with such different water sources as New York City; Sacramento, California; and Denver, Colorado. Metering, in fact, is a twentieth century phenomena for many municipalities, East and West. Even today, most cities have failed to install meters within individual apartment units (the meters instead are read for the apartment as a whole) or make a distinction between different kinds of users (for example, office buildings, single-family homes, apartment buildings, or industries). This limited ability to distinguish between different uses or even to record in some cases how much water is being used, has made it difficult for utilities to provide for an equitable rate and a more efficient use of the water.

The rate problem has been further compounded by nearly all water agencies utilizing a historical average cost, or "postage stamp" pricing system rather than one defined by marginal or incremental use. This issue was highlighted in the early 1970s by the National Water Commission, though changes in rate setting have been slow to occur. Under the postage stamp systems, a water utility that increased its costs, say by obtaining a new water source, building a new facility, or serving new hookups, would simply meld those costs with all previous costs to determine the new rate. A marginal pricing system, on the other hand, would calculate the costs for the new facilities and then develop a new rate that would be based on the additional or incremental costs. The additional charges would be paid by those responsible for incurring the costs—for example, a new residential development. That way, the new development would be obliged to more fully pay its way, rather than, as happens today with nearly all utilities, receiving a subsidy through the existing "postage stamp" rates.

Over the years, water agencies have employed a number of other mechanisms as well to disguise or soften the impact of the cost of water for their various constituencies. Utilities, for example, have often relied on property tax revenues or revenues from the general fund, particularly in financing the expansion of a system to accommodate new growth. They have taken great pride in keeping water rates extremely low, both for their favored customers such as industry or new developments and for the general residential customer. This ability to prevent the "rate shock" the electrical utilities experienced when the cost of oil or nuclear power increased dramatically during the 1970s was considered a crucial political asset in keeping the water agencies removed from critical review or public opposition. The desire to keep rates low, in fact, was one of the factors contributing to water utility resistance to the imposition of new water quality standards and more costly treatment methods.

These various pricing policies have clear winners and losers. Those who have most benefited are the largest users in the system, particularly big industrial plants and the outlying, newly developing areas. In Southern California, for example, the "inner city" of Los Angeles has provided more than $300 million in subsidies to the new growth areas of Orange, San Diego, and Riverside counties over the last forty years, according to calculations put together by the Los Angeles City Administrative Office in the early 1980s. Those who have benefited from this system, particularly San Diego interests, have argued that the use of tax revenues and average cost pricing have generated benefits for the region as a whole, which in turn create benefits for the city of Los Angeles. This argument has been widely employed by agencies using another kind of tax break, "zone of benefit" charges, to justify one area subsidizing another. Such justification, however, identifies an inherent value in expansion and development that would outweigh any disadvantages associated with pricing subsidies and inequities. But those values, ironically, have come to be questioned even in high-growth areas like San Diego and Tucson.

THE INTERRUPTED MARCH TOWARD PRIVATIZATION

Such arguments are equally applicable to residential users subsidizing industry. From the outset of the industrial revolution in the mid-nineteenth century, the water agencies, particularly in urban areas, have treated industry as a primary constituency. Some utilities, in fact, combined jurisdiction over sewage treatment and potable water service. As a consequence, utilities became directly linked to industrial interests. This was expressed both in terms of rates for fresh water (flat or declining blocks favoring industry) as well as discharge and wastewater treatment issues (utilities resisting discharge restrictions and seeking out federal block grants rather than user fees to pay for secondary treatment plants). For a number of years, moreover, at least until the passage of the Clean Water Act, water agencies tended to ally with industry in dismissing concerns regarding the nature and extent of contamination resulting from discharges.

Once the federal monies became available, billions of dollars were spent for the construction of long overdue treatment facilities. The Construction Grants Program, administered by EPA, became one of the largest transfer of funds, outside of the military budget and agricultural price-support programs, from the federal government to local utilities and governments.

The Reagan administration, led by the OMB, immediately saw this area as potentially fertile ground for cutbacks, with the simultaneous encouragement of a shift toward privatization. The new tax provisions enacted during 1981 and 1982 further stimulated that development by providing important subsidies for private companies doing business with public entities. Unlike municipal water utilities, the private companies were also able to obtain such tax breaks as capital depreciation, investment tax credits, and tax-exempt industrial development bonds, or IDBs. Although the IDBs were issued through the public utility or municipality, the advantages accrued to the private recipient, who was able to cash in on both its tax-exempt status *and* the tax credits and depreciation reserved only for private entities. IDBs became the private sector's form of double dipping.

By the early 1980s, a number of small and medium-sized private firms with such names as U.S. Pollution Control Inc. and American Ecology had already established themselves as consultants or subcontractors to federal agencies, water utilities, or municipalities in the water and waste treatment business. With the new Reagan tax breaks and the push for privatization, a number of even larger consulting, service, and construction companies, such as Bechtel, CH$_2$M Hill, Signal, and the Ralph M. Parsons Company, began to explore their involvement in the potentially lucrative wastewater market.

Parsons, in particular, decided to make a major effort in this direction. The company was a spin-off of the giant Bechtel construction and engineering firm that during the 1930s had been involved in the construction of Hoover, Parker, and Grand Coulee dams. Based in Pasadena, California, Parsons had a long history in water development. During the 1960s and 1970s, however, it was more likely to be involved in dam projects in Saudi Arabia than in California. Its one major effort to devise a water plan—the North American Water and Power Alliance project, to bring water down from British Columbia to the southwestern U.S.—became by the 1970s more a public relations exercise designed to show how the company could "think big" than a project that was presumed to merit serious consideration.

In the early 1980s, the Parsons company decided that the "privatization" market, including the water area, was worth exploring in a major way. The company conducted a study in 1982 on privatization opportunities called "Build, Own, Operate," and concluded there was room for expansion in several areas: an engineering role, financing, operations, and environmental review. "Some of this type of work had been done in international settings," declared Parsons Executive Vice-President Robert Davidson. "What was new here was extending the concept into the domestic markets."

In that same period, Parsons had established a subsidiary, Parsons Municipal Services, Inc., after acquiring Engineering Science, a smaller company that had hooked into the growing environmental business field by becoming involved in environmental impact reports, sewer systems, hazardous waste treatment facilities, and other projects for government agencies. In 1983, Parsons got its first big opportunity in the field when the city of Chandler, a suburb of Phoenix, decided to turn to the private sector to handle its wastewater problem.

Chandler was a fast-growing community in one of the fastest growing metropolitan areas in the country. It knew it had to expand its wastewater treatment facilities, yet it was only seventy-fifth in Arizona's funding priorities for EPA money. Given the Reagan cutbacks and the slowdown at EPA during the Gorsuch period, the situtation for Chandler didn't look promising. The city hired the investment banking house of Boettcher & Company to come up with a financing recommendation, but Boettcher suggested instead that private companies be solicited on how such companies would approach the problem. It was an invitation to privatization.

When the solicitations went out in late 1983, it was already clear to a number of companies besides Parsons that privatization was becoming a lucrative possibility, given the tax breaks and the favorable disposition of the Reagan administration. Several companies responded, including Signal, the large construction firm of Metcalfe-Eddy, and several regional firms from Texas, Colorado, and elsewhere. Parsons won the bid and ended up constructing the facility, with the city maintaining its ownership interest in the reclaimed water.

The Chandler arrangement seemed at first to be a sign of things to come. The Reagan administration continued to push the idea, and one of its commissions, headed by businessman J. Peter Grace, suggested that the government actually begin to divest itself of key assets in the water area, including Bonneville Dam. By February 1986, the *Journal of the American Water Works Association* would devote an issue to the theme of privatization, including a separate article on the Chandler arrangement. The AWWA editors contrasted the private companies with their "well-trained staffs," "streamlined management," and "experts respected throughout the world," with "fiscally and politically constrained water suppliers." "There is little doubt that as new water crises are faced," the AWWA editors concluded, "more municipal utilities . . . will opt to form public-private partnerships. The marriage of public service to private enterprise may well be the logical arrangement that enables many cities to supply the quantity and quality of water so vital to the general well-being."

By the late 1980s, the meetings of various water utility and water industry groups such as AWWA and the National Water Resources Association were besieged by private sector companies looking for a piece of the action. The revolving door between public agencies and private sector companies had become more extensive than ever, and the companies became adept at extending contacts and lobbying for business. At one meeting of the NWRA in December 1986, for example, several dozen companies were present, displaying exhibits, hosting cocktail parties, and, in one instance, offering a dinner cruise on a yacht. NWRA, in fact, had established a separate caucus that came to be dominated by the "privatization" companies.

The privatization effort was also, however, plagued by problems. The new tax law of 1986, for example, eliminated a number of key privatization subsidies such as investment tax credits while placing restrictions on the key factor, the use of IDBs. Companies like Parsons continued to insist that privatization was still an attractive proposition for companies and utilities alike, but the early enthusiasm had been dampened by the less attractive economics.

By the waning years of the Reagan administration there had occurred a retreat on several fronts, including the privatization area. In the case of the renewal of the Clean Water Act, with its provisions for continued funding for wastewater treatment, the Reaganites suffered a major defeat in 1987 when Congress overrode a presidential veto. The Grace Commission recommendations, especially the proposed "fire sale" of assets, as they came to be called, also came under attack from a variety of interests, including members of the water industry who preferred the existing arrangements with BuRec. The big dams and the power plants never did get sold, though the Reagan administration still continued to evoke the rhetoric of privatization.

The tentative forays of the privatization companies into other water-related areas aside from wastewater treatment also ran into difficulties. Parsons, for example, had made a proposal to manage the publicly owned Pasadena Water and Power Department, but was quickly met with strong resistance from utility management and directors. This proposal eventually died a quiet death. Furthermore, Parsons' involvement in the Imperial Irrigation District's plans for a water swap, its plum contract for the company's subsidiary operation, Parsons Water Resources Inc., lasted only a couple of years, as the company itself became a subject of controversy and contention. Privatization, once the jewel in the big engineering company's eye, had become a diminished, though still important, area of interest.

TROUBLED MARKETS

The initial enthusiasm and subsequent difficulties in the privatization area paralleled the situation regarding the development of water markets. This catchall phrase had come to signify any number of possible transactions: transfer arrangements, the sale or lease of water rights or the land for which the water rights attached, or some form of exchange agreement involving the construction of conservation or related facilities. Interest in the issue had been stimulated during the mid- and late 1980s in a number of states throughout the West and even in the Plains States. There was a great deal of talk about new possibilities, complete with conferences, forums, public meetings, and back room exchanges. Water markets, if you believed publications like *Time* magazine, the *Washington Post*, the *New York Times*, and the *San Diego Union*, had arrived.

Water sales and transfers of rights are as old as the Anglo settlement and development of the West. The early markets of the late nineteenth and twentieth centuries often involved the purchase of water rights by private parties as part of the consolidation of land holdings. One major exception was the Owens Valley, where the city of Los Angeles, with the complicity of certain federal agents, successfully acquired sufficient land and water rights along the Owens River in order to pursue its plan for an aqueduct to the city. This "theft" of the water and "rape" of Owens Valley, as some critics characterized Los Angeles's actions, would later give cause to public agencies and municipalities who feared that any purchase of land or water rights might become associated with the Owens Valley tag.

Once the era of large-scale water development began in earnest with the construction of Hoover Dam in 1935, the use of private water transfers to facilitate development became a minor factor in the water picture. Government intervention, including the purchase of land and allocation of water rights, was now primarily responsible for determining the patterns of development. Those "market" transfer arrangements that did exist, such as the active trading of rights that took place in the Northern Colorado Water Conservancy District, were made possible in part by the feds constructing new facilities, such as the Colorado Big-Thompson project in the case of Colorado. By the 1950s and 1960s, transfers of rights between different parties also reflected the gradual economic decline of various users of surface water and groundwater, particularly agricultural interests in Utah, Colorado, and Arizona.

There was a brief flurry of water market activity during the first and second energy crises (1973–74 and 1979 respectively) when a number of companies sought to purchase or lease water rights in anticipation of a continuing energy boom. The sale price of the water immediately skyrocketed, ranging as high as fifteen hundred to two thousand dollars per acre foot. In Sevier County, Utah, for example, water rights were purchased at a price of $1750 an acre foot for the Intermountain Power Project, a coal-fired plant mostly designed for Southern California utilities. When the power plant was later scaled down, the price for water rights dropped to a level of $300 to $500 an acre foot, a situation that paralleled the decline in prices through much of the Intermountain West when the energy boom collapsed in the 1980s.

The apparent inverse link between "markets" and water development—the greater the number of publicly subsidized water projects, the fewer the number of market transfers—became a truism among observers of the water industry. During the 1960s, when market transfers were still limited to a handful of areas, proposals for new development projects involving massive interbasin transfers of water reached an unprecedented scale. There were schemes to bring water to West Texas and eastern New Mexico from the lower Mississippi, proposals to transfer water from the James Bay Basin in Canada to the Great Lakes, and of course the NAWAPA plan to bring water from the Pacific Northwest, northwest Canada, and possibly Alaska to California and the Southwest. These plans were monumental in their cost, complexity, and environmental impact. They contrasted sharply with the "market" notion of *reallocating* existing supplies to their highest use, which had become so attractive to critics of water industry economics.

This contrast of the big projects with a market alternative was widely employed by a number of water market advocates, including the National Water Commission. In its report, the commission had urged that local beneficiaries pay full costs for any water transfer project. This would mean cash payments instead of some kind of political deal to buy off the "area-of-origin" where the water supply had originated. By being obliged to pay full costs, it was hoped that the water industry would begin to see market arrangements in much more favorable terms. The commission ultimately wanted to reorient water users toward "consideration of the question that would dominate the decision in a private transaction: what is the water worth to the seller and what is it worth to the buyer?"

This concept of water markets, as applied by the National Water Commission and advocates such as the Rand Corporation, offered a narrowly defined view of the economic or "commodity" value of the water. Their studies attempted to demonstrate the cost-effective value of markets by contrasting big project economics with market economics. But in the process they failed to address any social, environmental, or equity concerns related to market transfers, presuming that those could be taken care of in the political or legislative arena.

During the 1970s, the water industry tended to dismiss market advocates such as Rand and the NWC as irrelevant to their water agenda. Yet the water industry's troubles with Congress, the OMB, the press, and the growing environmental movement were increasingly focused on project economics. By the late 1970s and early 1980s, some conservative voices, including the group of new resource economists such as Terry Anderson and John Baden, joined the chorus of criticism around economic subsidies. These conservative opponents of water development focused on government intervention as the source of the problem and the establishment of markets and efforts toward privatization as the best way to achieve both efficiency and environmental protection. When the Reagan administration came to power, it was these arguments especially that were looked on with favor at OMB and even among some in the Interior Department. Several new resource economists took positions in the new administration and became champions for the development of policy initiatives to help encourage these trends.

By the mid-1980s, the water industry, slowly and haltingly, began to shift positions. This was due less to the logic of the arguments or even the debates within the Reagan administration than to the growing realization that new supply projects were becoming increasingly problematic in economic terms. The severe economic crisis in agriculture that extended throughout the country by the mid-1980s also contributed to this shift. Certain agricultural users hardest hit by the economic downturn seemed to change their perspectives about the attractiveness of markets—overnight in some cases. The interest in markets was further stimulated by the simultaneous repositioning of the urban water interests who were rapidly becoming the key player in the search for new water supplies.

At first, it appeared that markets would be quickly established during the Reagan years. In 1982, the Supreme Court ruled in *Sporhase* v. *Nebraska* that water was an article of commerce and that sales across state lines could not be restricted. This legal justification of interstate markets was complemented that same year by legislation passed in California. The California bill allowed water that resulted from conservation efforts to be "sold, leased, exchanged or otherwise transferred."

Within a couple of years, a number of legislators, state officials and congressional representatives had jumped on the water market bandwagon. The Western Governors Association issued a policy document calling for the establishment of markets. Legislation was enacted in several states, either facilitating transfers or laying out certain conditions to guide the establishment of markets.

By the mid-1980s, market possibilities were widely discussed throughout the western and midwestern states. There were proposals concerning interstate transfers (from Nebraska to Colorado, New Mexico to Texas), transfers from the upper to the lower basin in the Colorado River system (the Galloway proposal), and transfers within states, primarily from agriculture to urban users (in California, Arizona, Colorado, and Utah, among others).

The talk about markets had become so extensive that in 1985 a group was organized to purchase water rights solely for investment purposes. The group, Western Water Rights Management Inc., headed by water investor/speculator Albert Parker, Jr., convinced a small number of investors from East Coast financial institutions to put up $35 million for the purchase and eventual sale of water rights in Colorado. Parker's idea was to have the group purchase these rights, manage them in the interim, and then, when the timing was propitious, sell them to another party, thus providing a favorable return on the investment. Within a year after he had established his fund, Parker had purchased nearly $10 million worth of water rights, primarily along the eastern slope of the Colorado Front Range in the urban stretch that reached from Fort Collins through Denver to Colorado Springs.

Water marketing deals continued to flourish in those areas that had already experienced active trading of water rights, especially

Colorado and Utah. Prices fluctuated rapidly, and for a time the sale price became heavily inflated in several areas, going as high as eight thousand dollars an acre foot in Park City, Utah, on one occasion. In Arizona, several cities in the Maricopa Valley—such as Phoenix and Scottsdale—became active buyers, following Tucson's lead of purchasing water rights in the nearby Avra Valley for more than a decade.

In late December 1986 Phoenix purchased fourteen thousand acres of farmland in the McMullen Valley in La Paz County (southwestern Arizona) so as to obtain rights to the land's groundwater. The purchase price was $30.5 million with the expectation that the acquisition of the land would yield between thirty thousand to fifty thousand acre feet of water a year for the city. Phoenix figured that it, like Tucson, would become water short after the turn of the century because of the continuing explosion in population. Furthermore, the McMullen Valley purchase, the city manager's office announced, would be only one of several such "market" acquisitions to supplement Phoenix's existing supplies, which included the additional supplies from the Central Arizona Project.

The Phoenix deal, which generated concern in both Phoenix and the McMullen Valley, highlighted a number of the problems beginning to be associated with market transactions. Though the purchase price for the land was $30.5 million, the overall cost of actually delivering the water to Phoenix was expected to increase to $66 million, due to the pumping costs and the cost of building a twenty-five-mile canal to carry the water to the Central Arizona Project canal.

Some Phoenix council members questioned the high price and the limited public discussion that had preceded the decision. The purchase in fact had been arranged quickly in 1986, without much prior public notification. This had happened so that the twenty-three owners of the McMullen Valley land parcels acquired by Phoenix could take advantage of lower capital gains tax rates before they were changed in 1987 under the new tax laws. Though the Phoenix city manager's office suggested that the transaction could be financed in part by water hookup fees charged to new developments, the major part of the deal was to be financed by straight water rate hikes. Ultimately, Phoenix, like Tucson, was turning to the alternate route of "markets" in order to stretch supplies to meet its anticipated growth. By choosing the "supply-side" path of markets, Phoenix had decided to avoid directly confronting the economic—and social—costs of growth.

The area's rapid pace of development reflected in part the actions of the Phoenix developers for whom water was simply not a limiting factor in their expansionary plans. "We get into situations," one Phoenix economic consultant noted, "where land developers are first interested in marking out turf and then later in dealing with the issues—is there sufficient water, is there sufficient market support for this development?"

The Phoenix purchase greatly affected the McMullen Valley, particularly the two unincorporated communities of Wenden and Salome, which were surrounded by the fourteen thousand acres just purchased. Furthermore, land and water rights had already been acquired by other outside parties in La Paz County. These new La Paz landowners included the city of Scottsdale, which had purchased an 8,400-acre ranch along the Bill Williams river; Arizona Public Service, the largest utility in the state and the lead agency for several nuclear power plants fifty miles east of Phoenix, which had purchased 12,500 acres in the county; and even a developer, Continental Homes, which had made some speculative acquisitions to obtain water rights. By the time the Phoenix deal went through, La Paz County manager Neta Bowman pointed out that of the 140,571 acres of fee land in the county, 44,413 acres had either "been bought or speculated on"—31.6 percent of the total amount that could be taxed.

The Phoenix sale brought to a head fears in the county and particularly among the twelve hundred rural residents of Wenden and Salome that these market transactions would ultimately benefit the sellers, but not the local area. There were concerns over possible declining groundwater levels and perhaps more significantly, a shrinking tax base for the area, since most of the acquisitions took those lands off the tax roll. The Arizona legislature had passed legislation earlier in 1986 allowing cities to pay "voluntary" contributions to an affected community in lieu of taxes. But, as Bowman pointed out, the operative word was "voluntary." There was no binding, contractual commitment. The legislature, in the wake of these fears, established further study committees, but the issues raised by the McMullen Valley transactions did not appear to be easily resolved.

Less than a year after Phoenix arranged its deal for the La Paz land and water rights, the state's retired longtime water "czar," Wes Steiner, proposed a new policy on water transfers. "Arizona cities should harbor no guilt about exercising their moral and legal obligations to respond to the water challenges of the twenty-first century," he told the annual meeting of the Arizona League of Cities and Towns. Steiner's proposal called for a moratorium on water transfers throughout the state—except for western Arizona, which primarily meant La Paz County. This area, Steiner declared, was fair game for water transfers because of the area's small population and "negligible" potential for future development. At the time he made the speech, Steiner was working for a water marketing company that was seeking to buy land—in La Paz County.

The maneuvering around the water rights in La Paz County raised for some, such as Neta Bowman, the specter of Owens Valley. There were in fact both similarities and differences. Back at the turn of the century in the Owens Valley, local farmers had hoped that the new Reclamation Service could transform their valley, much of which was undeveloped, into an agricultural growth area, similar to what had happened to the south in the Imperial Valley with its attempts to harness the Colorado River. The McMullen Valley in Arizona, however, was already developed. Its land was primarily used for cotton, grains, and nuts. After the Phoenix purchase, the land was to be leased back until Phoenix began to draw on the water supply. Ultimately, the market transactions and proposals like those of Wes Steiner made La Paz County an area in decline, controlled by outside landowners or speculators who wished to extract its primary resource. In that way, the comparison with

Owens Valley, which had become a rural colony to Los Angeles, seemed appropriate.

The impact on rural areas was not limited to counties with less concentrated landholdings. In places like California's Kern County, the Imperial Valley, and the Westlands Water District, it was the large landowners like the Tejon Ranch or Berrenda Mesa's Blackwell Land Company that were also expressing interest in such sales. Some of these landowners had profited enormously over the years from the availability of subsidized federal or state water. Others had guessed that by acquiring future rights to the water for their lands that would have been marginal without the water, they would ultimately realize a profitable return on such speculation. When the agricultural industry went into its decline and the price of water rose simultaneously, many of these companies wanted to cash out, to at least cover their costs or perhaps even realize a profit. Markets became a form of bailout, particularly when they absorbed the costs of a speculation turned sour, as in the case of the Tejon Ranch's lands north of the dividing line between Kern and Los Angeles counties.

Not all farmers interested in selling their water rights were necessarily large landowners. But the major players who had emerged by the mid- and late 1980s to dominate the talk about markets almost entirely were. Furthermore, though enormous wealth (and power) had accrued to these landowners in places like Kern, Tulare, Fresno, and Imperial counties in California, these same counties were also among the poorest in the country. By the 1980s, it had become increasingly clear that the advent of industrialized agriculture, especially in California, Arizona, Texas and Florida, had also created some of the most economically depressed communities in the U.S.

This two-tier structure of wealth and poverty threatened to duplicate itself with water market transactions. Those who sold or benefited from a sale, as in the IID-MET exchange, would be those bailing out or cashing in on their profits. The losers would likely be the small farmers, farmworkers, and nonfarm rural residents who

269

would experience the negative economic and social impacts of a decline in farm activity, without realizing a share in the profits.

As for the buyers, the advent of markets allowed urban areas like Phoenix and Tucson to put off equity and economic considerations regarding their own future expansion and growth. Water markets also provided a kind of progressive veneer, similar to Tucson's conservation-oriented Beat the Peak campaign, to the pursuit of development.

Although both the potential buyers and sellers within the water industry had begun accepting markets as an attractive possibility, they still proceeded slowly and cautiously. Despite the talk, there were few deals that had actually been completed during the 1980s, other than where markets had long been established. The continuing ambivalence within the Reagan administration paralleled the ambivalence within the water industry. Market advocates, such as the Western Governors Association, frustrated by the lack of deals, urged the Bureau of Reclamation, the federal agency most capable of facilitating market transactions, to shift its role away from "supplying capital for large new water projects to helping the West enhance the efficiency of use of the water that the Bureau already provides"— that is, by establishing markets.

The bureau had in fact been approached several times to intervene in possible market arrangements, including the IID-MET situation. The bureau's policy, in that instance, reflected its ambivalence. At one point, Joseph Findaro, the acting assistant secretary of science and water, was approached by Imperial, for whom he offered his support in interpreting any such transaction as a sale. MET of course didn't like this one bit, so it pressured Findaro to reverse his position to support MET's claim that such a transaction would simply constitute payment for conservation facilities. Findaro ultimately adopted a more neutral stance as Interior Department officials tried to walk a fine line between the two parties. The failure to develop "any clearly established Bureau of Reclamation policy on voluntary transfers of project water," commented Richard Wahl, the one-time head of the Interior Department Office of Policy in the Reagan administration, "raises the cost of transferred water and discourages transfers."

While the bureau and the water industry remained tentative in their approach to markets, they still claimed to be interested in such "alternate" supply measures. This interest, which California BuRec director David Houston called "enlightened environmentalism," in reality simply turned the old criticisms about subsidies on their head. "Water marketing in its simplest form," *California Farmer* magazine commented, "just means finding ways to share surplus water." This interpretation had also been adopted by BuRec. In this context, markets simply became another way to extend the subsidies rather than eliminate them. According to Houston, for example, transfers of surplus water could mean a shift or transfer of water from the Central Valley Project to the California State Water Project.

Such an idea had circulated during the spring and summer of 1987 when the BuRec attempted to sell "excess" CVP water to State Water Project users within the Kern County Water Agency. The proposal was being explored while California was in the midst of an extremely dry year. This so-called "market" transfer would have involved the export of water from the Delta—something which, at that time, would have harmed the environment. Furthermore, while some Kern contractors were attempting to sell their "expensive" State Water Project entitlements, others in Kern were simultaneously seeking to buy the cheap CVP water. The deal was tentatively blocked only at the last minute by the intervention of environmental groups who insisted the bureau had to prepare an environmental impact report.

Both water marketing and privatization ultimately can be seen as efforts to extend a system in trouble. While these efforts have not yet become fully accepted as the best approaches available, market deals and private sector arrangements have nevertheless secured a niche within the water industry. And as "reallocations" begin to replace "new allocations" as the primary mode for water development, they are likely to further aid the key objectives of water industry activity—to support the expansion of urban areas and to maintain the agro-industrial system. The delivery of water to sustain development, whether marketed or imported, is still central to the system.

VALUES AND IDEOLOGIES

There have emerged over the years, particularly in the West, a series of stock phrases about water. Many of these have a kind of macho ring to them, portraying the control of water as a source of power. "Whisky is for drinking, and water is for fighting about," Mark Twain commented a hundred years ago about this western attitude. Others have not only celebrated that phrase but also extended it. Former Arizona Senator Barry Goldwater, for one, has been quoted as saying, "A Westerner's priorities are, in order 1) water, 2) gold, 3) women; you may tamper with the other two, but not the first." In a similar vein, the term "water wars" has become an overused phrase.

The key for the water industry has been how to control this elusive and valuable resource. In the West, such efforts have primarily involved policies designed to deal with scarcity, such as drought conditions, and the ways in which surpluses can be created by transferring water from one area to another. In the East, these efforts have largely referred to situations where there is an overabundance of supply, with such problems as flooding, and the ways in which water sources can be tamed and harnessed.

The water industry arose in part to exercise this control. It began to flourish after the turn of the century when a conservationist ideology about eliminating waste and controlling resources came to dominate the thinking of policymakers in the Bureau of Reclamation and elsewhere. It reached the heights of its power after World War II when control efforts seemed pervasive and the big dreams of water industry engineers appeared to coincide with the needs of the industry's primary players: agriculture, industry, and urban interests. Even in the more recent period, when the water industry's plans and goals have come under criticism, it has continued to push for control through water development, albeit in a somewhat modified form. And, with the rise of markets, the concept of control has evolved further along the lines perhaps best expressed by another water industry truism: "Water flows uphill—toward money."

In 1968, the *New Yorker* staff writer John McPhee arranged a rafting trip on the Colorado River with a leading environmentalist, Sierra Club executive director David Brower, and Floyd Dominy, the indomitable head of the Bureau of Reclamation. McPhee saw this encounter—and two others he set up for Brower, the "arch-druid" holding forth as the protector of Nature—as indicative of conflicting images and ideologies. These contending points of view not only presented different ways to formulate policy about water development, but also suggested how the issues over "control" of water fit into larger issues of the society.

Those images offered different and contrasting paradigms, ones that are still largely applicable today. Where Brower saw the majesty of the white water rapids and the beauty of the free-flowing river, Dominy saw a great source of water and power that needed to be harnessed. While Brower wished to see the river move uninterrupted toward its destination in the Gulf of California, Dominy wanted to "tame" the river and construct great dams, creating for the recreation industry peaceful, artificial lakes—perhaps the strongest symbol of controlling the water of the West. These differences were matters of both perception and substance. Scenic resources were in the eye of the beholder. "I see a certain beauty when I see those giant pumps in the desert," one longtime Southern California water industry figure said of the pumps for the California Aqueduct.

What had become most disturbing to the water industry, as it increasingly came under attack during the 1970s, was that its engineering "marvels," as they were once commonly referred to, were now objects of contention. Popular novels, such as Edward Abbey's *The Monkey Wrench Gang*, saw the giant dam, the most magnified instrument of control, as a source of violation, a kind of "rape" of the land. It was, to these critics, the clearest indication of an abuse of power. In his book, published in 1975, Abbey's fictional eco-terrorists, later celebrated by such groups as Earth First!, design an

273

elaborate plot to blow up Glen Canyon Dam, an action that could permanently cripple the dam. Only by these means, the activists decide, can they undo the damage to nature.

Abbey's eco-fantasy, it turned out, has provided for some both literal and symbolic significance. Twelve years after the publication of *The Monkey Wrench Gang*, a group of real-life eco-activists, sympathetic to the Earth First! concept of direct action or "ecotage," painted a streak down the front of O'Shaunnessy Dam in the Hetch-Hetchy Valley, creating the impression of a sizable fissure in the dam. Below the streak they wrote, "Free the Rivers," and signed it "J. Muir." That action was roundly condemned by the water industry.

But then, just a few months later, in what some critics saw as a ploy to deflect criticism from the administration's environmental track record while at the same time isolating liberal, environmentally inclined San Francisco, Interior Department Secretary Donald Hodel suggested publicly that perhaps O'Shaunnessy could, after all, be dismantled. By doing so, Hodel claimed, the Hetch-Hetchy Valley could be restored in a relatively short period of time. This in turn could take some pressure off the overcrowded and adjacent Yosemite Valley. It would also, Hodel well knew, oblige the city of San Francisco to seek a new supply of water, with one possible candidate the troubled Auburn Dam project.

The Hodel scheme, on the face of it, seemed preposterous, as water industry leaders commented in private. Such an effort, for one, would involve a substantial cost, unlikely in an era of limited budgets. The amount of concrete to be disposed of would be vast, and the combination of dismantling and removal could require the expenditure of hundreds of millions of dollars.

While Hodel's trial-balloon scheme created a flurry of interest—could Hetch-Hetchy be revived?!—it also served to detract from several bureau policies, undertaken on behalf of various water industry interests, that were a reminder of the continuing realities of water development. As opposed to restoring valleys and saving rivers, new projects, like the San Felipe unit of the Central Valley Project, were going on line. The water industry's primary concern was not for a nostalgic encounter with the past but how to sell—and buy—cheap water that would otherwise flow to the sea. The Hetch-Hetchy Valley, Donald Hodel and monkey wrenchers notwithstanding, was not likely to be saved without a related attempt to fundamentally restructure the practices of the water industry. In the end, this reconstructed valley will likely remain a historic casualty of one of the first water industry efforts to control the flow of water in the urban West.

As the big water projects entered their period of decline in the 1970s and 1980s, images of water development began to change. Different fictional treatments, for example, came to be structured around a particular puzzle of water or resource development, where development interests sought control over resources for private gain. This approach, which was popularized with the film *Chinatown* (a composite of the events at Owens Valley), had, for example, entered mainstream detective fiction by the mid-1980s. The water industry was fast becoming an object of suspicion, much in the way that government officials and business figures had also become suspect in the popular culture.

As these new images proliferated, the water industry attempted to regroup, relying on its most successful and long-standing arguments. Numerous water officials would evoke well-known conservationist arguments about waste, while warning of the dire consequences resulting from any loss of control. "Wasted" water was water that wasn't put to a beneficial use by either urban interests or agriculture and thus ended up "lost" by flowing out to sea. Failure to develop free-flowing rivers and streams was similarly perceived as waste.

These images repeated throughout the country, in places like California, Texas, Louisiana, North Dakota, Colorado, Utah, Arizona, and New Mexico. The water industry had found itself donning the mantle of the conservationists of the progressive era, arguing for a certain "rationality" and "efficient" redistribution of resources from water surplus to water deficient regions, in the face of powerful public sentiment in favor of saving those lands and waters from development.

"Keep the water in the streams, let it flow to the sea," became the rejoinder to the "waste" argument. By the 1970s and 1980s, such attitudes would resonate for an urbanized and wilderness-deprived public. At one point in his "encounters," David Brower, on a trip to Glacier Peak Wilderness in the state of Washington, tells of a friend, the well-known environmentalist Garrett Hardin. Hardin, who wore leg braces, argued against building an access road into the wilderness area, even though he would thus be prevented from ever seeing the site. Hardin, Brower commented, said that it would be "enough for him to just know that these mountains exist as they are." It was a sentiment that Brower and many of his allies shared: a nostalgic celebration of wilderness in this highly urbanized and industrialized age.

Even more than wilderness yearnings, the concerns about growth had placed the water industry on the defensive. Through much of the 1970s and 1980s, the water industry joined with other industrial interests in sharply attacking growth-control advocates, suggesting that such "no growth" sentiments were both elitist and akin to promoting unemployment and economic decline. Many of the environmental organizations shied away from growth-control arguments, suggesting instead that with conservation and greater efficiencies future growth could be accommodated while still protecting nature.

Yet the growth issue continued to reappear. Slow growth positions were increasingly adopted by local community groups operating either on the edges of or separate from the mainstream environmental organizations. The concerns they raised were primarily urban ones, such as congestion, pollution, the lack of green space, and the deterioration of everyday life. These movements focused on how their neighborhoods and communities were affected by housing and transportation, toxic dumps, and air and water quality, issues not ordinarily found within the traditional environmental agenda. Growth control initiatives succeeded in a number of communities, reflective of this emerging new urban politics. The link between growth and water development, moreover, began to emerge as a key issue for slow growth advocates as well, while the water industry continued to hammer away at the need for additional supplies, warning that expanding regions such as Denver, Phoenix, Albuquerque and San Diego would face severe economic consequences in the event of a shortfall.

The possibility of drought was the longest standing and most effective argument in the water industry's arsenal. "Drought in the West is as certain as death and taxes"; thus water development was "fundamental," the *Salt Lake Tribune* had editorialized. But while the water industry warned about shortfalls, it continued to devise rate structures and build oversized projects that created a dependence on high sales. These dependencies were exacerbated during dry cycles. "Pray for rain" became in this setting "pray for drought," in order that bills be paid through high-volume water sales and the public mobilized around further water development. When the rains came and sales dropped off, some agencies found themselves in a financial squeeze, since their fixed capital costs, a large component of the annual costs of an agency dependent on imported water, still had to be paid.

"Drought" also came to be recognized, in certain situations, as a political fiction. This was particularly true in urban areas such as Los Angeles and Denver, which had overbuilt systems with multiple sources of water. If a drought signified massive reductions in available water rather than simply an extremely dry weather cycle, such events were more likely to occur in places like New York or Wisconsin than California or Arizona. Yet, it was in the West especially that the fears of drought were constantly evoked, with future water development, including the idea of water markets, offered as a solution.

The once-powerful fear of drought, however, was beginning to be offset by counter images of growth and the environment— the crowded freeways, new tract housing, polluted air and water. These negative associations now carried weight even in Southern California, where growth advocacy had been considered impregnable. In San Diego, the fear of "Los Angelesization" paralleled the emergence in Los Angeles of the group "Not Yet New York." Fear of drought was coming up against "quality of life" considerations.

The contrast of "environments"—polluted and pristine—had also entered the popular culture through ad campaigns and marketing devices concerning the taste and quality of water. This was a new consideration for the water industry. It had long touted its water as different from and superior to water outside the United States, particularly in Third World countries such as Mexico, where "el turista" was associated with inadequate treatment of water supplies. Now the water in cities and on farms was being judged by newer standards, with issues of contamination by synthetic organics and the by-products and wastes of industrialization becoming the concern.

Commercial advertising for such products as bottled water and beer emphasized that their source of water could be found in places like mountain streams and uncontaminated springs, located in rural, rustic settings. This high-quality water helped differentiate the product, so this marketing strategy suggested. "Water—as it used to be," one Illinois bottled-water ad jingle announced.

The water industry was often at a loss about how to respond. Water agency managers had, at first, dismissed the concerns as exaggerated fears that would eventually fade once they were placed in context. The water industry's depiction of trace levels of contaminants as minimal and insignificant was a frequent rejoinder; so was placing the blame on more sophisticated measuring techniques. Even the standard one-in-a-million cancer risk estimate was frequently trivialized as insignificant.

Yet these arguments were not particularly successful with the public—or even with the press and the policymakers to whom they were primarily addressed. "We have been saying that there's just a little bit of cancer that's likely to occur," one water industry figure said of the problem, "but the public is telling us in turn that even a little cancer is still cancer, and thus cause for concern." Ultimately, the water agencies were obliged to develop their own public relations program to proclaim that tap water was "safe," while suggesting that some of its critics, from bottled-water operators to citizen movements, were engaged in making unscrupulous, deceptive, or overblown statements.

The differing images about water, from the waste versus free-flow argument to the sharply contrasting conceptions about "clean" or "safe" water, reflected different priorities, different interpretations of the role of the water agencies. The water industry had long defined its role as the attempt to excercise control over water resources on behalf of its key constituents—agriculture, industry, and urban interests. Consequently, water development had become the industry's paramount activity, and an engineering bias had emerged to fulfill the objective. With the decline in the big water projects, that engineering bias came to be modified. Water utility managers were beginning to redefine themselves as ersatz chief executive officers, schooled in legal, political, and economic matters. Water was seen as both a resource and a commodity. The "supply-side" orientation remained intact, with a focus on "stretching" supplies rather than developing new ones, reallocation as opposed to new allocations.

These concepts of the role and the objectives of the water agencies are today being challenged. In limited ways, but with increasing intensity, other concepts have come to the fore. These alternative views, in turn, signify other approaches and other priorities. Instead of the focus on new water development or even stretching supplies, there are those who have raised the concept of the management of demand, with a focus on pricing issues, equity considerations, and growth implications. Instead of the strong organizational and economic weight placed on water supply, considered by the water industry so essential to the requirements of growth, many insist that an organizational and economic priority be placed on the quality of the water. Instead of defining agencies as development-centered institutions, water industry critics have begun to insist that agencies should be seen primarily as public health oriented. Instead of seeking to control water, whether as resource or commodity, there are those who emphasize harmony with this "living" resource, as the Ute Indians say of water, and of nature. And instead of a water industry where the lines between public and private blur, there has emerged a conception of accessible and accountable public utilities, where democratic and participatory goals are considered preeminent.

Soon after I joined the board at MET and entered the world of the water industry, my first child was born. He had a favorite record by the Canadian singer Raffi, a wonderful assortment of old and new tunes. One of these songs became a favorite. I would sing it to my son, not paying attention at first to the words. But as I sang and listened, Raffi's words became a little hypnotic. "All I really need is a song in my heart, food in my belly, and love in my family," he would sing. And then, with a young girl's voice in harmony, Raffi would repeat the refrain:

> *And I need some clean water for drinkin'*
> *And I need some clean air for breathin'*
> *So that I can grow up strong and*
> *Take my place where I belong*

Clean water for drinking, water for living, these are the new stock phrases emerging today. The issues of the water industry, a group so crucial yet still sufficiently obscure, are issues about how to address our environments—urban and rural, natural and social, industrial and postindustrial. They are issues about decision making and priority setting, about our values, and our social objectives. To a certain extent, the conflicts around these issues suggest there will continue to be a period of transition in water policy and politics. How we resolve such conflicts may tell us much about what things remain essential and in what kind of society we will live.

ACKNOWLEDGMENTS

In gathering the material for this project, I was fortunate to have some special assistance from several colleagues and students of mine who reviewed the manuscript, offered criticisms, undertook additional research, and provided insights for a subject that was at once absorbing, difficult to communicate, and intricate in its language and structure. I want to especially thank Cathy Wharton, Louis Blumberg, and Rubell Hegelson for their assistance, perseverance, and enormously helpful research efforts. Helen Ingram reviewed the manuscript and offered her usual sage and thoughtful comments; her extensive and crucial work in this area is a starting point for any serious analyst of the ways of the water industry. Don Villarejo—who reviewed the manuscript, offered comments and research leads, and continually showed himself to be a model of how to combine research and action—contributed in important ways to the development of this book. Pete Carlson, who also read the manuscript and offered comment and criticisms, has for many years been a key link and an important and tireless source of information about the world of Washington, D.C.–based water policymakers and critics.

There were many friends, activists, and colleagues in and around the water industry, at UCLA, and in the media who provided advice and support for this work. Tim Brick, whose friendship and common political activity long predated our "insider-outsider" involvement in the water industry, has shared many of the same hopes and thoughts about the limits and possibilities of change, as has Dorothy Green who deserves enormous respect for her self-taught mastery of the subject and ability to see the importance of new issues and movements. Tom Graff remains a very special person within the world of water politics for his knowledge and bravura, and I've always wanted to know his thoughts and insights even when we disagreed sharply. Margaret FitzSimmons, with whom I've done extensive work on the structure and processes of water agencies, has been a close and warm friend and colleague. And even though we have now completed separate books, Peter Wiley and I will always remain special friends and writing partners, loving that special combination of investigation and analysis; reporting, commentary, and engagement that are the heart of the passion of journalism.

Laura King, Lawrie Mott, and Penny Newman all reviewed parts of the manuscript, providing suggestions and support. Erika Roos helped in countless ways and Marsha Brown, Debbie Jolly, and Ets Otomo were also there to help and hear me out. Carolina Butler, a one-woman whirlwind of activity and criticism of the water industry, is a great friend, activist, and source of information. Mike Picker, Emily Durbin, and Patti Prickett, and those I know less well, such as Ron Krupicka and Will Collette, not only helped with information but also gave me a sense that a network of activism, despite the hurdles, is out there and growing. I had lots of help from several staff members of the Metropolitan Water District and would especially like to thank Karen Dorff, Dawn Chim, Jay Malinowski, Dora Lee and Lillian Wood at the MWD library, Dan Ashkenaizer, Fred Vendig, and Wiley Horne. Beth Willard at the UCLA Water Resources Library was especially helpful. There were others both inside and outside the water industry who helped and contributed: Carl Boronkay, Cheryl Clark, Michael Dennis, Lee Kapaloski, Dan Luecke, Michael McGuire, Dick Miller, Larry Michaels, Mike Nolan, John Means, Stuart Pyle, Julian Rhinehart, Sue Ruddick, Pam Schilling, Stan Scholl, Deborah Sewell, Charles Shreves, Jacqueline Warren, to name just a few.

Finally, I would like to thank my agent, Bob Cornfield, and especially my editor, John Radziewicz, whose capabilities in editing, commenting and criticizing, and parenting are all skills to relish and enjoy.

·

NOTES

Research for *A Life of Its Own* was based both on personal experience—relationships and information developed within and through the water industry—and on investigation of documents, records, and various primary and secondary sources. My activity on the MET board allowed me to attend conferences, engage in banter and informal conversations, and pick up details and information not usually afforded a researcher from the outside looking in. However, I also wanted to systematically pursue the issues and analysis as any "outside" researcher would also do, albeit with the advantage of access to certain documents and materials that often escape the public's notice.

The following notes draw on these various methods involved in gathering information and checking sources. In several instances, I refer to speeches or talks given at conferences or meetings I attended. In some cases, I also have alluded to information that was initially derived from statements made in informal conversations, though all the direct quotes stem from formal interviews. Most of those interviews were undertaken directly for this book. There are several, however, that were originally related to articles prepared for the Points West newspaper column that Peter Wiley and I wrote for nearly five years. Similarly, some of the documents that have been used or referred to include memos and correspondence not intended for public consumption. Most of the material cited, however, including several of the voluminous number of reports issued continuously by water agencies, has been published and is available directly to the public.

PREFACE

xv "the role of the Chandler family": *Thinking Big: The Story of the Los Angeles Times, Its Publishers, and Their Influence on Southern California*, Robert Gottlieb and Irene Wolt, New York, 1977

xvi "our book *Empires in the Sun*": *Empires in the Sun: The Rise of the New American West*, Peter Wiley and Robert Gottlieb, New York, 1982

xvii "given his previous work at the Denver-based Mountain States Legal Foundation": "The Watt Report," *The Nation*, January 17, 1981; "New Voice in the Wilderness: James Watt," Ron Wolf, *Rocky Mountain Magazine*, March–April, 1981; Interview with James Watt (1979)

CHAPTER 1

4 "In the letter": Mailing sent by "Californians Against Higher Water Bills," February 1982

4 "Blais ordered the legal staff": Minutes of the Metropolitan Water District Board of Directors, March 9, 1982

5 "aggressive and forceful 'water seekers' ": *The Water Seekers*, Remi Nadeau, Santa Barbara, 1974

8 "The landowners in the area": See "Conjunctive Use Water Management Programs in Kern County, California," Stuart Pyle, presented at United Nations Seminar on Conjunctive Use of Surface and Groundwater Resources, New Delhi, India, February 1986; "Water Scarcity and Gains from Trade in Kern County, California," H. J. Vaux, Jr., in *Scarce Water and Institutional Change*, Kenneth D. Frederick (editor), Washington, D.C., 1986

8 " 'Land is just land' ": *Developing California's Natural Resources*, Joseph Jensen, Oral History Program, UCLA, 1970

9 " 'Pat Brown deserves the credit' ": Interview with William Gianelli (1986)

9 "In the give-and-take": Interviews with Donald Brooks (1986), John Lauten (1987), Henry Garnett (1987); see also *Aqueduct Empire*, Erwin Cooper, Glendale, California, 1968

9 "MET, on the other hand": Minutes of the Metropolitan Water District Board of Directors August 9, 23, 25; September 13, 27; October 4, 11, 18, 25; November 1, 1960; Interviews with Don Brooks, John Lauten, Robert Gough (1986)

10 " 'Los Angeles's primary industry' ": "The Undiscovered City," *Fortune*, June 1949

10   "The arguments in the north": *San Francisco Chronicle*, October 27, 29, 1960; see also *The Politics of Land*, Ralph Nader's Study Group Report on Land Use in California, Robert Fellmeth, NY, 1973

11   "It was a close election": *Los Angeles Times*, November 10, 1960; *Sacramento Bee*, November 10, 1960

11   "Pat Brown and others in the water industry": Interviews with Pat Brown (1980); William Gianelli: "The California Water Project: Personal Interest and Involvement in the Legislation, Public Support, and Construction, 1950–1966," Edmund G. Brown, Sr., University of California Oral History, Berkeley, 1979

12   "Kern and MET . . . were wary partners": Interviews with Henry Garnett, John Lauten, Don Brooks; see also "Overview of the State Water Project History and Background," Don Brooks, State Water Project Workshop, Metropolitan Water District, January 22, 1986; *The Price of Water: Surplus and Subsidy in the California State Water Project*, Michael Storper and Richard Walker, Berkeley, 1984

12   "For Kern, the deal set the stage": *New Lands for Agriculture*, Don Villarejo, Davis, 1981; "Large Landholdings in the History of California Agriculture," Ellen Liebman, Ph.D., Berkeley, 1981; "Conjunctive Use Water Management Programs in Kern County, California," Stuart Pyle; Kern County Department of Agriculture Annual Crop Report, 1976, 1981

12   "While Kern landowners claimed economic poverty": See "Quantitative Economic Study of Representative Kern County Farm Enterprises," Francis A. Moore, Jr., and Park J. Ewart, authorized by the Kern County Water Agency, Bakersfield, 1962

12–13   "The big urban district was most concerned": Interviews with Don Brooks; John Lauten; Memorandum from Assistant Engineer T. A. Rinn to Principal Engineer R. W. Thompson, Metropolitan Water District, February 21, 1975; Memorandum from Senior Engineer Glen W. Smith to Assistant General Manager, Metropolitan Water District, December 28, 1967

13   "a new crop of MET leaders": Interview with Howard Hawkins (1986); Form 730, "Statement of Economic Interests," Howard Hawkins, 1986, Fair Political Practices Commission, Sacramento

14   "the world's seventh-largest country": *Los Angeles Times*, November 15, 1987

14   "the final solution": Author's notes, Executive Committee meeting, Metropolitan Water District, March 9, 1982

14   "Gianelli . . . was in no rush": "William R. Gianelli, The California State Department of Water Resources, 1967–1973," Government History Documentation Project, University of California, Berkeley, 1986

15 "a cautious and respected water lawyer": Interview with Ronald Robie (1981); "What happens when the well runs dry?" Robert Gottlieb, *Student Lawyer*, November 1981

15 "In the midst of the drought": Annual Report, Metropolitan Water District, 1977, 1978; *Management of the California State Water Project*, Bulletin 132–77, 132–78, Department of Water Resources, Sacramento, 1977, 1978

16 "the agricultural contractors still needed to cut back": "Kern County Water Agency: Summary of 1977 Drought Conditions and Outlook for 1978," Stuart Pyle, presented to Water Problems Committee, Metropolitan Water District, December 13, 1977

16 " 'the missing link' ": Monthly Reports, Public Information Division, Metropolitan Water District, February 1981–May 1982; see for example Letter from the Director of Public Information to the General Manager, Metropolitan Water District, November 4, 1981

17 " 'The drought forced us to think' ": Interview with Gene Lundquist (1987)

17 "Yet Brown avoided constituency pressures": Interviews with Jerry Brown (1978); Tom Graff (1980)

17–18 "anathema to the agricultural interests": Interview with Stuart Pyle (1987)

18 "he was able to issue an executive order": *Management of the California State Water Project*, Bulletin 132–81

18 " 'the best anyone could get' ": Author's notes, discussion with Gerald Meral (1981)

19 " 'For the first time' ": Cited in Bulletin 132–81

20 " 'strange bedfellow' coalition": *Sacramento Bee*, March 26, 1981; *Los Angeles Times*, January 12, 1982; *San Diego Union*, April 9, 1981

21 " 'Money . . . makes politics' ": Author's notes, presentation by John Sterling, UCLA, November 18, 1982

21 "In one notable instance": Interview with Earle Blais (1986); "The Politics of Water," Jonathan Kirsch, *New West*, Vol. 4, No. 19, September 10, 1979; "Water: What We Don't Know and Why We Don't Know It," George L. Baker and Tom DeVries, *New West*, Vol. 5, No. 12, June 16, 1980

22 "At the very next meeting": Author's notes, Coalition to Stop the Peripheral Canal, Finance Committee meeting, April 1981

23 "The Consensus Group": Interviews with David Kennedy (1986), Earle Blais

23 "Some water industry participants": Letter from David Kennedy to Theo T. Nowak, July 14, 1981; see also "The Farm Bureau's big switch on the big ditch," Daniel Blackburn, *California Journal*, March 1981

23 "The environmentalists were at first": Author's discussions with Emily Durbin, Sandra Baldonado, Susan Rice (1981), and several other environmental and public interest group representatives at the time

24 "Press releases would appear verbatim": See "Clip Sheet," April, May, June 1981, Metropolitan Water District Public Information Division; see for example, Letter from the Director of Public Information to the General Manager, Metropolitan Water District, August 6, 1981

25 "1981 bond buyers' conference": "1981 Municipal Bond Buyers Conference: Response to Analysts' Questions and Comments," Prepared by the staff of the Metropolitan Water District of Southern California, January 27, 1981

25 "The Northern California newspapers": *San Francisco Chronicle*, March 5, 1982

25 "Even the *Los Angeles Times*": *Los Angeles Times*, May 9, 1982; see Tejon Ranch Co. Form 10K, for the year ended December 31, 1982, Securities and Exchange Commission

26 "the Water Watch campaign": See especially the minutes of the Special Committee on Public Information, Metropolitan Water District, July 7, 1981, November 10, 1981

26 " 'I was brand new' ": Interview with Gerald Lonergan (1986)

27 "A common refrain": See interview with E. Thornton Ibbetson (1986)

27 "One poll undertaken by MET": A *Survey of Public Opinion Toward Water Issues and Major Water Agencies*, Novick/Rappaport Associates, report prepared for the Metropolitan Water District, August 30, 1983

28 " 'Whom do you believe?' ": Author's notes, discussion with Tim Brick (1982)

28 "a pair of self-assured, media-oriented consultants": See memorandum from Russo Watts & Associates, Inc., to Steering Committee, California Coalition to Stop the Peripheral Canal, January 7, 1981

28 "The language of the poll": See memorandum and draft survey questionnaire from Russo Watts & Associates, Inc., to executive committee and interested parties, May 12, 1981; and Survey Questionnaire Responses, June 1, 1981

29 " 'Bash away' ": Author's notes, meeting of the executive committee, Californians for a Fair Water Policy, June 3, 1981

29 "I remembered a passage": *The Prophet Armed: Trotsky, 1879–1921*, Volume I, Isaac Deutscher, New York, 1954

30 "For months he dallied": See MWD *Speaker's Bureau Bulletin*, July 22, 1981; *Los Angeles Times*, March 5, 1981

30 "This official campaign": Interviews with Mike Neal (1986); Leo McElroy (1986); Earle Blais; *Water Currents*, Citizens for Water, September 1981

31 "The election results": *Los Angeles Times*, June 10, 1982

32 "a water crisis caused": Author's notes, meetings of the Finance & Insurance Committee, Metropolitan Water District, 1983; see especially minutes of the Special Meeting of the Finance & Insurance Committee, Metropolitan Water District, August 25, 1983; *Los Angeles Herald-Examiner*, October 10, 1983

CHAPTER 2

37 "Over the years, NWRA had achieved": See *The Bureau of Reclamation*, William Warne, New York, 1973

38 " 'The battle is not yet over' ": Author's notes, presentation by James Watts, National Water Resources Association Golden Jubilee Convention, Salt Lake City, October 24–27, 1982

39 " 'a whole lot of rhetoric' ": *Wall Street Journal*, October 27, 1982

41 "Established in 1802 as an engineering body": *The History of the US Army Corps of Engineers*, Army Corps of Engineers, EP 360-1-21, 1986

41 "Clean Water Act": This 1972 legislation was originally entitled the Federal Water Pollution Control Act, but soon became known as the Clean Water Act. Further references in the book use "Clean Water Act" as the common reference.

42 "three contrasting approaches to the land": See *Beyond the 100th Meridian*, Wallace Stegner, Lincoln, Nebraska, 1954

43 "Various legislative efforts": *From the Family Farm to Agribusiness: The Irrigation Crusade in California and the West, 1850–1931*, Donald Pisani, Berkeley, 1984; see also *Rivers of Empire*, Donald Worster, New York, 1986

43–44 "the new Reclamation Service": *The Magnificent Experiment: Building the Salt River Reclamation Project, 1890–1917*, Karen Smith, Tucson, 1986; see also *Cadillac Desert*, Marc Reisner, New York, 1986; *The Bureau of Reclamation*, William Warne; *Rivers of Empire*, Donald Worster

44 "In the early years of maneuvering": J. B. Lippincott Papers, University of California, Berkeley; see also *Thinking Big*, Robert Gottlieb and Irene Wolt; "Joseph B. Lippincott and the Owens Valley Controversy: Time for Revision," Abraham Hoffman, *Southern California Quarterly*, Vol. 54, No. 3, Fall 1972; *Water and Power*, William Kahrl, Berkeley, 1982

45 "In the space of five years": *Imperial Valley: The Land of Sun and Subsidies*, Paul Barnett, California Institute for Rural Studies, Davis, 1978; . . . *and the Desert Shall Rejoice: Conflict, Growth, and Justice in Arid Environments*, Arthur Maass and Raymond L. Anderson, Cambridge, 1978

45 "BuRec was bitterly attacked": "Water, Power, and Politics in the Central Valley Project, 1933–1967," Charles Eugene Coate, Ph.D., University of Cal-

ifornia, Berkeley, 1969; *They Would Rule the Valley*, Sheridan Downey, San Francisco, 1947; *Cadillac Desert*, Marc Reisner

47 "The Iron Triangle system especially dominated": *Muddy Waters: The Army Engineers and the Nation's Rivers*, Arthur Maass, Cambridge, 1951

47 "The group was especially supportive": See "Floods and Navigation; Surveys and Legislation," Address by Edgar Jadwin, chief of engineers, U.S. Army, in *Proceedings of the Twenty-Fourth Convention*, National Rivers and Harbors Congress, Washington, D.C., December 5 and 6, 1928

47–48 " 'every state and practically every congressional district' ": Cited in *Pork Barrel Politics: Rivers and Harbors Legislation, 1947–1968*, John A. Ferejohn, Stanford, 1974

48 "a 'subgovernment' ": Douglass Carter, *Power in Washington: A Critical Look at Today's Struggle to Govern in the Nation's Capital*, New York, 1964

48 "Corps projects were also notorious": *The Economic Performance of Public Investments: An Ex Post Evaluation of Water Resources Investments*, Robert Haveman, Resources for the Future, Baltimore, 1972; see also *Pork Barrel Politics*, John Ferejohn

49 "by the time Floyd Dominy": Interview with Bob Will (1986); see also *Cadillac Desert*, Marc Reisner

49 "The CVP had originally been conceived": "Water, Power, and Politics in the Central Valley Project," Charles Eugene Coate

49 "the bureau had effectively abandoned": *From the Family Farm to Agribusiness*, Donald Pisani

50 "A variety of techniques were successfully employed". See *Special Task Force Report on San Luis Unit*, Central Valley Project, California, Public Law 94-46, 1978

51 "Westlands became at once": "Westlands Water District: Land of Super-Farms and Super Subsidies," Don Villarejo, California Institute for Rural Studies, Davis, 1986; "Agricultural Land Ownership and Operations in the 49,000 Acre Drainage Study Area of the Westlands Water District," Assembly Office of Research, 060-A, 1985

51 "These 'paper farmers' ": *San Francisco Examiner*, January 11–15, 1976

51 "At the core of the criticisms": Interview with George Ballis (1986); see also *The Water Reporter*, August 28, 1986, Vol. 10, No. 24; *The Fresno Bee*, August 29, 1986

51 " 'new farms, new jobs, and increased production' ": "Role of Irrigation in the West's Expanding Economy," Floyd E. Dominy, *Journal of the Irrigation and Drainage Division*, Proceedings of the American Society of Civil Engineers, December 1968

53 "The campaign to save Dinosaur": Sierra Club Papers, University of California, Berkeley; *David R. Brower: Environmental Activist, Publicist, and Prophet*, University of California Oral History, Berkeley, 1980; *Dams, Parks, and Politics: Resource Development and Preservation in the Truman-Eisenhower Era*, Elmo Richardson, Lexington, Kentucky, 1973

54 "Brower, in a powerful self-criticism": *The Place No One Knew: Glen Canyon on the Colorado*, Sierra Club, San Francisco, 1963

54 "To get the CAP authorized": See *Patterns of Politics in Water Resource Development: A Case Study of New Mexico's Role in the Colorado River Basin Bill*, Helen Ingram, No. 79: Publications of the Division of Government Research, University of New Mexico, Albuquerque, 1969; *Empires in the Sun*, Peter Wiley and Robert Gottlieb; David Brower Oral History; Interview with Wayne Aspinall (1979)

56 "Udall . . . had a reputation": *The Quiet Crisis*, Stewart Udall, New York, 1963; *Pioneer Conservationists of Western America*, Peter Wild, Missoula, 1979; Interview with Stewart Udall (1980)

56 "The Interior Secretary finally settled on an ingenious solution": *Empires in the Sun*, Peter Wiley and Robert Gottlieb; Interviews with Floyd Goss (1979); Stewart Udall; Wayne Aspinall

56 "There had been other water commissions": See *History of Federal Water Resources Programs and Policies, 1961–1970*, Beatrice Hort Holmes, U.S. Department of Agriculture, Miscellaneous Publication No. 1379, Washington, D.C., 1979

57 "The National Water Commission Report": *Water Policies for the Future*, National Water Commission, Final Report to the President and the Congress of the United States, Port Washington, New York, 1973; see also interview with Bob Will

59 "In the eyes of the water industry": See interviews with John Lauten; Bob Will; Howard Hawkins

60 "based on ninety-five 'theses' ": *95 Theses*, Prepared by the American Rivers Conservation Council and the Environmental Policy Center, 1974, Washington, D.C.; See also "Dig They Must: The Army Engineers, Securing Allies and Acquiring Enemies," Don Moser, *Smithsonian*, December 1976

60 "a serious decline in this ecological resource": *Wetlands: Their Use and Regulation*, Office of Technology Assessment, OTA-O-206, March 1984; *Wetlands of the United States: Current Status and Recent Trends*, Ralph W. Tiner, Jr., Fish and Wildlife Service, U.S. Department of the Interior, March 1984

61 "Under the leadership of Colonel John 'Jack' Morris": *Can Organizations Change? Environmental Protection, Citizen Participation, and the Corps of*

Engineers, Daniel A. Mazmanian and Jeanne Nienaber, The Brookings Institution, Washington, D.C., 1979

61 "the corps created an environmental advisory board": *History of Federal Water Resources Programs and Policies, 1961–1970*, Beatrice Hort Holmes

61 "would 'have an unacceptable adverse effect' ": "Permits for Dredged or Fill Material," Section 404, Public Law 92-500, October 18, 1972, Federal Water Pollution Control Act (Clean Water Act)

61 "Two environmental groups": See *Natural Resources Defense Council* v. *Callaway*, No. 74-1242 (D.D.C. March 27, 1975)

62 " 'an implicit distinction' ": Cited in *Can Organizations Change?* Daniel Mazmanian and Jeanne Nienaber

62 "One chief of a permit section": Cited in *Can Organizations Change?* Daniel Mazmanian and Jeanne Nienaber

62 "At one point it issued a press release": "Dig They Must," Don Moser, *Smithsonian*

63 "Carter was interested in demonstrating": *Empires in the Sun*, Peter Wiley and Robert Gottlieb; Interviews with Cecil Andrus (1981); Joseph Browder (1981); Guy Martin (1980); *Keeping Faith: Memoirs of a President*, Jimmy Carter, Toronto, New York, 1982

63 " 'prudent and responsible use' ": Cited in *Out of Balance*, Scott Matheson, Salt Lake City, 1986

63 "enabled the water industry to launch": "Recent Trends in Federal Water Resource Management: Are the 'Iron Triangles' in Retreat," Tim R. Miller, *Policy Studies Review*, November 1985, Vol. 5, No. 2; Interviews with Felix Sparks (1979); Wes Steiner (1980); Myron Holburt (1981); Bob Will

63 " 'spelled the difference' ": *Out of Balance*, Scott Matheson

64 "Andrus used the threat": Interviews with Cecil Andrus; Kathy Ferris (1980); Bruce Babbitt (1980); Bob Moore (1980); Bob McCain (1980)

65 "The OMB became a strong advocate": *Sacramento Bee*, November 25, 1982; Interviews with Peter Carlson (1986); Bob Will

66 " 'I found myself questioning' ": *Water Resources: People and Issues*, William R. Gianelli, U.S. Army Corps of Engineers, EP 870-1-24, August 1985

67 "Through these debates": *Sacramento Bee*, March 14, 1984; Interviews with William Gianelli; Bob Will; Peter Carlson

67 "a safety of dams bill": *Reclamation Safety of Dams Act Amendments of 1984*, Public Law 98-404, 98 Stat. 1481, August 28, 1984

67 "the new math applied to projects": See *An Analysis of the Animas–La Plata Project*, Peter Carlson and Spencer Wilson, Environmental Policy Institute, Washington, D.C., July 1987; *New York Times*, June 20, 1987

68 "At one 1985 water conference": Author's notes, remarks by Edwin Dale, "Water in the West: Understanding the New Era," conference sponsored by the Institute for Resource Management, Sundance, Utah, October 18–20, 1985

69 "This legislation, HR 6": "Section by Section Summary: 'Water Resources Development Act of 1986' (HR-6)," U.S. Army Corps of Engineers, November 7, 1986; Interviews with Robert Dawson (1986); William Gianelli

69 " 'This creates a bright future' ": Interview with Robert Dawson

70 "as a lead article in *Engineering News-Record*": "BuRec searching for a new role after 83 years," *Engineering News-Record*, September 12, 1985

70 "first outlined in a 1984 letter": Ronald Reagan to Paul Laxalt, January 24, 1984; See also *Sacramento Bee*, March 14, 1984

71 " 'they can't afford it' ": Interview with C. Dale Duvall (1987)

71 "The protracted conflict": "The Westlands Settlement: The Alleged Pros and the Real Cons," Hamilton Candee and Laura B. King, Natural Resources Defense Council, September 12, 1986, San Francisco; *Sacramento Bee*, July 25, 1986; *Los Angeles Times*, July 25, 1986; *ACWA News*, August 11, 1986, Vol. 14, No. 16

72 " 'The water industry does have to change' ": Interview with C. Dale Duvall

72 " 'an agency based on federally supported construction' ": *National Water Line*, National Water Resources Association, October 1987

72 " 'more a fact of life than a real change' ": Author's notes, oral presentation by Bob Will, Executive Committee, Metropolitan Water District, October 13, 1987

72 "water industry allies within the Interior Department": *Sacramento Bee*, April 19, 1987

73 " 'the building of a great empire' ": "Water, Power, and Politics in the Central Valley Project," Charles Eugene Coate

73 " 'The old days, the pork barrel days' ": Interview with C. Dale Duvall

CHAPTER 3

75 "When the phone rang": Interview with Don Villarejo (1987)

75 "AgOreo is the arm": Interviews with Gary Pevey (1987); Don Kington (1987)

77 "the active efforts of Giannini's Bank of America": *Biography of a Bank: The Story of Bank of America N.T. & S.A.*, Marquis James and Bessie R. James, New York, 1954

77 "it suddenly found itself holding title": *Sacramento Bee*, November 18, 1984

78 "The example was strongly symbolic": See *California's Finest: The History of Del Monte Corporation and the Del Monte Brand*, William Braznell, Del Monte Corporation, 1982

79 "the bank announced a series of auctions": *Sacramento Bee*, September 23, 1986

81 " 'use all their influence' ": Cited in *From the Family Farm to Agribusiness*, Donald Pisani

81 "Huge land empires": See *The Cattle King: A Dramatized Biography*, Edward Treadwell, Boston, 1931; *Land, Water and Settlement in Kern County, California, 1850–1890*, Margaret Aseman Cooper, New York, 1979

82 "the 'stepchild of land speculation' ": *From the Family Farm to Agribusiness*, Donald Pisani

83 "The centerpiece for reform": See "Water, Land, and Environment: Imperial Valley—Law Caught in the Winds of Politics," Paul Taylor, *Natural Resources Journal*, Vol 13, No. 1, January 1973; *The Magnificent Experiment*, Karen Smith

84 " 'factories in the field' ": *Factories in the Field*, Carey McWilliams, Santa Barbara, 1971

85 "land irrigated with bureau water": Figures cited in *The Bureau of Reclamation*, William Warne

86 " 'To have a farm out there' ": *Bernie Sisk in the House: An Oral History*, University of California, Berkeley, California Government Series II, No. 17, 1981

86 "California's irrigated land nearly doubled": U.S. Department of Commerce, Bureau of the Census, *1982 Census of Agriculture, Vol. 1, Part 5, California State and County Data*, June 1984; see also *How Much Is Enough? Federal Water Subsidies and Agriculture in California's Central Valley*, Don Villarejo, California Institute for Rural Studies, Davis, 1986

86 "which had far surpassed Iowa": *Economic Indicators of the Farm Sector, Income and Balance Sheet Statistics, 1985*, U.S. Department of Agriculture, September 1986

86 "or even, according to some critics": See *Turning off the Tap on Federal Water Subsidies: Volume I, The Central Valley Project: The $3.5 Billion Giveaway*, E. Phillip LeVeen and Laura B. King, Natural Resources Defense Council, California Rural Legal Assistance Foundation, San Francisco, August 1985

86 "a 'strictly business' approach": *The Bureau of Reclamation*, William Warne

87 "But the system as it evolved": See *Special Task Force Report on the San Luis Unit*, Bureau of Reclamation, Washington, D.C., 1978; also *Review of*

the Central Valley Project, Office of Audit and Investigation, Department of the Interior, Washington, D.C., 1978

87   "The CVP system became the most pronounced example": See *Turning off the Tap on Federal Water Subsidies*, E. Phillip LeVeen and Laura B. King

87   "One study that compared landownership data": *How Much Is Enough?* Don Villarejo; see also *Agricultural Land Ownership and Operation in the Southern San Joaquin Valley*, Edwin Wilson and Marion Clawson, U.S. Department of Agriculture, Bureau of Agricultural Economics, Berkeley, 1945

87   "a little less than a billion dollars was spent": See *Turning off the Tap in Federal Water Subsidies*, E. Phillip LeVeen and Laura B. King

88   "A series of audits": *Review of the Central Valley Project*, Office of Audit and Investigation, Department of the Interior; *Special Task Force Report on the San Luis Unit*, Bureau of Reclamation

88   "a whole new set of surplus-crop programs": *Sacramento Bee*, July 20, 1983; *National Water Line*, Vol. 7, No. 8, April 15, 1983; *U.S. News and World Report*, May 30, 1983; *Wall Street Journal*, July 19, 1983; "Agriculture," *California Outlook*, Bank of America, May 20, 1983; see also *Production of Surplus Crops on Irrigated Land Served by the U.S. Bureau of Reclamation*, Austin Fox, Charles Moore, Harold Stults, Economic Research Service, U.S. Department of Agriculture, February 1984

88   "The double-dipping effect was most revealing": *Water Age*, Kern County Water Agency, May 1983; *Sacramento Bee*, July 20, 1983; Interviews with Laurence Wold (1983); John Sterling (1983)

89   " 'Every farm structure' ": Cited in *Tehama County News*, Aug. 29, 1987; see "The Effect of Agricultural Scale on Communities," Dean MacCannell, in *Sustainability of California Agriculture*, Symposium Proceedings, 1986, Davis; "Agribusiness and the Small Community," Dean MacCannell, in *Technology, Public Policy, and the Changing Structure of American Agriculture.* Volume II—Background Papers, Office of Technology Assessment, 1986, Washington, D.C.

91   "the district was represented by Bernie Sisk": *Bernie Sisk in the House*, UC Berkeley; Interviews with Bernie Sisk (1985); Tony Coelho (Peter Wiley interview) (1985)

91   "It didn't take Tony Coelho long": Interviews with Bernie Sisk; Tony Coelho; Roy Greenaway (1985); Ken Maddy (1985); see also "Ass Backward," Robert Kuttner, *New Republic*, April 22, 1985; "Power in the House," Bob Sector, *Los Angeles Times Magazine*, January 11, 1987

92   " 'hyper as a hummingbird' ": Interview with Jim Wright (Peter Wiley interview), 1985

92   " 'always wanting to move very rapidly' ": Interview with Bernie Sisk

92 " 'the business of politics' ": Author's notes (with Peter Wiley), presentation by Tony Coelho to Southland Corporation executives, Washington, D.C., March 1985

92 " 'If I were chairman of the [DCCC] or not' ": Interview with Tony Coelho; see also "Money to Burn: How Chicago's Commodity Traders Get Their Way on Capitol Hill," Florence Graves and Lee Norrgard, *Common Cause Magazine*, January–February 1985

93 "the 'Pleasant Valley Massacre' ": *Washington Post*, November 1, 1984; *Fresno Bee*, October 21, 1984; *Sacramento Bee*, February 24, 1987

94 "Miller continually railed": Author's notes, presentation by George Miller at the "Water in the West, Understanding the New Era" conference, Institute for Resource Management, October 1985

95 "For more than one hundred years": *The Imperial Valley and the Salton Sink*, H. T. Cory, San Francisco, 1915; *The Water Seekers*, Remi Nadeau; "Imperial Valley: Triumph and Failure in the Colorado Desert," Helen Hosmer, *American West*, Vol. 13, No. 1, Winter, 1966; *Imperial Valley: The Land of Sun and Subsidies*, Paul Barnett

95 "The IID, created in 1911": *Prospects for Accountability and Innovation in Six Public Water Agencies*, Robert Gottlieb and Margaret FitzSimmons; *From Desert Wasteland to Agricultural Wonderland: The Story of Water and Power*, Imperial Irrigation District, 1977

96 "Swing . . . had initially attempted to exempt Imperial": See *Bryant* v. *Yellen*, 447 US 352, 65 L Ed 2d 184, 100 S Ct 2232; *Imperial Valley: The Land of Sun and Subsidies*, Paul G. Barnett

96 "a Mexican land syndicate": *Thinking Big: The Story of the Los Angeles Times*, Robert Gottlieb and Irene Wolt; "Estudio general sobre el aprovechamiento de las aguas del Río Colorado, en el Valle de Mexicali, Baja California y San Luis, R. C. Sonora," Luis Soleno Benavente, Tesis que para obtener el Título de Agrónomo presenta el pasante, Ciudad Juarez, 1972

96 "The district, teetering on the edge of bankruptcy": *Imperial Valley: The Land of Sun and Subsidies*, Paul Barnett

97 "IID became an active player in land dealings": Interviews with Lester Bornt (1987); Stephen Elmore (1986); "Miracle Salton City by the Desert Sea," *District News*, Imperial Irrigation District, June 1959; "Many District Facilities Used for Recreation in Imperial County," *District News*, July 1960; *District News*, October 1958

97 "flush out the salts": *Wall Street Journal*, June 17, 1986; Interview with Charles Shreves

98 "The Elmores . . . also brought complaints": See *Investigation under California Water Code Section 275 of Use of Water by the Imperial Irrigation District*,

Department of Water Resources, Southern District, Los Angeles, December 1981; Interviews with David Osias (1986); John Elmore (1986); Stephen Elmore

98 "according to the district's own later estimates": Final Environmental Impact Report, *Proposed Water Conservation Program and Initial Water Transfer, Imperial Irrigation District*, California State Clearinghouse, No. 86012903, October 1986; see also *Water Requirements and Availability Study and Water Transfer Study, Water Conservation Program, Imperial Irrigation District*, Parsons Water Resources Inc., November 1985

99 "EDF released a report": *Trading Conservation Investments for Water*, Robert Stavins, Environmental Defense Fund, Berkeley, 1983

99 " 'a win-win situation' ": Author's notes, discussion with Tom Graff (1985)

99 " 'Nobody, either within the valley' ": Interview with David Osias

99 " 'the finest in the country' ": Testimony by Wiley Horne, September 29, 1983 in *Hearing on Alleged Waste and Unreasonable Use of Water by the Imperial Irrigation District*, State Water Resources Control Board

100 "Ibbetson . . . was a major real estate developer": Form 730, E. Thornton Ibbetson's "Statement of Economic Interests," 1986, Fair Political Practices Commission; *Imperial Valley Press*, May 19, 1987; Interview with E. Thornton Ibbetson (1986)

100 "The ties were not simply limited": "Water, Land, and Environment, Imperial Valley," Paul Taylor; Interviews with Willy Morris (1987); Stephen Elmore

101 " 'Parsons suggested to us' ": Interview with John Benson (1986)

101 "The Parsons-IID relationship was fraught": Interviews with Charles Shreves (1987); Robert Davidson (1986); Mel Brown (1986); Tom Havens (1987); Bill Condit (1987); John Benson (1986)

101 "a strong outcry within the valley": *Imperial Valley Press*, April 30, 1986; May 14, 1986; May 27, 1986; "When Water Kingdoms Clash," Ed Marston, *High Country News*, September 29, 1986

102 "the MET/IID negotiations became jumbled": "Memorandum of Understanding—Imperial Irrigation District," Letter from the General Manager to the Board of Directors, Metropolitan Water District, July 5, 1985; "Imperial Irrigation District Negotiations on a Water Conservation Agreement," Letter from General Manager to the Board of Directors, Metropolitan Water District, August 5, 1986; Letter from Leroy Edwards, president, IID Board of Directors, to E. Thornton Ibbetson, Chairman, MWD Board of Directors, July 15, 1986; Interviews with Carl Boronkay (1987); Bill Condit; Lester Bornt

102 "taxed in the form of a water charge": Interview with Charles Shreves (1987)

102 "two key pests": *Los Angeles Times*, December 14, 1987; *California Farmer*, November 6, 1982; *California-Arizona Farm Press*, August 3, 1985; *Los Angeles Times Magazine*, September 20, 1987; Interview with John Benson

103 "take their lands out of production": Annual Crop Report, Imperial Valley Agricultural Commissioner, 1981, 1983, 1986

103 "the situation had reached crisis proportions": *Six-State High Plains Ogallala Aquifer Regional Resources Study*, High Plains Associates, a report to the U.S. Department of Commerce and the High Plains Study Council, Austin, March 1982; "Ogallala: Half Full or Half Empty," Dick Russell, *Amicus Journal*, Fall, 1985

104 "The situation was most critical for the Texas High Plains": "Land and Water Management Issues: Texas High Plains," Ronald Lacewell and John Lee, paper developed for the World Resources Institute, October 1985

105 "irrigated acreage in Nebraska": *A Report on the High Plains Study*, The Working Group on the Ogallala Aquifer of the Missouri Basin–Great Plains Caucus, Walthill, Nebraska, October 1982

105 "The rise of the center-pivot system": *Wheels of Fortune: A Report on the Impact of Center Pivot Irrigation on the Ownership of Land in Nebraska*, Center for Rural Affairs, Walthill, Nebraska, 1976; "Changes in Farming in Nebraska: The Role of Center Pivot Irrigation," Steve Hopkins, paper prepared for the Small Farm Resources Project, Hartington, Nebraska, 1987

106 " 'It appeared to many people' ": "Changes in Farming in Nebraska," Steve Hopkins

106 "outside investors . . . entered the state": *Wheels of Fortune*, Center for Rural Affairs; *Report on the High Plains Study*, Missouri Basin–Great Plains Caucus

107 " 'forced the farmer to abuse the land' ": Interview with Ron Krupicka (1987)

108 "the bailout came in the form": *Omaha World-Herald*, October 5, 1986; *Omaha Journal-Star*, April 28, 1985

108 "there was now talk of water markets": *Omaha World-Herald*, November 9, 1986

109 "This federally subsidized project": "Fact Sheet: San Felipe Division, Central Valley Project," Bureau of Reclamation, mid-Pacific region, Sacramento, May 1977; *San Francisco Examiner*, March 4, 1979; February 18, 1979

109 "the longtime California head": Interview with Ray Corley (1987)

109 "there were potential conflict-of-interest problems": *Washington Post*, April 14, 1987

109 "The critics objected to the fact": Interviews with Tom Graff (1987); Laura King (1987)

109–110 "Lindgren was temporarily suspended": *New York Times,* July 25, 1987; *Washington Post,* January 16,1988; *Los Angeles Times,* March 16, 1988; letter from Assistant Attorney General John R. Bolton to Congressman George Miller, December 17, 1987

110 "a number of western farm operations . . . restructured their form of ownership": "Acreage Limitation: Proposed Rules 43 CFR Part 426, U.S. Department of Interior, Bureau of Reclamation," Don Villarejo, California Institute for Rural Studies, Davis, January 29, 1987

110 "Miller called BuRec's decision on FMAs a 'fraud' ": *Los Angeles Times,* April 11, 1987; see also *National Water Line,* March 1987; ACWA *News,* January 26, 1987; *Bakersfield Californian,* March 15, 1987; March 16, 1987

110 " 'Flat defiance of the law' ": *Los Angeles Times,* April 11, 1987

111 " 'the actions of a few farmers' ": *National Water Line,* July 1987

112 "that process of buying and selling was first associated": *Water for the Energy Market,* John A. Folk-Williams and James S. Cannon, Volume Two of *Water in the West,* Western Network, Santa Fe, 1983

CHAPTER 4

113 "The Honey Springs plan": Environmental Impact Report, Honey Springs, LSP81-096, P81-096, TM4306; see also "Proposed concurrent annexation of Honey Springs Ranch Annexation to San Diego County Water Authority and Metropolitan Water District," Letter from General Manager to the Board of Directors, Metropolitan Water District, December 29, 1980; *General Plan Amendment Report for Honey Springs,* Presenting Inc., 1980

115 "The CH$_2$M Hill study": *Preliminary Study of Potable Water System for Honey Springs Ranch,* Presenting Inc., CH$_2$M Hill, San Diego, March 1980

115 "Local residents were furious": *The Metropolitan Water District: The Institution and Water Supply Planning,* Robert N. Blanche et al., UCLA School of Architecture and Urban Planning, report prepared for the city of Santa Monica, 1980; Interview with Dianne Jacob (1981)

115 "A local San Diego newspaper": "Honey Springs' developers turn on the juice," Gerry Ollodart, *San Diego Newsline,* Vol. 4, No. 18, February 4–11, 1981

118 "The political leadership of cities": See *Water for the Cities: A History of the Urban Supply Problem in the United States,* Nelson Blake, Syracuse, 1956;

The Urban Wilderness: A History of the American City, Sam Bass Warner, New York, 1972

118   "one-tenth of all new corporations": *Water for the Cities*, Nelson Blake

118   "a high-powered ersatz banking combine": *Water for a City: A History of New York City's Problem from the Beginning to the Delaware River System*, Charles Weidner, Newark, 1974; *Water for the Cities*, Nelson Blake

120   "most large cities had been forced": See *Northern California's Water Industry: The Comparative Efficiency of Public Enterprise in Developing a Scarce Natural Resource*, Joe S. Bain, Richard E. Caves, Julius Margolis, Resources for the Future, Baltimore, 1966; "Historical Development of Municipal Water Systems in the United States, 1776–1976," J. Michael LaNier, *Journal of the American Water Works Association*, Vol. 68, No. 4, April 1976

120   "Per capita water consumption had increased": See *History of Public Works in the United States, 1776–1976*, American Public Works Association, Ellis L. Armstrong (editor), Chicago, 1976

121   "In New York": *Water for a City*, Charles H. Weidner; "Historical Development of Municipal Water Systems in the United States," J. Michael LaNier

122   "Chicago had a vast supply": "Unfouling the Public's Nest: Chicago's Sanitary Diversion of Lake Michigan Water," Louis P. Cain, *Technology and Culture*, Vol. 15, No. 4, October 1974; *Man and Epidemics*, C-E A. Winslow, Princeton, 1952; interview with Harry Pawlowski (1985)

122   " 'As a result' ": *Chicago Water System*, Department of Water, City of Chicago, 1984

123   " 'its magnificent and manifest destiny' ": *Los Angeles Times*, September 8, 1905

124   " 'the future development and prosperity' ": Cited in the *Los Angeles Times*, September 2, 1905

124   "the early water industry in Los Angeles": See *Thinking Big: The Story of the Los Angeles Times*, Robert Gottlieb and Irene Wolt; Moses Sherman papers, the Sherman Foundation, Corona del Mar, California

125   "the city dramatically increased its land area": See *The American City*, July 1916; *Water and Politics: A Study of Water Policies and Administration in the Development of Los Angeles*, Vincent Ostrom, Los Angeles, 1953

125   "The organization created for the purpose of securing that supply": *Developing California's Natural Resources*, Joseph Jensen

126   "Opposition to the water industry's plans": "Does the Colorado River Aqueduct Mean Economic Suicide for the City of Los Angeles," F. E. Weymouth, Metropolitan Water District Report No. 4, Los Angeles, April 3, 1933

126 "so much surplus water was available": *1976 Analysis of Annexation Policy of Metropolitan Water District; Developing California's Natural Resources,* Joseph Jensen

127 " 'So I joined the water board' ": Interview with E. Thornton Ibbetson

127 "the MET board established its new policy": "Statement of Policy," Laguna Declaration; Metropolitan Water District, December 16, 1952; see also *Prospects for Accountability and Innovation in Six Public Water Agencies,* Robert Gottlieb and Margaret FitzSimmons

129 " 'We were more MET than MET' ": Interview with Linden Burzell (1986)

129 " 'a big opportunity to make some money' ": *William H. Jennings: Water Lawyer,* William Jennings Oral History, University of California at Los Angeles, 1967

130 " 'a very risky type of economy' ": Cited in *William Jennings: Water Lawyer*

130 "The local San Diego water industry undertook a systematic campaign": Interviews with Mike Madigan (1987); Larry Michaels (1986); Art Bullock (1986); Emily Durbin (1985); *San Diego Union,* March 21, 1982; March 5, 1982; March 6, 1982; June 22, 1981; March 9, 1981

131 "one Japanese firm in particular": *Economic Value of Reliable Water Supplies,* State Water Contractors Exhibit No. 51, Bay-Delta Hearings, D-1485 Proceedings, State Water Resources Control Board, Sacramento, 1987; "Economic Value of Reliable Water Supplies for Industrial Water Users," Thomas C. Thomas and Richard C. Carlson, prepared for the Metropolitan Water District, June 9, 1987, State Water Contractors Exhibit No. 57, SWRCB Hearings; Interviews with Mike Madigan; Larry Michaels

131 "The situation was ripe": Interviews with John Musick (1987); Paul Engstrand (1987); Phil Pryde (1986); Linden Burzell; Mike Madigan; Larry Michaels

132 "an 'enterprising group' ": *San Diego Union,* August 30, 1984

133 " 'I saw CWA as fundamental to San Diego' ": Interview with Mike Madigan

133 "MET staff were livid at the idea": Interviews with Carl Boronkay (1987); Larry Michaels; *San Diego Union,* August 30, 1987; August 31, 1987

133 "MET staff provided a barrage of materials": "Analysis of Option Agreement between the Galloway Group Ltd. and the San Diego County Water Authority," Letter from the General Manager and the General Counsel to the Board of Directors, Metropolitan Water District, September 11, 1984; "Analysis of Legal Opinion Re: Proposed Water Service Agreement Between the Galloway Group Ltd. and the San Diego County Water Authority," Letter from General Counsel to the Board of Directors, Metropolitan Water District, November 9, 1984

133 " 'actually smoke [controlled substances]' ": *San Diego Union*, August 30, 1984; see also Letter from Carl Boronkay to Nat Eggert, August 31, 1984; Interview with Cheryl Clark (1986)

133 " 'a malevolent leader' ": Interview with John Musick

134 " 'You have to take risks' ": Interview with Mike Madigan

134 "the Pamo Dam storage facility": Interviews with Dale Mason (1986); Larry Michaels; Emily Durbin; "Transcript of Proceedings, Public Hearing: Pamo Reservoir," San Diego, Army Corps of Engineers, November 19, 1986; *Draft Environmental Impact Report/ Environmental Assessment for the PAMO Reservoir*, Mooney-Lettieri and Associates, prepared for the San Diego County Water Authority, November 18, 1983; "Pamo Reservoir Feasibility Study," Letter from the General Manager to the Board of Directors, Metropolitan Water District, June 17, 1982

135 "the emergence of a 'slow growth' movement": *San Diego Evening Tribune*, October 9, 1987; *San Diego Union*, September 13, 1987; *New York Times*, June 28, 1987

136 "Since its organization in 1918": *The Denver Water Department: 1918–1978; Sixty Years Young*, Denver Water Department, 1978; *Empires in the Sun: The Rise of the New American West*, Peter Wiley and Robert Gottlieb; "Water Management Issues in the Denver, Colorado Urban Area," J. Gordon Milliken, World Resources Institute, Washington, D.C., 1985; Interviews with James Ogilvie (1979); Bill Miller (1979); David Getches (1987); Charles Jordan (1987)

137 "the Blue Line policy had a curious mix": Interviews with Ken Ruetz (1987); James Ogilvie; Charles Jordan; "Water Management Issues in the Denver, Colorado Area," J. Gordon Milliken

138 "like the city of Aurora": Annual Report, Utilities Department, Aurora, Colorado, 1986

138 "Despite an impressive array": "Financing Water Development Programs in an Ecological Age," James Ogilvie, *Journal of the American Water Works Association*, February 1976, *Rocky Mountain News*, July 7, 1972; July 8, 1972; October 24, 1973; October 26, 1973; October 30, 1973

138–139 "The water board, despite substantial funds for lobbying": "Eagle's Nest: An Overview," Patricia Schroeder (D-Denver), July 3, 1976

139 "the Poundstone Amendment": Interviews with Charles Jordan; Ken Ruetz; Virgil Hill (1987); David Getches

139 " 'Something had been done to the city' ": Interview with Charles Jordan

140 " 'Black Wednesday' ": Interviews with Virgil Hill; David Getches; Ken Ruetz; "Denver Plays Its Water Card," John Aloysius Farrell, *Denver Post Magazine*, June 22, 1986

140   "the Metropolitan Water Providers": Annual Report, Denver Water Department, 1986; *Denver Post*, July 15, 1981; Interview with Virgil Hill; David Getches; Charles Jordan

140   "Two Forks had become the centerpiece": "Denver Plays Its Water Card," John Aloysius Farrell; "Environmental Caucus Recommendations to the Denver Board of Water Commissioners Regarding Future Water Supply Scenarios," Colorado Environmental Caucus, Denver, January 16, 1986

141   " 'The old order in delivering water' ": "Denver Plays Its Water Card," John Aloysius Farrell

141   " 'The perception of the Denver Water Department' ": John Aloysius Farrell, *ibid.*

142   "For critics of the Denver water industry": See *Water for Denver: An Analysis of the Alternatives*, John R. Morris and Clive V. Jones, Environmental Defense Fund, Denver, 1980; *Denver Water Department Staff Review of Water for Denver*, Denver Water Department, October 1980; Interview with Daniel Luecke (1987); "Evaluation of SEIS Population Projections," memorandum from John Morris and Daniel Luecke to U.S. Army Corps of Engineers, October 9, 1985

142   "That argument had become more compelling": Interviews with Tim Holman (1987); David Getches; *New York Times*, May 12, 1988; *High Country News*, March 14, 1988

144   "the CAP was the water industry's link": *Empires in the Sun: The Rise of the New American West*, Peter Wiley and Robert Gottlieb; *The Central Arizona Project: 1918–1968*, Rich Johnson, Tucson, 1977

144   "the CAP had become the BuRec's most expensive project": "Project Data Sheet," Central Arizona Project, Public Law 90-537, Public Law 97-373, Bureau of Reclamation, Department of the Interior, January 31, 1987

144   " 'find themselves worse off with the CAP' ": See *Potential Costs and Benefits to Arizona Agriculture of the Central Arizona Project*, David B. Bush and William E. Martin, Technical Bulletin Number 254, University of Arizona College of Agriculture, Tucson, 1986

145   "water availability in Tucson": *Saving Water in a Desert City*, William E. Martin et al., Resources for the Future, 1984; *Planning for Growth in the Southwest*, William E. Martin and Helen M. Ingram, National Planning Association, Washington, D.C., 1985; "The Californiaization of Water Politics," William W. Parsons and Douglas W. Mathews, Presented at the Annual Meeting of the Western Political Science Association, Anaheim, March 26–28, 1987

145–146   "In elections for the Tucson City Council in 1975": *Saving Water for a Desert City*, William Martin et al.; *Arizona Daily Star*, November 5, 1975

146 "that *should,* as a department memo advised": cited in *Saving Water for a Desert City,* William Martin et al.

147 " 'the single most important educational undertaking' ": Minutes of Water Education meeting, Tucson City Council, March 28, 1977, cited in *Saving Water for a Desert City,* William Martin et al.

148 "Even when per capita use began to increase": See *Water Words,* Southern Arizona Water Resources Association, Vol. 5, No. 5, July–August, 1987

CHAPTER 5

156 " 'As we enter an era of uncertainty' ": "Meeting the Challenges of the New Water Quality Arena," George Britton, presented to the National Water Resources Association Municipal Caucus, San Diego, December 3, 1986

156 " 'a drop of vermouth in a sea of gin' ": Author's notes, comments by Richard Balzersak, Board of Director's meeting, Metropolitan Water District, June 12, 1984

157 " 'well below the standard' ": Author's notes, comments by Duane Georgeson, "Water in the West" conference, Sundance, Utah, October 19, 1985; see also "L.A.'s Troubled Water," Michael Balter, *Los Angeles Weekly,* October 11–17, 1985

157 "Such an event would be a major undertaking": Author's notes, discussion with George Britton, NWRA Annual Meeting, December 3, 1986

159 "To have water 'pure and plenty' ": Cited in *Water for the Cities,* Nelson Blake

160 "water service was a public-utility function": *The Evolution of American Urban Society,* Howard P. Chudacoff, Englewood Cliffs, New Jersey, 1975; see also *The Urban Wilderness,* Sam Bass Warner

160 "The first clear indication": *Man and Epidemics,* C-E. A. Winslow

161 "By the 1890s, a social movement had emerged": See *Pollution and Reform in American Cities, 1870–1930,* Martin Melosi (editor), Austin, 1980

162 "it would be importune to 'interfere' ": Cited in *Water for the Cities,* Nelson Blake

163 " 'all the characteristics of an open sewer' ": "*Triumph and Failure: The American Response to the Urban Water Supply Problem, 1860–1923,*" Stuart Galishoff, in *Pollution and Reform in American Cities*

163 "The Izaac Walton League, a Midwest-based group": See *John Muir and His Legacy: The American Conservation Movement,* Stephen Fox, Boston, 1981; *Disaster by Default,* Frank Graham, Jr., New York, 1966

163 " 'streams are nature's sewers' ": Cited in *The Politics of Ecology*, James Ridgeway, New York, 1970; see also "Urban Wastewater Technology: Changing Concepts of Water Quality Control, 1850–1930," Joel A. Tarr, James Mc-Curley, and Terry Yosie, in *Pollution and Reform in American Cities*

163–164 " 'regardless of how one may feel' ": "The Development and Impact of Industrial Wastes and Water Supplies," Ralph Evans, *Journal of the American Water Works Association*, May 1, 1965

165 " 'moving to and fro' ": Cited in *Disaster by Default*, Frank Graham, Jr.

165 "The chemical industry bitterly attacked": *Silent Spring*, New York, 1962; *Since Silent Spring*, Frank Graham, Jr., Boston, 1970; *John Muir and His Legacy*, Stephen Fox

165 " 'Today the new challenge facing the water supply profession' ": See Panel Discussion: "Effects of Pollution in Water Supplies," *Journal of the American Water Works Association*, November 1960

166 " 'one of the major deterrents to energetic state enforcement' ": *Public Regulation of Water Quality in the United States*, N. William Hines, Prepared for the National Water Commission, Report # NWC-L-72-036, Washington, D.C., 1971

166 "the use of synthetic laundry detergents": See *History of Federal Water Resources Programs and Policies*, Beatrice Hort Holmes; "ABS Contamination," Graham Walton, *Journal of the American Water Works Association*, November 1960

167 "In 1969, the Cuyahoga River": *Cleveland Plain Dealer*, June 23, 1969; *New York Times*, October 8, 1969; December 19, 1970; "Threat to Man's Only Home," Gordon Young, *National Geographic*, Vol. 138, No. 6, December 1970

168 " 'Although it is generally accepted' ": *Water Quality and Treatment: A Handbook of Public Water Supplies*, American Water Works Association, New York, 1971

168 "Nitro's water source": See "Carbon Bed Design Criteria Study at Nitro, West Virginia," Kenneth A. Dostal, Rex C. Pierson, Donald G. Hager, and Gordon G. Robeck, *Journal of the American Water Works Association*, May 1965

169 "One of the more widely publicized cases": *The Reserve Mining Controversy: Science, Technology, and Environmental Quality*, Robert Bartlett, Bloomington, 1980; *Judgment Reserved: A Landmark Environmental Case*, Frank D. Schaumburg, Reston, Virginia, 1976

170 " 'the dullest issue he could possibly research' ": Interview with Robert Harris (1986)

170 "a three-part series for *Consumer Reports*": "Is the Water Safe to Drink?" Robert H. Harris and Edward M. Brecher, *Consumer Reports* (3 parts), June, July, August 1974

170 " 'the identities and the quantitative concentrations' ": Cited in "A History of the Attempted Federal Regulation Requiring GAC Adsorption for Water Treatment," James M. Symons, *Journal of the American Water Works Association*, August 1984

171 " 'the petrochemical corridor' ": See "Who is Killing the Great Rivers of the World: Part I, the Mississippi," Zack Nauth, *In These Times*, December 24, 1986

171 "At the same time that EPA issued its findings": "The Implications of Cancer-Causing Substances in Mississippi River Water," Robert H. Harris, with assistance from The Ecology Center of Louisiana, Edith Vermeij, Samuel S. Epstein, A Report Submitted to James A. Moreau, Councilman-at-Large, New Orleans, November 6, 1974; *Safe Drinking Water: Current and Future Problems*, Clifford S. Russell (editor), Resources for the Future, Washington, D.C., 1978; "Drinking Water and Cancer Mortality in Louisiana," Talbot Page, Robert Harris, Samuel Epstein, *Science*, July 1976

171 "When the head of the Cincinnati utility": Interview with Robert Harris; see also "Cincinnati Research in Organics," Charles M. Bolton, *Journal of the American Water Works Association*, August 1977

171 "one key group of organics, trihalomethanes": See "A History of the Attempted Federal Regulation Requiring GAC Adsorption for Water Treatment," James Symons; "The Age of Trace Contaminants," Michael J. McGuire, *WATER/Engineering and Management*, February 1981; *Trihalomethanes in Drinking Water*, American Water Works Association, Denver, 1980

172 "The Safe Drinking Water Act was signed into law": Public Law 93–55, December 14, 1974

172 " 'serious implications for the water supply industry' ": See "Opening Remarks," R. B. Hilbert, *Proceedings, AWWA 95th Annual Conference*, American Water Works Association, Denver, 1975

173 "A major spill of carbon tetrachloride": "Carbon Tetrachloride Contamination of the Ohio River: A Case Study of Federal Efforts to Insure the Availability of Safe Drinking Water," report by the Subcommittee on Oversight and Investigations of the Committee on Interstate and Foreign Commerce, 95th Congress, 1st Session, September 1977

173–174 " 'When we set out to do the research' ": Interview with Richard Miller (1986); see also "Cincinnati Research in Organics," Charles Bolton

174 "The costs would be considerable": "Design of the GAC Treatment Facility at Cincinnati," Garret P. Westerhoff and Richard Miller, *Journal of the Amer-*

ican Water Works Association, April 1986; "Feasibility Study of Granular Activated Carbon Adsorption and On-Site Regeneration," 2 Volumes, Richard Miller and David J. Hartman, Cincinnati, 1982

174–175 "EPA's eighty-city survey discovered": *Final Community Water Supply Survey*, Environmental Protection Agency, 1981

175 "Coalition for Safe Drinking Water": Interviews with Foster Burba (1986); Jacqueline Warren (1986); "A History of the Attempted Federal Regulation Requiring GAC Adsorption for Water Treatment," James Symons

175 " 'pseudo-science' ": Interview with Foster Burba

175 " 'The best solution' ": Cited in *Troubled Water*, Jonathan King, Emmaus, Pennsylvania, 1985

176 " 'took place outside the public eye' ": Interview with Jacqueline Warren

176 " 'bankrupt the treasury' ": Author's notes, comments by Michael McGuire, Special Committee on Water Quality, Metropolitan Water District, April 9, 1987; see also "Safe Drinking Water Issues—What the Water Utility Manager Can Do," Joseph Goss, *Journal of the American Water Works Association*, February 1976

177 "But even those water agencies": See "Optimization and Economic Evaluation of Granular Activated Carbon for Organic Removal," 4th Quarter Progress Report (July 16, 1987–October 15,1987), Metropolitan Water District; "AWWARF Trihalomethane Survey," Michael J. McGuire and Robert G. Meadow, *Journal of the American Water Works Association*, January 1988

177 "More than 80 percent of the country's water systems": See *The Quest for Pure Water*, Volume II, compiled by Michael J. Taras, American Water Works Association, 1981

178 "Then, in December 1979, the Aerojet Corporation": See *Final Community Relations Plan, San Gabriel Sites, Los Angeles County, California*, Environmental Protection Agency, San Francisco, 1984

178 "TCE is a solvent": See *Serious Reduction of Hazardous Waste: For Pollution Prevention and Industrial Efficiency*, Office of Technology Assessment, OTA-ITE-317, Washington, D.C., September 1986; "Chlorinated Solvents: Market Interactions and Regulations," Katy Wolf and Thomas W. Chesnutt, *Journal of Hazardous Materials*, 15, Amsterdam, 1987

178 "EPA established for TCE": "National Primary Drinking Water Regulations: Volatile Synthetic Organic Chemicals," Environmental Protection Agency, *Federal Register*, July 8, 1987

179 "Hundreds of wells were shut down": "Water, Water Everywhere," Jacqueline Warren, *Amicus Journal*, Vol. 3, No. 1, Summer, 1981

180 "the Department of Health Services was directed": *Organic Chemical Contamination of Large Public Water Systems in California*, California Department of Health Services, Sacramento, April 1986

180 " 'a significant and widespread problem' ": "Federal and State Efforts to Protect Groundwater," U.S. General Accounting Office, GAO/RCED 84–80, February 21, 1984; "Groundwater Contamination in the United States," Environmental Assessment Council, Academy of Natural Sciences, Council on Environmental Quality, 1981; "Contamination of Groundwater by Toxic Organic Chemicals," Council on Environmental Quality, 1981

181 " 'as a complaint center' ": "Revisions in Cancer Policy," Eliot Marshall, *Science*, April 1, 1983

181 " 'good science' ": "Revisions in Cancer Policy," Eliot Marshall; *Beauty, Health, and Permanence*, Samuel Hays

182 " 'And see,' Hawkins told his audience": Interview with Howard Hawkins

183 " 'chemophobia' ": "Ranking Possible Carcinogenic Hazards," Bruce N. Ames, Renae Magaw, Lois Swirsky Gold

183 "Ames's argument was based": "Ranking Possible Carcinogenic Hazards," Bruce N. Ames, Renae Magaw, Lois Swirsky Gold, *Science*, April 17, 1987; "Caveat," Bruce Ames, *ACWA News*, October 19, 1987; "Testimony of Bruce N. Ames," California Senate Committee on Toxics and Public Safety Management, November 11, 1985; see also "Prediction of Chemical Carcinogenicity in Rodents from in Vitro Genetic Toxicity Assays," Raymond Tennant et al., *Science*, May 22, 1987

183 "Ames became a favorite speaker": For example, several water agencies reprinted Ames's articles or opinion pieces for newspapers, including the Metropolitan Water District, which printed two hundred and fifty thousand copies of one *Los Angeles Times* article by Ames. See Letter from the General Manager to all Directors and Member Public Agencies, Metropolitan Water District, June 30, 1986

183–184 "Following Ames's lead": See "Cancer Paranoia vs. Common Sense," Elizabeth M. Whelan, *Los Angeles Times*, October 14, 1985; "The Environmental Snowball: DDT, EDB, PCB and Love Canal," Jay H. Lehr, *Water Well Journal*, March 1986

184 " 'Who should bear the burden?' ": *Silicon Valley Toxic News*, Summer, 1987, Vol. 5, No. 2; see also "Drinking Water and Public Health: Policies and Principles for Ensuring Safe Drinking Water," Health Officers Association of California, Sacramento, 1985

185 " 'adversaries in this battle' ": Testimony by Bruce Young, cited in *Epidemic and the Children of Woburn, Mass.*, Paula diPierna, St. Louis, 1987

185 "in a 1986 out-of-court settlement": *Los Angeles Times*, September 23, 1986; see also *New York Times*, July 29, 1986

186 "reluctantly signed into law by President Reagan": *Safe Drinking Water Amendments of 1986*, Public Law 99-339, June 19, 1986

186 "EPA . . . indicated to the water industry": "Regulating Organics: An Interview with Michael Cook, EPA," *Journal of the American Water Works Association*, January 1987

186 " 'support additional controls' ": See "Changing Views of Water Quality," Anne T. Thomas, presented at the fall conference of the Association of California Water Agencies, Lake Tahoe, October 16, 1986

186 "water industry was 'overreacting' ": Comments by John De Vito at California Water Resources Association Winter Conference, Palm Springs, November 21, 1986

187 "In March 1985, the California Assembly Office of Research": *The Leaching Fields: A Nonpoint Threat to Groundwater*, Assembly Office of Research, 064-A, Sacramento, 1985

187 "the two small farming towns of McFarland and Fowler": *Los Angeles Times*, October 17, 1987; November 19, 1987; December 1, 1987

187 "Nitrate contamination": "Water Quality Trends in the Nation's Rivers," Richard A. Smith, Richard B. Alexander, M. Gordon Wolman, *Science*, March 27, 1987; *U.S. Water News*, August 1986; January 1987

188 "The growing use of pesticides": See "Pesticides, Insects in Foods, and Cosmetic Standards," *BioScience*, Vol. 27, No. 3, March 1977; "Hooked on Pesticides," Bob Gottlieb and Peter Wiley, *St. Louis Post-Dispatch*, April 21, 1984; "America's Pesticide-Permeated Food," Anne Montgomery, *Nutrition Action*, Vol. 14, No. 5, June 1987

188 "the center-pivot spray frequently includes a mix": *It's Not All Sunshine and Fresh Air: Chronic Health Effects of Modern Farming Practices*, Center for Rural Affairs, Walthill, Nebraska, 1985; Interview with Michael Dennis (1986)

189 " 'It's got to a point' ": Cited in "Stopping the Pesticide Treadmill," California Agrarian Action Project, Davis, 1981

189 "The banning of DBCP": "Testicular Function in DBCP Exposed Pesticide Workers," Donald Wharton et al., *Journal of Occupational Medicine*, Vol. 21, No. 3, March 1979

190 "In 1976, FDA investigators accidentally discovered": "Faking It: The Case Against Industrial Bio-Test Laboratories," Keith Schneider, *Amicus Journal*, Spring, 1983; "Comments of the Natural Resources Defense Council on the Environmental Protection Agency's Summary of the IBT Review Program," Lawrie Mott and Simon Frankel, San Francisco, July 11, 1983

190 "In states as diverse as Hawaii and Kansas": See "Honolulu's Unique Ground-water Sources," *Journal of the American Water Works Association*, June 1984; August 1984; *National Water Line*, April 1987; January 1987; *Christian Science Monitor*, March 23, 1987

191 "a groundwater pollutant study in Kern County": Interviews with Stuart Pyle; John Means (1986); Michael Rector (1986); Flore Korn (1987); Pauline Larwood (1986); *Groundwater Pollutant Study: San Joaquin Valley Basin, Kern County, California*, Kern County Health Department, 1980; *Groundwater Quality Report: San Joaquin Valley, Kern County, California*, Groundwater Pollutant Study Review Committee, in Cooperation with the Kern County Health Department and the Kern County Water Agency, 1982

193 "Within just a decade, per capita consumption of bottled water": "Annual Industry Survey: 1985," Beverage Marketing Corporation, New York; "Beverage Data Bank," Beverage Marketing Corporation, New York, 1985; "Beverage Market Index," *Beverage World*, May 1987

193 " 'a play on the pollution industry' ": Interview with Larry Hickey (1987); see also *New York Times*, May 25, 1986

193 "The expansion of the industry also reflected a change": Interview with William Deal (1987); *New York Times*, May 25, 1986

194 "As early as the 1880s": "Triumph and Failure: The American Response to the Urban Water Supply Problem: 1860–1923," Stuart Galishoff

194 "there have been a number of abuses": See *Bottled Water and Vended Water: Are Consumers Getting Their Money's Worth?* California Assembly Office of Research, 061-A, Sacramento, 1985; *Bottled Water and Vended Water: Industry Responds*, International Bottled Water Association, Alexandria, Virgina, n.d.; *Los Angeles Times*, October 30, 1987; April 20, 1979; *San Diego Union*, May 5, 1987; *Sacramento Bee*, September 14, 1986

195 " 'might erode the mystique' ": "Mineral Water Could Drown in Regulation," *Business Week*, June 11, 1979

195 " 'well below the levels found in decaffeinated coffee' ": *Long Beach Independent Press Telegram*, June 14, 1987; see also *Los Angeles Times*, September 20, 1986

195 "compounded by recent scientific studies": See "The Role of Skin Absorption as a Route of Exposure for Volatile Organic Compounds (VOCs) in Drinking Water," Halina Szejnwald Brown, Donna R. Bishop, and Carol A. Rowan, *American Journal of Public Health*, Vol. 74, No. 5, May 1984; "Volatilization of Organic Chemicals from Indoor Uses of Water," Julian B. Andelman, Steven M. Meyets, and Lynn C. Wilder, in *Chemicals in the Environment*, J. N. Lester et al. (editors), London, 1986; "Inhalation Exposure in the Home to Volatile

Organic Contaminants of Drinking Water," Julian Andelman, *The Science of the Total Environment*, Amsterdam, 47, 1985

196 "A *Los Angeles Times* poll suggested": *Los Angeles Times*, September 20, 1986

196 "if people 'can afford it' ": *Los Angles Times*, September 20, 1986

196 "Water quality advocates, on the other hand": See *New York Times*, August 31, 1981; "The Selling of H2O," *Consumer Reports*, September 1980

197 "the solution of the marketplace": Author's notes, comments by Michael McGuire and William Dahlmann at a meeting on the bottled-water industry, Southern California Water Conference, Los Angeles Chamber of Commerce, June 16, 1986

CHAPTER 6

199 " 'We need a balance' ": Author's notes, comments by Robert Redford, "Water in the West: Understanding the New Era" conference, October 18, 1985

200 " 'New winds are already blowing' ": See "Water in the West: Understanding the New Era," Symposium Background Paper Prepared by Jim Butler for the Institute for Resource Management, Sundance, Utah, 1985

201 " 'Is it the nature of the issue?' ": Interview with Lee Kapiloski (1986)

204 "There shall be no private ownership": Cited in *Great Basin Kingdom: Economic History of the Latter-Day Saints, 1830–1900*, Leonard J. Arrington, Lincoln, 1966

204 "The utopian character of the Mormon settlement": *Building the City of God: Community and Cooperation Among the Mormons*, Leonard J. Arrington, Feramorz Y. Fox, and Dean L. May, Salt Lake City, 1976; *America's Saints: The Rise of Mormon Power*, Robert Gottlieb and Peter Wiley

205 "The preservationist perspective, best embodied": *John Muir and His Legacy: The American Conservation Movement*, Stephen Fox

206 "conservationist ideas came to be associated": *Breaking New Ground*, Gifford Pinchot, New York, 1947

207 " 'to save resources from use' ": Cited in *Conservation and the Gospel of Efficiency*, Samuel Hays

208 "Under Franklin Roosevelt and Secretary of Interior Harold Ickes": See *The Autobiography of a Curmudgeon*, Harold Ickes, New York, 1943

210 "an 'ecotopia' ": *Ecotopia: The Notebooks and Reports of William Weston*, Ernest Callenbach, Berkeley, 1975

210   " 'Green' became the symbol of this new politics": "A New Environmental Politics," Margaret FitzSimmons and Robert Gottlieb, in *The Year Left*, Volume 3, Mike Davis (editor), New York (forthcoming)

210   "During the Nixon and Ford years": See *Striking a Balance: Environment and Natural Resources in the Nixon-Ford Years*, John Whitaker

211   "One important new organization, the Environmental Policy Center": "Environmental Policy Institute, 15th Anniversary Report," Environmental Policy Institute, Washington, D.C., 1987; Interviews with Louise Dunlap, Brent Blackwelder, Joseph Browder (with Peter Wiley), (1980)

212   "major industrial interests, led by the Business Roundtable and the Western Regional Council": See Author's notes from discussions and presentations at "The Future of the American West: A Vision of the '80s," Third Annual Meeting, The Western Regional Council, Phoenix, November 29–December 1, 1979

213   "RFF published a series of books and monographs": See *Attainment of Efficiency in Satisfying Demands for Water Resources*, Irving K. Fox and Orris C. Herfindahl, Resources for the Future, 1964; *Environmental Improvement through Economic Incentives*, Frederick Anderson et al., Resources for the Future, 1977; *Getting the Most out of Resources*, Irving K. Fox and Henry P. Caulfield, Jr., Resources for the Future, 1961; *Multiple Purpose River Developments: Studies in Applied Economic Analysis*, John V. Krutills and Otto Eckstein, Resources for the Future, 1958

213   "The EDF position, as it evolved": *Los Angeles Times*, February 5, 1984; Interview with Tom Graff (1981, 1985); "What Happens When the Well Runs Dry?" Robert Gottlieb (1981); "Graff: PERC Challenges Mythology," *PERC Reports*, Vol. 2, No. 2, July 1984

214   "wrote approvingly in the *Wall Street Journal*": *Wall Street Journal*, September 30, 1983

214   "the 'conservationist-conservative alliance' ": *Los Angeles Times*, June 13, 1982; see also "Environmental Quality, Water Marketing, and the Public Trust: Can They Coexist?" Tom Graff, Presentation at a Political Economy Research Center Symposium, Bozeman, May 17, 1986

214   " 'absence of private property rights' ": Comments by Roger Sedjo from congressional staffer's conference, Political Economy Research Center, December 1986, cited in *PERC Reports*, Summer, 1987

215   "EDF had modified that criticism": See "Potential Areas of Cooperation Between Environmentalists and Water Developers in California," Testimony of Thomas Graff before the California Water Commission, San Francisco, April 12, 1985; also, "Memorandum of Understanding between Berrenda Mesa Water District and the Environmental Defense Fund," July 9, 1987; "Pilot Study on

Source Reduction of Toxic Substances," Letter from the General Manager to the Board of Directors, Metropolitan Water District, December 1, 1986

215 "a 'third stage of environmental advocacy' ": "New Environmentalism Factors in Economic Needs," Frederic Krupp, *Wall Street Journal*, November 20, 1986

215 "The fear of being tagged an obstructionist": See the Sierra Club Papers, Bancroft Library, University of California, Berkeley

216 " 'to do the job that the water agencies' ": Discussion with Tom Graff (1987)

216 "Figures like Harris Sherman and Joseph Browder": Conversations with Harris Sherman and Joseph Browder (1985)

216 "or 'chief executive officers' as one environmental document called them": *An Environmental Agenda for the Future*, Washington, D.C., 1985

217 " 'We're looking for a person' ": Cited in *Los Angeles Times*, December 27, 1984

217 "one of the leading environmental lobbyists": Interviews with Mike Clark (1987); Peter Carlson (1987); "15th Anniversary Report," Environmental Policy Institute

217 "In the Kesterson situation": Interviews with Don Villarejo; Elizabeth Martin (1987); George Ballis (1985)

218 "And, with the MWD source reduction study": Discussions with Patti Prickett (1987)

218 " 'to do for us what we couldn't do without them' ": Conversation with Jerald Butchert and Carl Boronkay, Annual Meeting of the National Water Resources Association, San Diego, December 3, 1986; see also "California Water Agreement Shows Progress is Possible," Ron Khachigian and Tom Graff, *Orange County Register*, August 23, 1987

219 " 'Water is part of living' ": Cited in *Water and Poverty in the Southwest: Conflict, Opportunity, and Challenge*, F. Lee Brown and Helen Ingram, Tucson, 1987

219 " 'which arise upon, border, traverse, or underlie a reservation' ": *Winters v. United States*, 207 U.S. 564 (1908)

220 "proceeded without Indian participation": See "Indian Water Rights in Theory and Practice: Navajo Experience in the Colorado River Basin," Monroe E. Price and Gary D. Weatherford, *Law and Contemporary Problems*, Vol. 40, No. 1, Winter, 1976; *Water and the West: The Colorado River Compact and the Politics of Water in the American West*, Norris Hundley, Berkeley, 1975

220 " 'practically irrigable acreage' ": *Arizona v. California*, 373 U.S. 546, 555 (1963)

221 "The quandary for the Indian tribes": "The Mirage of Definitive Solutions to the Problem of Indian Reserved Water Rights," Charles DuMars and Helen Ingram, *Natural Resources Journal*

222 " 'By selling the water' ": Cited in "Cultural Differences and the Political Economy of Water in the United States West," Joanna L. Endter, Presented at the Western Social Science Association, El Paso, April 1987

223 "The Chandler syndicate controlled 860,000 acres": *Thinking Big: The Story of the Los Angeles Times*, Robert Gottlieb and Irene Wolt; *The Desert Revolution: Baja California, 1911*, Lowell Blaisdell, Madison, 1962; "United States Interests in Lower California," Eugene Keith Chamberlin, Ph.D., University of California, Berkeley, 1949

223 "Chandler's *Los Angeles Times*, meanwhile, became a major opponent": *Los Angeles Times*; "Imperial Valley's Most Essential Need Is a Flood Control and Storage Dam in the Colorado River," Harry Chandler, in Harry Chandler Papers, Sherman Foundation, n.d.

224 "This water industry reluctance": See *Dividing the Waters: A Century of Controversy Between the United States and Mexico*, Norris Hundley, Berkeley, 1966

224 "Within five years, 50 percent of the Mexicali Valley": See "An Excess of a Scarce Resource: Flooding of the Colorado River and the Rules of Crisis Creation and Management," Scott Whiteford, Laura Montgomery, Jesus Roman, presented at the meeting of ANUIES and PROFMEX, Tijuana, 1983

225 "the problems emerged with a vengeance": Interviews with Richard Balzersak (1983); William Plummer (1983); *Los Angeles Times*, June 28, 1983; June 29, 1983; June 25, 1983; August 1, 1983; *Desert Star* (Needles, California), June 29, 1983; *Arizona Republic*, June 23, 1983; *Long Beach Independent Press-Telegram*, June 24, 1983

226 " 'far more than just a means of water distribution' ": Cited in *Water and Poverty*, F. Lee Brown and Helen Ingram

226 "The key to the New Mexico water industry": *Patterns of Politics in Water Resource Development*, Helen Ingram; *Water in New Mexico: A History of Its Management and Use*, Ira G. Clark, Albuquerque, 1987

227 "spelled out in John Nichols's novel": *The Milagro Beanfield War*, John Nichols, New York, 1974

227 " 'a political and economic commodity' ": Cited in *Water and Poverty*, F. Lee Brown and Helen Ingram

229 "He became one of the most insightful analysts": *The Education of Carey McWilliams*, Carey McWilliams, New York, 1978; *Factories in the Field*, Carey McWilliams; *California: The Great Exception*, Carey McWilliams, New York, 1949; Interviews with Carey McWilliams (1975); Robert W. Kenney (1975)

229 "an equally disliked and targeted opponent": "Paul Taylor: The Power of a Tenacious Man," Mary Ellen Leary, *The Nation*, October 12, 1974; "Reclamation: The Rise and Fall of an American Idea," Paul Taylor, *American West*, Vol. 7. No. 4, July 1970; "Water, Land, and People in the Great Valley," Paul Taylor, *American West*, Vol. 5, No. 2, March 1968; "Water, Land, and Environment—Imperial Valley: Caught in the Winds of Politics," Paul Taylor, *Natural Resources Journal*

230 "This perspective formed the backdrop": *As You Sow: Three Studies in the Social Consequences of Agribusiness*, Walter Goldschmidt, Montclair, New Jersey, 1947

230 "One of Taylor's students": See "Flouting the Reclamation Act," Stanley Poss, *The Nation*, November 15, 1975; Interview with George Ballis

230 "One study undertaken in the mid-1980s": *How Much Is Enough: Federal Water Subsidies and Agriculture in California's Central Valley*, Don Villarejo

231 " 'It was like a revelation' ": Interview with Don Villarejo, 1987; see also "CAAP Founders Recall How It Was," Kelly Gould, *Agrarian Advocate*, Summer, 1987

232 "the Center for Rural Affairs was part": See A *Newsletter Surveying Events Affecting Rural Nebraska*, Center for Rural Affairs, Walthill, Nebraska, August 1987; "Integrating Equity into Ground Water Policy," Small Farm Resources Project, Center for Rural Affairs, 1986; *Who's Who in Nebraska Water Policy*, Steve Hopkins, Center for Rural Affairs, 1987; "Changes in Farming in Nebraska: The Role of Center Pivot Irrigation," Small Farm Resources Project, Center for Rural Affairs, Hartington, Nebraska, 1985; Interview with Ron Krupicka (1987); *General Plan* (1986–87), Center for Rural Affairs

233 " 'there is also a social mortgage' ": *Report on the High Plains Study*, Working Group on the Ogallala Aquifer of the Missouri Basin–Great Plains Caucus, October 1982, Walthill, Nebraska

233 "in 1982, Nebraska voters passed": *New York Times*, September 7, 1986

234–235 "most notably the League of Women Voters": See *The Big Water Fight: Trials and Triumphs in Citizen Action on Problems of Supply, Pollution, Floods, and Planning Across the United States*, League of Women Voters, Brattleboro, Vermont, 1966

235 "In 1981, Lois Gibbs, the housewife": *Five Years of Progress: 1981–1986*, Citizen's Clearinghouse for Toxic Waste, Fifth Anniversary Convention book, Arlington, Virginia, 1986; Interview with Will Collette (1987)

236 "The 'acid pits' of Stringfellow": "Engineering Case Study of the Stringfellow Superfund Site," G. J. Trezek, prepared for the Office of Technology Assessment, August 1984; *Santa Ana Register*, August 26, 1984; *Los Angeles Times*,

June 6, 1987; August 7, 1984; June 16, 1983; January 15, 1984; Interview with Penny Newman (1987)

239 " 'resulting from the migration of toxic wastes' ": "Engineering Case Study of Stringfellow Superfund Site," G. J. Trezek; see also *Riverside Press Enterprise,* September 5, 1984

239 "immediately mobilized to attack Trezek": See "Stringfellow Toxic Waste Dump," letter from Carl Boronkay to the author, November 8,1984; Interview with Penny Newman

239 " 'The mere fact that my small community' ": "Interview with Penny Newman

240 "When Trezek did a followup report": "Cleanup Strategies for the String-fellow Site," G. J. Trezek, prepared for the Office of Technology Assessment, April 1987

CHAPTER 7

243 "When the measure first came to the attention of the MET": "Safe Drinking Water and Toxics Enforcement Act Initiative," Letter from the General Manager to the Board of Directors, Metropolitan Water District, September 24, 1986; Interview with David Roe (1986)

244 " 'I recently received a letter' ": Author's notes, comments by E. Thornton Ibbetson, Special Committee on Water Quality, Metropolitan Water District, August 9, 1986; Letter from E. C. Giermann, Corporate Counsel, J. G. Boswell Company to "Ibbey" Ibbetson, August 7, 1986

245 "Business interests had already contributed": *Los Angeles Times,* October 15, 1986; November 10–14, 1986; *Legislative Agenda,* Sierra Club, Vol. 8, No. 19, August 15, 1986

245 " 'If we oppose Prop 65' ": Comments by Ray Corley, Annual Retreat, Board of Directors, Metropolitan Water District, September 17, 1986

245 "This fact was noted": Letter from Michael Belliveau to Metropolitan Water District Board of Directors Regarding: "Potential Conflict of Interest Involving MWO Director E. L. Balmer," October 7, 1986

245 "The agricultural agencies, on the other hand": *Valley Grower,* Fall, 1986; *California Farmer,* October 4, 1986

247 "These agencies are the mainstay": See *Prospects for Accountability and Innovation in Six Public Water Agencies,* Robert Gottlieb and Margaret FitzSimmons

249 "In Onandaga County": *The Big Water Fight,* League of Women Voters

249 "the press helped define water issues": See "Reclaiming the Reclamation Beat," Roger Morris, *Columbia Journalism Review*, March/April, 1986; see also, "The Politics of Information: Constraints on New Sources," Helen Ingram in *Water Politics and Public Involvement*, John C. Pierce and Harvey P. Doerksen (editors), Ann Arbor, 1976

250 " 'The water industry is managed mostly' ": "The Necessity and Importance of Changing the Water-Utility Image," Clark Casken, *Journal of the American Water Works Association*, February 1975

250 " 'Public involvement' firms": Interview with Gene Lundquist; *Riverside Press Enterprise*, August 27, 1987

251 " 'Citizens of the 1970s' ": "Financing Water Development Programs in an Ecological Age," James L. Ogilvie, *Journal of the American Water Works Association*, February 1976

251 " 'It's like a safety program' ": Author's notes, presentation by James L. Creighton, California Municipal Utilities Association convention, Monterey, February 26, 1987

253 "Environmental mediators": See "Metropolitan Water Roundtable Formed to Build Consensus on Meeting Denver's Long-term Water Needs," *Resolve*, The Conservation Foundation, Summer, 1982; Author's notes, presentations by John Huyler and Joan Kovalic, "Water in the West" conference, October 19, 1985

254 " 'In the past, these prices have included' ": Letter from Wayne Marchant to Steve Lanich, July 13, 1987; see also Letter from Wayne Marchant to Senator Bennett Johnston, July 13, 1987; see also Letter from George S. Dunlop, Assistant Secretary Natural Resources and Environment, Department of Agriculture, to Peter Carlson, July 1, 1987 and July 8, 1987

255 "Many of the initial rate structures": *Municipal Water Systems*, David Holtz and Scott Sebastian (editors), Bloomington, 1978; *Water for the Cities*, Nelson Blake; *Water Rates*, American Water Works Association, AWWA Manual M1, 1972

255 "The rate problem has been further compounded": "Water Rates: An Assessment of Current Issues," Steve H. Hanke, *Journal of the American Water Works Association*, May 1975

256 "the 'inner city' of Los Angeles": "Ramifications of the City Withdrawing from the Metropolitan Water District," Keith Comrie, City Administrative Officer, report to the Energy and Natural Resources Committee, Los Angeles City Council, September 9, 1982; *Los Angeles Herald-Examiner*, February 25, 1982

257 "Once the federal monies became available": See "Dirty Water: A Federal Failure," Patrick Tyler, *Washington Post*, May 10–14, 1981

258   "Parsons, in particular": "Historical Highlights," The Parsons Corporation, 1978; "Annual Report," The Parsons Corporation, 1985; Interviews with Robert Davidson; Melvyn Brown; Kline Barney, Jr. (1986); Dennis D. Parker (1986), *Los Angeles Times*, February 10, 1980

258   "Its one major effort to devise a water plan": Interview with Nathan Snyder (1980)

259   " 'Some of this type of work' ": Interview with Robert Davidson

259   "Chandler was a fast-growing community": "An Engineer's View of Privatization: The Chandler Experience," Garret P. Westerhoff, *Journal of the American Water Works Association*, February 1986

259   "The Reagan administration continued to push the idea": "Reagan's Budget: Selling off the Government," Lee Smith, *Fortune*, March 3, 1986; "New Reagan Privatization Concept: Industry Input Needed," Frank Sellers, *The Privatization Review*, Vol. 2, No. 3, Summer, 1986

260   "The AWWA editors contrasted the private companies": "Privatization: Trend of the Future: Theme Introduction," *Journal of the American Water Works Association*, February 1986

260   "the privatization effort was also plagued by problems": "Questions shroud privatization," John J. Kosowatz and Barbara Lamb, *Engineering News-Record*, January 9, 1986

261   "Parsons, for example, had made a proposal": *Pasadena Star-News*, September 7, 1986

262   "This 'theft' of the water and 'rape' of Owens Valley": See *Los Angeles*, Morrow Mayo, New York, 1933

262   "There was a brief flurry of water market activity": See "Reallocating Water in the West," Gary Weatherford and Steven J. Shupe, *Journal of the American Water Works Association*, October 1986

263   "There were schemes": See *The Coming Water Famine*, Jim Wright, New York, 1966; *The Water Crisis*, Frank E. Moss, New York, 1967; *Interbasin Transfers of Water: Economic Issues and Impacts*, Charles W. Howe and K. William Easter, Resources for the Future, Washington, D.C., 1971

263   " 'consideration of the question that would dominate the decision' ": *Water Policies for the Future*, National Water Commission

264   "in the process they failed to address": See "Information and the Role of the Analyst in Contemporary Water Transfers," Susan C. Nunn and Helen Ingram, *Water Resources Research* (forthcoming)

264   "These conservative opponents of water development": See *Water Crisis: Ending the Policy Drought*, Terry Anderson, Baltimore, 1983; "Selling Water Rights Will End Shortages," Richard Stroup, *San Francisco Chronicle*, May

15, 1987; "Water Marketing: An Idea Whose Time Has Come," Terry Anderson, Presented at a Congressional Research Service Seminar, March 12, 1987

265 "In 1982, the Supreme Court ruled": *Sporhase* v. *Nebraska*, 458 US 941 (1982)

265 "The Western Governors' Association issued a policy document": "Western Water: Tuning the System," Report to the Western Governor's Association from the Water Efficiency Task Force, Denver, 1986

265 "a group was organized to purchase water rights": *Water Market Update*, Vol.1, No.1, January 1987

266 "In late December 1986, Phoenix purchased fourteen thousand acres": *Arizona Republic*, December 24, 1986

267 " 'We get into situations' ": Presentation by Eric Rasmussen at "Water Transfers and the Quality of Rural Life," conference held at Casa Grande, Arizona, April 8, 1987

267 "The Phoenix purchase greatly affected": See "Water Transfers and the Quality of Life" conference; *Water Strategist*, Vol. 1, No. 3, October 1987; *Parker Pioneer*, December 24, 1986; *Arizona Republic*, September 1, 1987

267 "The Phoenix sale brought to a head": *Parker Pioneer*, June 3, 1987

268 " 'Arizona cities should harbor no guilt' ": Cited in *Arizona Republic*, October 18, 1987

269 "This two-tier structure of wealth and poverty": See "Report on the Structure of Agriculture and Impacts of New Technologies on Rural Communities in Arizona, California, Florida, and Texas," Dean MacCannell and Edward Dolber-Smith, prepared for the Office of Technology Assessment, 1985; *Technology, Public Policy, and the Changing Structure of American Agriculture*, Office of Technology Assessment, OTA-F-285, March 1986

270 " 'supplying capital for large new water projects' ": "Western Water: Tuning the System," Water Efficiency Task Force

270 "At one point, Joseph Findaro": See Joseph T. Findaro to Thomas S. Levy, August 5, 1986; *Brawley News*, October 8, 1986

271 " 'any clearly established Bureau of Reclamation policy' ": "Voluntary Transfers of Federally Supplied Water: Experiences of the Bureau of Reclamation," Richard W. Wahl, in *Water Marketing: Opportunities and Challenges of a New Era*, Steven J. Shupe (editor), Denver, 1986

271 " 'enlightened environmentalism' ": Cited in "What Would Make Water Marketing Work," Antoinette LaForce, *California Farmer*, October 4, 1986

271 " 'Water marketing in its simplest form' ": *California Farmer*, October 4, 1986

271 "when the BuRec attempted to sell": *The Water Coalition Newsletter*, July 1987; see John Krautkraemer and Hamilton Candee to Raymond Walsh, February 13, 1987; April 17, 1987

272 "a series of stock phrases": See "Community Values in Southwest Water Management," Stephen Mumme and Helen Ingram, *Policy Studies Review*, Vol. 5, No. 2, November 1985

273 "McPhee saw this encounter": *Encounters with the Archdruid*, John McPhee, New York, 1971

273 " 'I see a certain beauty' ": Interview with John Lauten

273 "Popular novels, such as Edward Abbey's": *The Monkey Wrench Gang*, Edward Abbey, Philadelphia, 1975

274 "Below the streak they wrote": *Los Angeles Times*, May 23, 1987

274 "The Hodel scheme": *Los Angeles Times*, August 8–11, 1987; "Undamming Hetch-Hetchy," Carl Pope, *Sierra*, Nov.–Dec. 1987

275 "entered mainstream detective fiction": See "Crime in Every Hamlet," Marilyn Stasie, *New York Times Book Review*, August 2, 1987; *Dancing Bear*, James Crumley, New York, 1983; *Ground Money*, Rex Burns, New York, 1986; *Skinwalkers*, Tony Hillerman, London, 1986; *Fish Story: A John Denson Mystery*, Richard Hoyt, New York, 1985

276 " 'enough for him just to know' ": *Encounters with the Archdruid*, John McPhee

277 " 'Drought in the West is as certain' ": Cited in "Community Values in Southwest Water Management," Stephen Mumme and Helen Ingram

277 " 'Pray for rain' became in this setting": *Los Angeles Herald-Examiner*, October 10, 1983

278 " 'We have been saying' ": Author's notes, comments by Burton Jones, Board of Directors Meeting, Metropolitan Water District, October 14, 1986

280 " 'All I really need is a song in my heart' ": "All I Really Need," D. Raffi, B. Pike, and B. Simpson (words); copyright, Homeland Publishing (CAPAC); from the United Nations *Rights of the Child*

Index

Abbey, Edward, 273–74
ABS (Alkyl benzene sulfonate), 166
Accountability, 218, 280
Acequias, 226
"Acid pits" (Stringfellow, CA), 236–40
Acreage restrictions, 208; and Kern Co. landowners, 8, 9; and BuRec, 45–46, 49–51, 83; evasion of, 51, 87, 93, 96, 110; and land concentration, 230–31. *See also* "Practically irrigable acreage"
"Acre foot," 6n
Aerojet Corporation, 178, 181
Aflatoxin mold, 183–84
Agribusiness, 75–103; defined, 80; disparity between rich and poor in, 89, 102–3, 269. *See also* Land ownership patterns
Agricultural Chemical Use Council, 191
Agriculture: growth of, and the water industry, xv, 67–68; decline in, 73–74, 111; disparity between rich and poor in, 89, 102–3, 269; lobby for, 90–94. *See also* Acreage restrictions; Agribusiness; Center pivots; Contamination: agricultural; Export markets; Farms; Farm workers; Irrigated agriculture; Land ownership patterns; Overproduction; Pesticides; Surplus crops

Albuquerque (NM), xv, 227
Aldicarb (insecticide), 190
Alkyl benzene sulfonate (ABS), 166
All-American Canal, 96–97, 223
Allen, Howard, 200
American Ecology (company), 258
American Iron and Steel Institute, 163
American Petroleum Institute, 163
American Rivers Conservation Council, 60
American Water Works Association (AWWA), 165, 168, 172, 175, 260
Ames, Bruce, 182–83
Anderson, Terry, 214, 264
Andrus, Cecil, 64
Animas-La Plata Project (CO), 55, 67, 220
Annexation battles: in California, 125–28, 130. *See also* Denver
Aqueduct: for Los Angeles, 124–27, 262; for San Diego, 129
Arizona. *See* Central Arizona Project; *Names of Arizona cities*
Army Corps of Engineers: and Gianelli, xvii, 9; role of, in water development, xviii, 37, 40–43, 46–49, 58, 252; and environmental issues, 59–62, 134, 162, 206, 233; during Reagan administration, 65–66, 68, 72–73, 150;

320

and Indian claims, 220; and the press, 64, 249–50
Arthur Kill area: pollution in, 165
As You Sow (Goldschmidt), 230
Asbestos fibers: in drinking water, 169
Ashland Oil: spill by, 197–98
Aspinall, Wayne, 55, 90
Associated Farmers, 229
Association of National Water Utilities, 248
Audobon Society, 210
Aurora (CO), 138, 140, 142
AWWA. *See* American Water Works Association

B of A (Bank of America), 75–79, 84
Babbitt, Bruce, 133, 201
Baden, John, 264
Ballis, George, 217, 230–31
Balmer, E. L. ("Les"), 245
Baltimore (MD), 118
Bank of America, 75–79, 84
Bay Delta. *See* Sacramento Bay Delta
Beard, Dan, 94
"Beat the Peak" campaign (Tucson), 147–48, 270
Bechtel (company), 258
Benson, John, 101
Berrenda Mesa Water District (CA), 215, 217, 269
Berry, Doyle Galloway, 131. *See also* Galloway Group
Beverly Hills (CA), 125
Blackwell Land Company, 269
Blais, Earle, 4, 13–14, 16, 23, 26, 244
Blue baby syndrome, 187–88
Blue Line policy (Denver), 137–38
Boettcher & Company, 259
Bonneville Indians. *See* Indian tribes
Boronkay, Carl, 133
Boston (MA), 121, 122, 159
Boswell Company. *See* J. G. Boswell Company
Bottled water, 174, 192–97, 278; price of, compared to filtration system, 194, 197; standards for, 194–95; statistics on use of, 196
Boulder Canyon Act, 96, 223
Bowman, Neta, 267–68
Bradley, Tom, 243

Brawley (CA), 101–2
Brecher, Edward, 170
Brick, Tim, 20, 30
Britton, George, 155–58, 196
Broadbent, Robert, 66–67, 69–70, 72
Browder, Joseph, 216
Brower, David, 54, 273, 276
Brown, Jerry, 15, 17–20, 23, 28–30, 238
Brown, Pat, 9–11, 18
Burba, Foster, 175
Bureau of Indian Affairs, 221, 222
Bureau of Reclamation, 64, 108, 200, 261; and growth of agribusiness, xviii, 37, 40–41, 44–52, 83–85, 87, 89, 90, 109, 110, 208; budgets of, 59, 65–73; and urbanization, 123, 144, 150, 208; and Mexican and Indian rights, 220–22, 224–26; and the press, 249–50; and water markets, 270–71
BuRec. *See* Bureau of Reclamation
Burford, Anne. *See* Gorsuch, Anne
Burns-Porter Act (CA), 9, 17
Burr, Aaron, 118–19
Bush, David, 144
Bush, George, 181
Business Roundtable, 23, 212
Butchert, Gerald, 218

Cabinet Council on Natural Resources, 38, 67
California: water industry in, 3–33; survey of well contamination in, 180, 187–92. *See also* Agribusiness; Land ownership patterns; Metropolitan Water District of Southern California; *Names of cities and counties*
California: The Great Exception (McWilliams), 229
California Action Network (CAN), 76, 231–33
California Agrarian Action Project, 189
California Business Roundtable, 23
California Central Valley Flood Control Association, 109
California Chamber of Commerce, 23
California Department of Health Services, 187, 188, 195, 238
California Department of Water Resources, 98

California Development Corporation, 95

California Farmer, 271

California Institute for Rural Studies, 75–76, 217

California State Water Project, xvii, 20, 32, 65, 271; and agribusiness, 6–12, 15–16, 86, 232; and annexation, 127, 128. *See also* Peripheral Canal

California Water Resources Control Board, 98, 100

CAN (California Action Network), 76, 231–33

Cancer: difficulties of proving causes of, 169; fears about, 171; risk of, 181–85; clusters of cases of, 187–88. *See also* Carcinogens; "Falling bodies" approach

CAP. *See* Central Arizona Project

Carbon tetrachloride, 173–74, 178

Carcinogens: in public water supplies, 156–57, 173, 175, 177, 195, 243. *See also* Cancer; Organic compounds; Pesticides; *Names of particular chemicals*

Carlson, Peter, 217

Carruthers, Garrey, 67, 70

Carson, Rachel, 165, 189

Carter administration, xvii; its "hit list," 63–65, 146, 211–12, 250–51

Catino, Michael, 109

CDC (California Development Corporation), 95

Center pivots, 103–8, 188, 232–34

Center for Rural Affairs, 107, 232–34

Central Arizona Project, 266; difficulties with, 39, 53–56, 64, 67, 71–73, 143–49, 211; and Indian claims, 220–21

Central Utah Project, 39, 53–54, 71–72, 211, 220

Central Valley (CA): contending water interests in, 6, 8; agriculture in, 75–79, 81. *See also* Central Valley Project

Central Valley Project (CA): and agribusiness, 6–8, 84, 86–89, 91, 93, 109, 217, 229–31; and BuRec, 45, 49–51

CH$_2$M Hill (company), 114–15, 258

Chandler, Harry, xv, 96, 223–24

Chandler (AZ), 259–60

Chase Manhattan Bank, 120

"Chemigation," 188

Chevron Corporation, 93

Chicago (IL): water industry in, xv, 121–22; contamination in, 177

Chinatown (film), 275

Chino Basin, 239–40

Chlorination (of public water supplies), 158–65, 71–72, 176. *See also* "Disinfection byproducts"

Chloroform, 238

Cincinnati (OH): water industry in, xv, 170–74

Citizen's Clearinghouse on Hazardous Wastes, 235

Citizens for a Better Environment, 245

Citizens for a Safe Drinking Water, 218

Citizens for Water, 28, 31

Clark, William, 67, 70

Clawson, Marion, 230–31

Cleanup (of public water supplies): failure of, 197; costs of, and privatization, 257–61

Clean Water Act, 41, 58, 61–62, 167, 193, 257, 260

Clean Water Act Amendments (1972), 60

Cleveland (OH), 121

Clinton, DeWitt, 118

Coalition for Safe Drinking Water, 175–76

Coelho, Tony, 90–94, 111

Colorado Big-Thompson project, 45, 50, 262

Colorado River: as MET supplier, 15, 45, 125–26, 129; and the Corps, 42–43; Bureau development of, 53, 71, 85; and the Salton Sea, 95–96; salt in, 97–98; and Arizona, 143–44; and Denver, 137; and Indians, 220; Mexican interests in, 223–26; storage levels on, 225–26; and Hispanics, 226–28

Colorado River Compact (1922), 223

Commodity exchanges, 92

Commoner, Barry, 218

Commonwealth Club, 27

Concerned Neighbors in Action, 237

Consensus Group, 4, 23

Conservation: in Tucson, 146–49
Conservationist Movement, 206–7
Construction Grants Program, 257
Consumer Reports, 170–71
Contamination: industrial, municipal, and agricultural, 159; industrial, 162–67; coastal, 167; chemical, 144–49, 162–67; agricultural, 107, 187–92; lack of cleanup strategies for, 197. *See also* Carcinogens; Dumping; Organic compounds; Water quality; *Names of contaminants*
Continental Homes, 267
Contra Costa County (CA), 20, 22, 93
Corn, 88, 105
Corn oil, 183
Corporate farming. *See* Agribusiness
Corps. *See* Army Corps of Engineers
Cost sharing, 64–72, 109, 149
Cotton production, 12, 51, 85, 88, 97
Croton (NY) Aqueduct, 120
Cuyahoga River (OH): fire on, 167
CVP. *See* Central Valley Project
CWA. *See* San Diego County Water Authority

Dale, Edwin, 68
Dallas (TX), 123
Daughters of the American Revolution, 207
Davidson, Robert, 259
Dawson, Robert, 69
DBCP (pesticide), 187–90, 232
DCCC (Democratic Congressional Campaign Committee), 92, 94
Decision-Making Inc. (DMI), 28
Del Monte peach orchard, 78–79
Delta. *See* Sacramento Bay Delta
"Delta facility," 11–12, 14–19. *See also* Peripheral Canal
Delta-Mendota canals, 50
Democratic Congressional Campaign Committee, 92, 94
Denver (CO), xv, xvi; and imported water, 121; growth of, 123; fights with suburbs over water development, 136–43, 150; water contamination in, 177; water company's public relations program in, 251
Denver Post, 141, 142, 250

Desert(s): irrigation of, 94–103; urbanization of, 143–49
Desertification: of agricultural land, 107
Desert Land Act (1877), 43, 95
Detergents, 166
Detroit (MI), 177
Deutscher, Isaac, 29
DeVito, John, 186
Diamond Bar (CA), 128
DiGiorgio (company), 50
Dinosaur National Monument, 53–54, 209
Discharge policies: and water companies, xv, 61
"Disinfection by-products," 171, 176, 186, 244
DMI (Decision-Making Inc.), 28
Dominy, Floyd, 49, 52, 59, 273
Dos Rios Dam (CA), 15
Double-dipping: and federal subsidies, 88–89, 258
Dow Chemical company, 157
Drainage: and Salton Sea, 97–98; in southern Arizona, 244. *See also* Dumping; Westlands Water District
Drinking water: public concerns about, 151, 156; industry concerns about, 158–61; bacterial contamination of, 159–61. *See also* Bottled water; Carcinogens; Chlorination; Organic compounds; Safe Drinking Water Act
Drought, 272, 277–78; in California (1976–77), 15–17, 27, 128
Dumping (of sewage and industrial wastes), 162–64, 168–69, 209, 236–40
Duvall, C. Dale, 70–72, 73
DWP. *See* Los Angeles Department of Water and Power

Echo Park Dam, 54
EDB (pesticide), 183, 190
EDF. *See* Environmental Defense Fund
Elizabethtown (NJ), 175
Elmore, John and Stephen, 98–99, 101
Ely, Northcutt, 96, 123
Empires in the Sun (Gottlieb and Wiley), xvi
Engineering News-Record, 70
Engineering Science (company), 259
Engle, Claire, 90

Engstrand, Paul, 100
Environmental Defense Fund (EDF), 63, 117; and State Water Project, 17, 98–99; history of, 209, 213–18
Environmental movement, 14–19, 150, 176, 201, 209–12, 235, 252. *See also* Grassroots organizations; *Names of specific environmental groups*
Environmental Policy Center (or Institute), 60, 63, 201, 211, 216, 217
Environmental Protection Agency (EPA), 134, 157, 257, 259; and water quality, 60–61, 167, 169–79, 184, 186, 192, 194; during Reagan administration, 180–82; and fraudulent test results, 290. *See also* Superfund
Epidemics: and polluted drinking water, 159–60
Equity concerns (about urban growth), 148, 150, 218, 253–57, 261–72
Erie Canal, 41
Erosion, 107–8
Export markets: and American agriculture, 78, 85, 94

Factories in the Field (McWilliams), 229
"Falling bodies" approach: to contaminated water allegations, 176, 185, 187
Farm(s): as land-development interests, 13–14. *See also* Agribusiness; Agriculture; Farm workers
Farm Bureau, 23, 99
"Farm management arrangements" (FMAs), 110–11
Farm workers: incomes of, 89, 102–3, 269; health problems of, 189; union activity among, 102, 229–32
FDA (Food and Drug Administration), 190
Federal Emergency Relief Appropriations Act (1935), 49
Federal government: and water. *See* Army Corps of Engineers; Bureau of Reclamation; Environmental Protection Agency; U.S. Congress; U.S. Interior Department
Federal Insecticide, Fungicide and Rodenticide Act (1972), 190

Federation of Southern Co-ops, 232
Felson, Jack, 113
Fertilizers, 107
FIFRA (Federal Insecticide, Fungicide, and Rodenticide Act), 190
Filtering systems, 160–61, 196. *See also* Granular activated carbon
Findaro, Joseph, 270
Fish and Wildlife Service, 134
Fisher, Jim, 244
Fishing interests, 26
Fish screens: Peripheral Canal, 18, 19, 21
Floods: control of, 52, 272; and Salton Sea, 98, 99; in Mexicali Valley, 225–26
FMA ("Farm management arrangements"), 110–11
FMC Corporation, 173
Food and Drug Administration, 190
Food for export programs. *See* Export markets
Ford administration, 59, 172, 210
Fowler (CA), 187–88, 192
Fraud: in industry chemical tests, 190
Fresno County (CA), 6, 85, 91, 93, 110, 188, 269. *See also* Westlands Water District
Friant-Kern canal, 50
Friedman, Milton, 183
Friends of the Earth, 20, 209, 211

GAC. *See* Granular activated carbon
Galloway Group, 131–35
GAO (General Accounting Office), 169, 180
Garrison Project (North Dakota), 39, 53, 54, 71, 211
General Accounting Office (GAO), 169, 180
Getty Oil Company, 30
Gianelli, William, xvii, 9, 14–15, 65–67, 69
Gibbs, Lois, 235
Giermann, Ed, 244
Glen Avon (CA), 236–40
Glen Canyon Dam, 53–55, 216
Goldschmidt, Walter, 230
Goldwater, Barry, 272
"Good science": Lavelle's conception of, 181–82

Gorsuch, Anne, 180–82, 186, 212, 237, 259
Grace, J. Peter, 259–61
Graff, Tom, 99, 213–14, 216
Graham, Ralph ("Mike"), 113–16
Grand Canyon dam, 55–56, 209
Grand Coulee Dam, 45
Granular activated carbon (GAC), 169, 173–74, 176–77, 179, 194, 197
Grassroots organizations: against water industry, xvi, 26, 53–54, 149, 234–40; against contaminants, 184, 217–18
Great Basin Kingdom (Utah), 38, 42, 204
Greeley, Horace, 81
Green, Dorothy, xvi–xvii, 20
"Green" politics, 210
Grimmer, Jack, 189
Groundwater: managements systems for, 17–18, 21–22, 72; overdrafting of, 32, 64; in Honey Springs, 114–15; in Tucson, 145; industrial contamination of, 176–87; statistics on use of, 177; agricultural contamination of, 187–92. See also Dumping; Plumes; Radiation
Growth. See Urbanization

Hamilton, Alexander, 118–19
"Hammer clause" (in Reclamation Reform Act), 109–11, 254
Hardin, Garrett, 276
Harriman, Job, 205
Harris, Robert, 170, 176
Hawaii, 190–91
Hawkins, Howard, 13, 182
Hayden, Carl, 90, 144
Hays, Samuel, 207
Hazardous wastes. See Contamination; Citizen's Clearinghouse on Hazardous Wastes; Dumping; *Names of particular contaminants*
Hedgecock, Roger, 113
Hernandez, John, 181
Hetch-Hetchy Valley (CA), 207, 274–75
Hightower, Jim, 232
Hilbert, Robert, 172
Hispanics, 219, 226–28
Hodel, Donald, 70, 274–75
Home filter systems, 196
Homestead Act (1862), 43, 81

Honey Springs (CA), 113–16
Hoover, Herbert, 45, 96
Hoover Dam, 50, 97, 125, 223, 262
Hotchkis, Preston, 3–4
House Interior and Insular Affairs Committee, 70, 94
House Water and Power Resources Subcommittee, 70, 93–94
Houston, David, 271
Houston (TX), 123
HR 6, 69

Ibbetson, E. Thornton, 100, 127, 243–45
IBT (Industrial Bio-Test Laboratories), 190
Ickes, Harold, 208
IDBs (Industrial development bonds), 258
IID. See Imperial Irrigation District
Illinois, 163–64. See also Chicago
"Image building": by the water industry, 155–58, 278
Imperial (CA), 101–2
Imperial Irrigation District (IID), 95–103, 134, 214, 261, 269–70
Imperial Valley (CA), 45, 50, 269; irrigation of, 94–103. See also IID
Imported water, xv, 32, 89, 109, 113–16, 129–36; definition of, 8. See also Interbasin transfers
Indianapolis (In), 175
Indian tribes: and water rights, 216, 219–23, 227–28, 279
Industrial Bio-Test Laboratories (IBT), 190
Industrial development bonds (IDBs), 258, 260
Industrial Workers of the World (IWW), 207
Industry: favorable treatment of, by water companies, xv, 164
Initiative 300 (NE), 233–34
Institute for Resource Management (IRM), 199–200, 216, 253
Interbasin transfers, 56–57, 94–103, 104–5, 265–72. See also SWAP
Intermountain Power Project, 262–63
Interstate Sanitation Commission, 165
Iowa, 191
IRM (Institute for Resource

IRM *(cont.)*
Management), 199–200, 216, 253
"Iron Triangle," 46–52, 58, 62–66,
68–70, 73
Irrigated agriculture: and water
development, xv, 5–14, 40–46, 50,
79–84; crisis in, xviii–xix, 68, 103–8,
232–34; development of, 42–46; in
Imperial Valley, 95–103; increase in
acreage due to, 104; and pesticides,
107, 188–89; Indian and Hispanic uses
of, 219–20, 226–28. *See also* Land
ownership patterns
Irrigation Age, 81
Irrigation congresses. *See* National
Irrigation Congresses
Irvine (CA), 128
Irvine Company, 30, 100
Izaac Walton League, 163, 201, 210–11

J. G. Boswell Company, 6, 21–23,
28–31, 89, 244
Jackson, Henry, 55
James Ragan Associates, 250
Jennings, William, 130
Jensen, Joseph, 8, 10, 126–27
Johnson, Bizz, 50–51, 91
Johnson, Eric, 175
Johnson, Lyndon Baines, 48
Jordan, Charles, 139
*Journal of the American Water Works
Association*, 165, 260

Kanawha River (WV), 168–69, 173
Kansas, 190, 191
KCWA. *See* Kern County Water
Authority
Kennedy, David, 23, 26
Kern County (CA), 25, 29, 134, 232;
agribusiness and water development
in, 6, 8–9, 12–16, 18–19, 23; and
federal programs, 85–86; and water
markets, 215, 269; contamination in,
187, 191–92, 245
Kern County Land Company, 8, 13
Kern County Water Authority (KCWA),
191–92, 271
Kesterson Wildlife Refuge, 51, 91, 94,
215, 217
Kovalic, Joan, 253

Krupicka, Ron, 107
Krupp, Frederic, 215

Laguna Declaration (of MET), 127–28,
130, 135, 141
Lake Erie: pollution of, 166
Lamm, Richard, 17, 216
Land ownership patterns: and trends
toward corporate farming, 12–13, 52,
77, 80, 84, 86–87, 97, 100, 108, 199;
and farm workers' unions, 229–31. *See
also* Farm workers; FMAs; Leasing
Land speculation: in the West, 81–82; in
Nebraska, 105–8
Las Vegas (NV), xv
Lathrop (CA), 189–90
Lavelle, Rita, 180–82
"Law of the River," 132, 133
Laxalt, Paul, 70
Leaching Fields, The (CA Assembly
Office of Research), 187
League of Women Voters, 24, 234–35
Leasing (of farmland), 77, 87, 93, 110
Lee, John Penn, 21
Lindgren, David, 109–10
Lippincott, J. B., 45, 124
Livermore, Norm ("Ike"), 15
"Logrolling," 48, 49
Lonergan, Gerald, 26
Long, Lorell, 21
Los Angeles (City of), 44–45, 96, 121,
123–28, 256, 262
Los Angeles (County of), 31, 178
Los Angeles Aqueduct, 45
Los Angeles Department of Water and
Power, xv, 124, 156–57
Los Angeles Times, xv, 10, 25, 96, 123,
196, 214, 223, 250
Louisville (KY), 175
Love Canal (NY), 178, 235
Lundquist, Gene, 16

MacCannell, Dean, 89
McClosky, Michael, 217
McFall, John, 51, 91
McFarland (CA), 187–88, 192
McIntyre, Robert, 31
McMullen Valley (AZ), 266–68
McPeak, Sunne, 20, 21, 26, 28, 29
McPhee, John, 273

McWilliams, Carey, 84, 229, 232
Madigan, Mike, 132–34
Manhattan Company, 119–20, 150
Manufacturing Chemists Association, 163
Markets (for water), 143, 200, 201; Reagan administration interest in, 68, 73, 149–50; and the IID, 101–3; and MET, 135; environmentalists' interest in, 213–18, 253; development of, 261–73
Marston, Arthur, 130
Martin, William, 144
Matheson, Scott, 63–64
Maxwell, George, 81
Meral, Gerald, 17–19, 23–24
Merced County (CA), 85, 90
MET. *See* Metropolitan Water District of Southern California
Metcalfe-Eddy (construction company), 259
Metering, 142, 255
Methylene chloride: in water bottled in plastic jugs, 195
Metropolitan Water District of Southern California: author's involvement with, xv–xvii, 3–4, 20; and development of Southern California, 6–9; and Delta facility, 15–16, 18, 24–27, 29–32; and water transfers, 99–102, 135, 214, 269–70; and urban growth, 113–15, 127–30, 150; and Colorado River, 125–27, 133; and drinking water standards, 177, 196, 215, 218, 239, 243–45. *See also* Laguna Declaration
Mexicali Valley (CA), 223–24
Mexican interests: in U.S. water, 223–26
Milagro Beanfield War (Nichols), 227–28
Miller, George, 70, 71, 93–94, 110–11, 201
Miller, Richard, 174, 186
Minnesota: pollution in, 169
Mississippi River: and Army Corps, 41, 42, 47, 53, 66; and pollution, 169–71
Moffat Railroad Tunnel, 137
Monkey Wrench Gang (Abbey), 273–74
Mormons, 42–43, 204–5
Morris, John ("Jack"), 61
Mothers of Glen Avon, 236
Mountain States Legal Foundation, xvii

Muir, John, 205–6, 274
"Multiple use" (of water), 206–9
Murphy, Lew, 147
Musick, John, 132

Nader, Ralph, 170, 176, 196
National Conservation Association, 207
National Environmental Policy Act, 58–59, 61, 209
National Irrigation Congresses, 43, 81, 82
National Rivers and Harbors Congress, 47
National Water Commission, 56–57, 62, 64, 166, 255, 263–64
National Water Commission Report (1973), 57, 213
National Water Resources Association (NWRA), 37–40, 49, 65, 90, 92, 155, 196, 260
National Wildlife Federation, 61, 201
Natural Resources Defense Council, 61, 71, 201, 209
Navajo Indian Irrigation Project, 222, 227. *See also* Indian tribes
NAWAPA. *See* North American Water and Power Alliance
Nebraska: as an irrigation state, 103–8; contamination in, 191
Nelson, Gordon, 91
New Deal, 84–85, 89, 208
"New Democrats" (in Tucson), 146–49
Newell, Frederick, 206
Newhall Land and Farming, 30
Newlands Acts (1902), 83
Newman, Penny, 236–40, 243
New Mexico: and Hispanic water rights, 226–28
New Orleans: water pollution in, 170–72
New York City, 118–122
Nichols, John, 227–28
Nitrates: groundwater contamination by, 187–88, 191
Nitro (WV), 168–69
Nixon administration, 59, 145, 210, 225
Nomellini, Dante, 21
North American Water and Power Alliance (NAWAPA), 263
Northern Colorado Water Conservancy District, 262

Norton Air Force Base, 236
NWC. *See* National Water Commission
NWRA. *See* National Water Resources
Association

Office of Governmental Ethics, 110
Office of Management and Budget, 201,
251; and water development projects,
59–60, 67, 145; and water policy, 65,
68, 177; during Reagan
administration, 181, 257, 264
Office of Technology Assessment, 180,
238
Ogallala aquifer, 103–8, 233
Ohio River, 169, 173
Olson, Culbert, 229
OMB. *See* Office of Management and
Budget
Onandaga County (NY), 249
160-acre restrictions. *See* Acreage
restrictions
Orange County (CA), 8, 14, 31, 126,
130, 256
Organic compounds: in drinking water,
168–77
O'Shaunnessy Dam, 274–75
Osias, David, 99
Overdrafting, 8, 13, 17; and center pivot
crisis, 103–8; in Denver, 140; in
Tucson, 143
Overproduction (farm), 75, 78, 111
Owens Valley (CA), 45, 124–25, 262,
268–69, 275
Ozone: as water purifier, 194

PACs. *See* Political action committees
Pamo Dam facility (CA), 134
Papagos. *See* Indian tribes
Parents of Jurupa, 236
Parker, Albert, Jr., 265
Parsons Corporation, 101–2, 258–61
Parsons Municipal Services, Inc., 259
Parsons Water Resources Inc., 261
Pasadena (CA), 125, 261
Pascoe, Monte, 141
Payment in Kind (PIK) programs,
88–89, 106
PCE (Perchlorethylene), 179
Peaches, 78–79
Peanut butter, 183–84

PERC (Political Economy Research
Center), 214
Perchlorethylene (PCE), 179
Peripheral Canal, 10, 98, 115, 215, 244;
description of project, xvii, 11;
author's opposition to, 4–5;
controversy over, 14–33, 128, 130–31.
See also "Delta facility"
Pesticides, 85, 90, 102, 107, 165, 183,
186–92, 244
Petrochemical companies, 186–87
Philadelphia (PA), 121, 159–62
Phoenix (AZ), xv, xvi, 123, 144–45,
155–56; bottled water use in, 196;
buying of water rights by, 266–68, 270
Phosphates, 166
PHS. *See* U.S. Public Health Service
PIK. *See* Payment in Kind programs
Pinchot, Gifford, 206–7, 208
PL 480, 85
"Pleasant Valley (CA) massacre," 93
Plumes: in groundwater, 179, 239
Pogue, Robert, 90
Political action committees, 92
Political Economy Research Center
(PERC), 214
Polls: on drinking water safety, 156, 186
Pollution, 57. *See also* Contamination;
Dumping; Water quality
Porter, Carley, 17
Poundstone Amendment (Denver), 139,
141
Powell, John Wesley, 42, 205
"Practically irrigable acreage," 220–21
Preservationists, 205–6, 207
Press, Bill, 113, 116
Press: as extension of water industry,
249–50
Pricing (of water), 12–13, 70–73, 78, 80,
90, 109, 218; of bottled water
compared to city water, 194, 197. *See
also* Equity questions; Subsidies
Privatization (of water industry), 68, 73,
101, 149, 247, 253, 257–61; of supply,
192–97. *See also* Bottled water
Production Credit Association, 106
Proposition 65 (CA), 192, 243–46
Prudential Life Insurance, 13, 106, 233
"Public participation": water industry's
interest in, 250–53

Public relations: water industry's, 155–58, 278
Public works projects: and BuRec, 45, 49
Pueblo Indians. *See* Indian tribes

"Quality of life" issues: and water development, 150, 278

Radiation: in groundwater, 238
Radionucleides, 177
Raffi (singer), 280
Ralph M. Parsons Company, 258–61
Rand Corporation, 263–64
Rates: favorable, for industry, xv, 164; and conservation, 146–49. *See also* Equity questions; Metering; Pricing
Reagan, Ronald, 9, 19, 28, 212; as governor, 14, 15; as president, 38–39, 65–74, 88–89
Reagan administration, xvii–xviii, 94, 101, 109; and EPA, 180–82; and environmental issues, 186, 213–18, 253–54, 257–61, 264–65, 270–71
Reallocations (of water). *See* Interbasin transfers; Markets
Reclamation Act, 86–87, 96
Reclamation Reform Act (1982), 93–94, 109, 110. *See also* "Hammer clause"
Reclamation Service, 43–44, 50, 83, 95, 268. *See also* Bureau of Reclamation
Reconstruction Finance Corporation, 97
Redford, Robert, 199–202, 216, 253
Refuse Act, 162
Regional concerns (about water), 54, 59–60, 73
Reserve Mining Company, 169
Resources for the Future (RFF), 213
Reynolds, Steve, 227
RFF (Resources for the Future), 213
Rice, 88
Rights (water), 81, 111, 131–32, 135, 214; and Tucson, 143–49; of Indians, 219–23; of Hispanics, 226–28; sale of, 262
Riverside County (CA), 8, 14, 31, 123, 126, 130, 256
Roberts Tunnel, 137
Robie, Ronald, 15, 17
Romer, Roy, 142

Roosevelt, Franklin, 208
Roosevelt, Theodore, 215
Runoff: contaminated, 187–92
Rural Coalition, 232
Rural Electrification Agency, 84, 97
Russo, Sal, 28, 29, 245

Sacramento Bay Delta, 6–7, 11, 27
Safe Drinking Water Act, 58, 172, 174, 177, 180, 185–86, 192–94
Safe Drinking Water and Toxic Enforcement Act of 1986 (Proposition 65), 243–46
Salome (AZ), 267
Salt contamination: in Colorado River, 97–98, 217; in Mexicali Valley, 224–26
Salt Lake Tribune, 250, 277
Salton Sea, 95, 97–98, 100–1
Salt River Project (Arizona), 143, 145
Salyer Land Company, 21–23, 28–31, 51
San Diego County (CA), 8, 14, 31; growth in, 123, 126, 128–36, 256–57, 277–78
San Diego County Water Authority, 100, 101, 113–15, 128–31, 133–35
San Felipe unit (CVP), 109
San Francisco, 31, 121
San Joaquin County (CA), 245
San Juan-Chama Project, 227–28
San Luis Drain (Central Valley Project), 91
Santa Barbara (CA), 31, 167
Santa Fe (NM), 227
Santa Monica (CA), xvi–xvii, 125
Save Lake Superior Association, 169
SAWARA (Southern Arizona Water Resources Association), 148
Schroeder, Pat, 139
Science (magazine), 181
Scottsdale (AZ), 267
Sedjo, Roger, 214
Selenium, 32, 51
Senate Select Committee on National Water Resources, 56
Set Aside programs, 88
Sevier County (Utah), 262
Sewage: disposal of, 162–64
Shasta Dam, 50, 86
Shell Oil Company, 30
Sherman, Harris, 216

Sierra Club, 19, 23–24, 54–55, 115, 200, 205, 208–10, 217
Signal (company), 258, 259
Silent Spring (Carson), 165, 189, 215
Silicon Valley Toxics Coalition, 184
Sisk, Bernie, 50–51, 86, 91–92
"Slow growth" movement, 148–49, 276–77
Snow, John, 160
Socialist Party, 207
SOCs (Synthetic organic compounds), 168
Soil Conservation Service Conservation Reserve Program, 108
Soil Conservation Service, 40
South Coast Basin (CA), 32, 123–28
Southern California Edison, 200
Southern Arizona Water Resources Association (SAWARA), 148
Southern Pacific Railroad, 50, 95, 96, 123
SP. *See* Southern Pacific
Sporhase v. Nebraska, 265
Standard Oil of California, 244, 245
State Water Project. *See* California State Water Project
Steiner, Wes, 268
Sterling, John, 21, 22, 28–29
Stockman, David, 65
Storper, Michael, 20
Stringfellow (CA), 178, 235–40
Subsidies, 218; and federal projects, 48, 52, 64; agricultural, 78, 85–90, 96–103, 108, 111; of suburban water, 256; of industries by residential users, 257. *See also* Double dipping; Payment in Kind programs
Superfund (EPA), 180–82, 237–38
Surplus crops, 109; and irrigation, 51, 104, 105; overproduction of, 78, 88–89
SWAP (water transfer), 99, 101–3, 134, 214
Swing, Phil, 96, 100, 129
Synthetic organic compounds (SOCs), 168

"Tap water replacement market," 193–94. *See also* Bottled water
Tarr, Ralph, 71, 72, 109, 254
Tax Reform Act of 1986, 107, 260

Taylor, Paul, 229–33
TCAA (Tetrachloroethylene), 179, 185
TCE (Trichloroethylene), 157
Tejon Ranch, 25, 269
"Tenants-in-common," 110
Tenneco, 13
Tennessee-Tombigbee project, 53, 54, 59, 69, 73
Tetrachloroethylene (TCAA), 179, 185
Texas High Plains, 103–8
"Third wave" (of environmental advocacy), 32, 215–18
THM. *See* Trihalomethanes
Thornton (CO), 140, 142
Thousand Oaks, (CA), 128
Times Beach (MO), 178
Tohono O'odham. *See* Indian tribes
Toxics. *See* Contamination; Hazardous wastes; Water quality
Trace organics. *See* Organic compounds
Trans-America Company, 84
Transfers (of water). *See* Interbasin transfers; Markets
Treatment (water). *See* Chlorination; Cleanup; GACs; Home filters
Trezek, G. J., 239–40
Trichloroethylene (TCE), 157, 178–79, 181–85, 195, 238
Trihalomethanes (THMs), 171–72, 175–77, 184, 186, 195, 244
Trotsky, Leon, 29
Tucson (AZ), xv, 143–49, 257, 266, 270
Tulare County (CA), 6, 269. *See also* Westlands Water District
Tulare Lake Basin, 88–89
Twain, Mark, 272
Two Forks Dam and Reservoir (Denver), 139–42

U.S. Congress, 61, 66, 72, 80, 86; and farm-water lobby, 90–94. *See also* House; Senate
U.S. Department of Agriculture, 79–80, 103
U.S. Forest Service, 206
U.S. Interior Department, 37, 38, 52. *See also* Tarr, Ralph
U.S. Justice Department, 110
U.S. Navy: and water development in San Diego, 129

U.S. Pollution Control Inc., 258
U.S. Public Health Service, 162, 166, 168–71
U.S. Supreme Court, 219, 265
Udall, Stewart, 55–56
Union activity (among farm workers), 102, 229–32
Union Development Corporation, 100
Upper Rio Grand Valley, 226–28
Urbanization: and water in Southern California, xv, xix, 5–6, 8, 31, 67–68, 74, 112–16, 123–36, 256; and agriculture, 80, 99–100; and early water systems, 116–22; in Denver, 136–43; in Tucson, 143–49. *See also* "Slow growth" movement
Utah, 37–38
Utes. *See* Indian tribes
Utopians, 204–5, 210

Van der Ryn, Sim, 113, 116
Ventura County (CA), 8, 123
Villarejo, Don, 75–79, 231
VOCs (Volatile organic compounds), 168

W. R. Grace & Co., 185
Wahl, Richard, 270
Wall Street Journal, 214, 215
Warren, Earl, 229
Warren, Jacqueline, 176, 196
"Wasted" water: as defined by water industry, 275–76, 279
Wastes: disposal of industrial, 162–64. *See also* Chicago; Contamination; Dumping
Wastewater market, 257–61
Water: as an economic commodity, 213–18; "Wasted" water, 275–76, 279
Water closet, 120
Water development, xv–xvi, xix, 279; in California, 5–14; federal involvement with, 46–58; troubles with, 251–52. *See also* Army Corps of Engineers; Bureau of Reclamation; Colorado River; Subsidies
Water industry: description of, xiii–xv, xviii–xix; early history of, 116–22; as water purveyors rather than public

utilities, 159, 184–85; opposition of, to regulation, 172; response to fears of contamination, 175–76; critics of, 202–9; political biases of, 246–53
"Water in the West" (1985 conference), 199–202
Water markets. *See* Markets
Water policy: effects of, xiii, xix, 4, 57–58
Water quality: concerns about, xviii–xx, 27, 32, 57, 149–51, 235; in Reagan years, 73; and lobbyists, 90; in Chicago, 122–23; and water industry's image, 155–58, 252, 256; U.S.'s, to Mexico, 224–26
Water Quality and Treatment (AWWA), 168
Water rates. *See* Rates
Water Resources Council, 56
Water supply, 58, 86. *See also* Water development
Water Watch campaign, 26
Watt, James, xvii, 38–40, 65, 67, 70, 92, 94, 212
Watts, Doug, 28, 29, 245
Weevils, 102
Wellton-Mohawk Valley drainage project, 224, 226
Well water: use of, from Texas to Nebraska, 103–8. *See also* Groundwater
Wenden (AZ), 267
Western Governors Association, 265, 270
Western Regional Council, 212, 220
Western Water Rights Management Inc., 265
Westlands Water District, 231; criticism of disaster at, 51–52, 217; price of water for, 71, 253–54, 269; governmental support for development of, 91, 109–10; and EDF, 215, 218
Wetlands issue, 60
White flies, 102
Wilbur, Ray Lyman, 96
Wilderness Act (1964), 56
Wilderness areas, 205–6
Wilderness Society, 208–10, 215
Will, Robert, 72

Wilson, Pete, 132–33
Winters Doctrine, 219
Wirthlin, Richard, 28
Woburn (MA), 185
Wolfe, Sidney, 196
Wright, Jim, 91
Wright Act (California), 82–83

Yampa River, 131–33
Young, Brigham, 28, 204

Zahniser, Howard, 215–16
Ziglar, James, 72
"Zuccolini," 21
Zuckerman, Tom, 21